Reading Paul's Mail

written and illustrated
by
Steven P. Thomason

Reading Paul's Mail

Steven P. Thomason

Published by:

Vibble Books

www.VibbleBooks.com

First printing
Hart Haus Resources, LLC ©2006

reprinted
Vibble Books © 2009

ISBN: 0-9840670-3-5
13-Digit: 978-0-9840670-3-9
Cover Artwork and Interior Illustration: Steven P. Thomason

Printed in the United States of America

Introduction

About This Study

This study was originally written in the fall of 2005 for a network of house churches in Southern Nevada called Hart Haus. Each week the members of the community would commit to spend 5 days studying the designated passage of scripture and then share what they learned with the group when they gathered in the various homes on Sunday.

About the Author

Steve Thomason is first and foremost a child of God that is committed to loving his wife and four children. He currently resides in the suburbs of Minneapolis, Minnesota.

Steve has two passions in life. The first is teaching people about God and how to grow in a relationship with the Creator. His second passion is art -- specifically cartooning and animation. Throughout his career he has sought to blend these two passions together to create visually interesting lessons that draw people closer to God.

From 1994-2002 Steve was in Adult Minstries at Central Christian Church in Las Vegas, Nevada. During those years Steve led small group ministries, adult education classes, and wrote curriculum for both settings. Along the way he earned a Masters of Divinity degree from Bethel Theological Seminary through their In-Ministry Program.

In 2002 Steve and his family joined with a group of friends to explore what it would look like to "do church" in a different way. For the next 5 years they experimented with being a community in a network of house churches called Hart Haus. During those years Steve wrote a daily Bible Study that combined cartoons and Bible Commentary.

In 2009 Steve set out on a new leg of his teacher/artist journey. He took the Hart Haus studies and used them as the foundation for creating Vibble Books. His desire is to see Vibble Books and VibbleSpace.com become a resource for his generation to engage with the reality of God's Love so that God's Kingdom can be realized in our world.

Discover more resources at www.vibblespace.com

Colorful Cartoons

At the beginning of each lesson you will find a cartoon illustration that attempts to encapsulate the letter. These illustrations were originally created in vibrant color. In order to keep the cost of this book to a minimum, the interior was printed in black and white. If you would like to see the illustrations in color, please visit *www.vibblespace.com/studies/pauls-letters/*

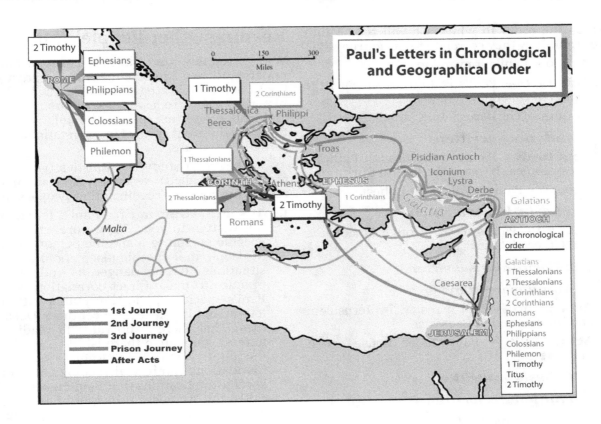

An Unfolding Story

Why are we so excited about a bunch of letters that were written 2,000 years ago? And, why are you asking me to devote sixteen weeks of my life to study them? Those are valid questions.

Next to Jesus Christ Himself, one of the most influential people in the formation of the Christian Church and its various interpretations of God, salvation, and daily living, is the Apostle Paul. In this study we will look at Paul's letters that have been preserved for us through time. Each of these letters was written to either a specific church or a specific individual during the years A.D. 50-64.

If you were to open the New Testament and begin reading Paul's letters in the order they are found there (called the 'canonical order') you would read them as follows: Romans, 1 Corinthians, 2 Corinthians, Galatians, Ephesians, Philippians, Colossians, 1 Thessalonians, 2 Thessalonians, 1 Timothy, 2 Timothy, Titus, Philemon. When the original compilers of the New Testament got together in the early 300's they decided to organize Paul's letters according to size and type. The first category was letters written to churches,

so they began with the big Daddy – Romans – and worked down to the smallest – 2 Thessalonians. The second category was letters to individuals. This, too, was organized by size.

While this method forms a nice, tidy organizational system (perhaps our early fathers worked for the Imperial Post Office!) it does little for us in regards to understanding the developing theology within the mind and ministry of Paul. In this study we will be reading Paul's letters in chronological order. When we organize his letters in this way we discover a beautiful correlation between them and the book of Acts. Ideally you would study Acts 9-28 in conjunction with the letters, observing how most of the letters were actually written while the story of Acts was unfolding. For example, if you want to understand the message to the church in Thessalonica then you must read Acts 15-17 to see how Paul was railroaded out of that town, prematurely, by some very irate politicians. Throughout the course of this study I will make reference to the appropriate sections of Acts and encourage you to go there for more context.

Here is the order in which we will read Paul's letters and how they correlate to his journeys

- **Acts 9** – Paul's conversion
- **Acts 13-14** – Paul's 1st Journey through the region of Galatia
- **Acts 15** – The Jerusalem Council

  Galatians written

- **Acts 16-18** – Paul travels through Philippi, Thessalonica, Berea, Athens, and Corinth
- **Acts 19** – Paul's ministry in Ephesus

  1 Corinthians written

- **Acts 20** – Paul sweeps through Macedonia and Greece (Corinth)

  2 Corinthians written

  Romans written

- **Acts 21-26** – Paul arrested in Jerusalem and imprisoned in Caesarea
- **Acts 27-28** -- Paul under house arrest in Rome

  Ephesians written

  Philippians written

  Colossians written

  Philemon written

After Acts

- Paul released from house arrest and sails to Spain

  1 Timothy written

  Titus written

- Paul arrested and imprisoned in Roman dungeon

  2 Timothy written

- Paul is executed

Reading Other People's Mail

When studying the Bible it is important to understand two important facts. First, not all books of the Bible are the same. Some books are histories, some are law codes, others are poems, and still others are personal mail. Secondly, there are different rules of interpretation for each genre of literature.

As we begin to study the Epistles (as they are traditionally called) we must take a moment to review the rules for reading other people's mail.

1. **It's not your mail.** Paul's letters were not written to you. They were written by a specific person to a specific person or group of people in a specific place about a specific situation. It is a dangerous and incorrect practice to make direct correlation between Paul's specific application points within the letters and life in the 21st century. Does that mean that there is no value in reading the letters? Of course there is! As a student of the letters it is your job to discern the deep, foundational, universal theology behind the specific applications that Paul makes. This is called the "timeless principle." For example, and most fundamentally, the message of the gospel is love: the unconditional, other-oriented love of God. What did love look like in each situation? What did love look like in Corinth? In Ephesus? In Colossi? In each city Paul knew the specific dynamic that was happening between human personalities, between the Gentiles and the Jews, between the church and the local government. In each case there was a different way in which Paul instructed the people to behave. And yet, there are also many, many universal and obvious things that Paul taught them as well. It is our job to be like the old 49ers of the Gold Rush who diligently dipped their pans in the river. We must sift through the cultural context of the letter and find the golden nugget for today.

2. **Its like playing telephone.** Have you ever been sitting in a room with someone who was talking on the phone? Sometimes its fun to try to guess what the person on the other end of the line is saying by listening to the responses the person in front of you is giving. That is what reading the epistles is like. Paul's letters were written in response to either specific questions that had been asked to him or to specific situations that had been brought to his attention. Here is an example scenario. Paul is living in Ephesus for nearly two years. While he is there some of his associates had sailed across the small Aegean Sea to visit the

church in Corinth that Paul had started a few years earlier. When they return they rushed into Paul's tent shop in disgust and alarm and rattle off a list of things that they had observed in Corinth that they knew would give Paul great cause for distress. Quickly Paul called for a scribe and some parchment. "OK, tell me again, one at a time, the things you saw..." then he proceeded to address those issues, with the faces of the people in his mind all the while. As soon as the ink was dry he sealed it up and gave it to the messenger saying, "Quickly, take this to them before it is too late!" As students of these letters it is our job to discern what the original questions/situations were that prompted Paul to write. Ascertaining this will give us a better ability to correctly interpret his instructions.

3. **The letters are not theology textbooks or instructional sermons.** When a teacher has the intention of sitting down to write an instructional document he generally tries to be comprehensive and thorough, building a clear and logical argument that takes into account as many aspects of the subject as possible. When you crack open a theology book you expect to find all of the "biggie" questions addressed in an integrated manner. We must remember that, with the possible exception of Romans, Paul's letters ARE NOT THEOLOGICAL TEXTBOOKS! Paul wrote the letters to his churches with a basic presupposition that his people already knew his theology and shared it as a common language. It is similar to a family that shares "inside jokes" or "family stories." When these things are shared within a family it is sometimes possible to communicate a very long and complicated story with a subtle shift of the eye or a simple phrase. Those outside the family would not have enough information to correctly interpret the look or simple phrase, yet the family would know exactly what they meant. In the letters Paul shares a theological language and understanding with his people that can only be developed through personal relationship. Not only did they share a theological language, they shared linguistic and cultural idioms as well. In writing, Paul alludes to his core theology, but does not present it deeply and thoroughly. The separation of time, language, and culture stands as a barrier between the true meaning in Paul's day and us as 21st century readers. In light of this, we must be careful to not build large theological constructs for our lives out of only one verse in Paul's letters. We must be careful to not take a verse "out of context." As

we do the work of theology we must draw from the whole of Paul's letters, distill the timeless principles, add them to the golden nuggets we have gleaned from the rest of scripture, fold them into the contemporary issues, catalyze them with the dynamic presence of the Holy Spirit in our lives, and DING! We have a working recipe for life in the 21st century.

A Response

There are at least three possible responses to the brief introduction that I have just presented to you. The first response may go something like this, "Oh, that's a bunch of liberal hogwash designed to undermine the authority of God's Word. The textual, literary, historical, form, and redaction critical methods that were developed in the 19th century and refined throughout the 20th century have led the church into a state of dissolution and decay[1]. We need to reject that kind of thinking and 'just get back to the Bible'" If that is your perspective, then I respect that. However, for the record, I do not align myself with the classical tradition called "Protestant Liberalism." While I do not agree with their anti-supernatural and demythologizing tendencies, I do think that their critical methods have shed new light on Scripture and have provided a wealth of tools and insights for the serious student of the most important, and authoritative, document ever written. Please be advised, however, that, if you fall into this first camp of reaction to my introduction, you may want to spare yourself the pain of reading the rest of my commentary on Paul's letters. Out of love for you, I'm giving you the 'out' right now.

There is a second possible reaction. You may get a little discouraged and think, "If it is that complicated or hidden behind cultural context, then is it even possible to figure out what the truth is? What's the point of studying the Bible? Can we really ever know the truth? I just want to know what is right and then do it." If that is your reaction then let me encourage you. First of all, take a deep breath....God is real. God is in control. The gospel is incredibly simple. God loves you. Jesus saves you. Just believe and love. There. It really is that easy. The reason we study the Bible is to grow in our ability to discern who God is, how He interacts with people, how people who have encountered Him have responded to His reality in practical ways, and then encounter God in our own lives, within our own culture, and respond authentically and appropriately so that the love of God can be spread to everyone we encounter. I don't believe the universe is like a big machine that runs in a linear fashion according to black/white, right/wrong rules and regulations. I believe the universe is much more subtle and "organic" than that. We don't follow an abstract theological idea or a religious system that is about being "right." Rather, we are engaged in a dynamic relationship with a loving Heavenly Father who is continually calling us forward to grow and develop and discover the depths of His love and the multifaceted nature of His eternal mysteries. Embrace the dance, persevere on the journey, and trust in the lover of your soul.

There is one more possible reaction that I'd like to address. You may think, "Ah, that feels like a breath of fresh air." Good. Breathe it in. Jesus said that the Spirit is like the wind. In the Old Testament the word for breath and spirit were the same and indistinguishable. The Spirit is the air we breathe. The love of God gives life to our bones. My prayer for you and for this study, to quote Paul's letter to the Ephesian church, is that God

> *may strengthen you with power through His Spirit in your inner being, so that Christ may dwell in your hearts through faith. And I pray that you, being rooted and established in love, may have power, together with all the saints, to grasp how wide and long and high and deep is the love of Christ, and to know this love that surpasses knowledge—that you may be filled to the measure of all the fullness of God.*

Introduction to Galatians

Paul's first journey took him through a region in Asia minor called Galatia. The story is found in Acts 13-14. During that trip he did the unthinkable. He interacted with Gentiles. More than that, God did the unthinkable. Uncircumcised people received the Holy Spirit.

To many of the Christian leaders in Jerusalem, this was intolerable. Paul was a threat that must be stopped. The debate between Gentile-lovers and "the circumcised" became so heated that it required a meeting of the minds. The church leaders met in Jerusalem and held the very first Church Council. The conversation is recorded in Acts 15.

James presided over the meeting. After hearing testimonies from Peter, Barnabus, and Paul about the miraculous things God was doing among the uncircumcised Gentiles, he was faced with a very difficult decision. Should uncircumcised Gentiles who profess to follow Jesus be welcomed into the church as equal members?

The question sounds silly to us, but to the 1st century Jew, this was a watershed moment. The implications of the debate would change the course of history forever. And it did.

James, and the other leaders of the church, officially declared that Jews and Gentiles should welcome one another as equals and work together as spiritual syblings in the family of God.

The dissenters were outraged and worked diligently to undermine this decision. This debate set the tone for the rest of Paul's life. He spent the majority of his ministry doing two things:

1. Sharing the Good News of Jesus with Gentiles.

2. Defending his authority to do this against those who believed his theology was heretical and dangerous.

The letter to the Galatians was his first document written in the wake of the Jerusalem Council. We will see the themes found in this letter refined and reformed throughout the course of his life and writing.

5

Lesson 1

- Galatians 1

Study Questions

What is happening to the church in Galatia?

Who is doing this to them?

How does Paul feel about it?

What accusation seems to be brought against Paul?

How does he defend himself against this accusation?

Food for Thought

Paul under fire

As we fade up from black on the opening scene of this drama that is Paul's life, we find Paul under heavy enemy fire. This is an appropriate place to start since Paul found himself being attacked throughout most of his career. Whenever Paul would enter a new town three things would inevitably happen. First, people would respond to his message and experience new found freedom in a relationship with Jesus and the indwelling of the Holy Spirit. Secondly, a large contingent of very angry people – typically the people who held control over the political/religious life of the city – would attack him, stone him, imprison him, run him out of town, or all of the above. Third, a contingent of people would follow after him and attempt to turn his newly formed churches against him and convince them to follow a legalistic form of Judaized Christianity. Such was the quality of life for the first foreign missionary of the church.

In Galatians we find Paul responding to the third event. During Paul's 1st missionary journey in Acts 13-14, he and Barnabus traveled through the region of Galatia and formed churches in Iconium, Lystra, and Derbe. The citizens of these cities were largely non-Jewish people that followed various forms of ancient Greek religions and rituals. When these Gentiles (a generic term used by Jews to denote non-Jewish people) responded to the message of Jesus they received the Holy Spirit.

To us that may seem passé, and we may think, "Well, duh, isn't that what happens when someone responds to the message of Jesus?" True, but, in order to grasp the full impact of Paul's ministry, and specifically this first letter to the Galatians, we must place ourselves into the time and perspective of the story and see Paul through the eyes of his enemies. In the time of Jesus and the Apostles, the Jewish people believed that they were the only people that God loved. As they read the book of Genesis and the story of God's promises to Abraham they believed that God's grace was poured out to him and to his family alone. This elevated place of being God's chosen was demonstrated through the physical act of circumcision. Having ones foreskin removed was a sign that you enjoyed this special position of election in God's Kingdom and that the rest of the world stood outside the promise and was eternally condemned. 430 years after God gave circumcision to Abraham's family, as found in the book of Genesis, the books of Exodus, Leviticus, Numbers, and Deuteronomy record that God then gave the Law to Moses to show His people how His holy people were to live. The 1st century Jews believed that the only way that a person could enjoy the blessings of God was to enter into the covenant that God made to Abraham by being circumcised (sorry women, this was a male only club, you had to trust in your husband's circumcision) and then to strictly follow the Law that was given to Moses.

In addition to this Jewish self-perception of elevated status, circumcision, and Law, they had a concept of the Holy Spirit that is important to highlight. The Holy Spirit was always viewed as a sign of God's anointing on the leadership of the nation. In other words, throughout the Old Testament the Holy Spirit would temporarily come upon one leader – a prophet, a judge, or a king – and empower him to lead the nation out of bondage and into freedom. It was absolutely unthinkable to the Jewish mind that the Holy Spirit would be poured out into the life of an uncircumcised Gentile.

Jesus was a Jew. His original apostles were also Jewish. The Jews had been long awaiting the promised deliverer – The Messiah – to arrive and lead them into the Kingdom of God. The first audience of the good news of Jesus was Jewish, so it was very easy for them to assimilate the theology of Jesus into their Jewish self-perception. So, the early Christians tended to continue thinking along these lines: God loves the Jews only, God promised a Messiah to lead the Jews to freedom, Jesus is the Messiah, faith in Jesus gives us access to the promised Holy Spirit of Israel and to spiritual freedom, therefore God still loves the Jews and has fulfilled us through Jesus. With this logic it made total sense for them to maintain all the customs, rituals, and traditions of the Jewish way of life. In the mind and theology of the Jewish Christians, ALL followers of Jesus would naturally want to be circumcised, observe the Sabbath, attend all the feasts, make the offerings at the temple, follow all the dietary laws of Leviticus, and stay far away from Gentile dogs and sinners.

Enter Paul. He began his life as a "Pharisee of Pharisees" – in other words, a legalistic self-inflated religious "right." He was thoroughly entrenched in the Jewish self-perception that was just described. Now however, something very strange was happening. Paul the Pharisee was doing the unthinkable. He was venturing into pagan cities. Not only was he going into these pagan cities, he also had the audacity to claim that God had poured out the Holy Spirit on these uncircumcised swine without any association with the covenant of circumcision or adherence to the

Law of Moses. This was impossible, unthinkable, an affront to God Almighty, and a work of Satan himself. This heresy must be stopped quickly before the very fabric of the universe was sent spiraling irreversibly down the slippery slope of syncretism, heresy, and idolatry. God save us all.

After all, who was Paul anyway? Was he there when Jesus walked the earth and trained his apostles? No. Was he trained by Peter, James, or John during the early days when Stephen and Philip were added to the team? No. In fact, he took part in the murder of Stephen and was raging against our brothers in the early days. We heard that he met Jesus on the way to Damascus, but then he vanished. He hasn't been back to Jerusalem since then. What has he been doing? How do we know he's telling the truth? How can we trust him? How do we know that he hasn't been deceived by Satan and is being used as his tool to desecrate the name of Jesus in Gentile regions? We must go to those cities in Galatia and show them the truth before it is too late. Those poor people need to be circumcised and be taught the truth of the Law before they hurt themselves and many other people. We owe it to God to right the wrongs that this imposter Paul has been doing!

That is how his enemies saw Paul. In light of that perspective can you imagine the struggle that Paul must have faced, both internally and externally, every day of his life? In this letter to the Galatian church we can feel the passion of Paul bursting through every line. At times he gets downright nasty and explodes in rash statements like "I wish those teachers would be eternally condemned!" "You foolish Galatians!" and, my personal favorite, "if they want to circumcise themselves, then I wish they would go ahead and cut the whole thing off!" OUCH!!!!

We can't really blame Paul. Here he was trying to demonstrate to the world that God loves everyone and that God's grace is, and always has been, accessible to anyone that simply has faith in Him. Now, made crystal clear through the ministry of Jesus, God was bringing healing and reconciliation to the world through the ministry of the Spirit in love. All Paul wanted was to show healing and peace to people who had been so long ostracized by God's "elect," but all he observed from the "religious" was a ministry of hatred, anger, and violence. That kind of religious abuse would take its toll on even the strongest person.

As we journey with Paul by reading his personal mail we will see that on more than one occasion he takes time to respond to his attackers by

Reading Paul's Mail

establishing his credentials as a legitimate apostle of Jesus. As you read 1:13-2:21 Paul explains his history in order to establish that he is a legitimate apostle and representative of Jesus. Put simply, in this passage Paul says,

"I completely understand the Jewish perspective, I was a hyper-Jew, remember. Yet, Jesus confronted me personally. Jesus removed me from the Jewish apostles and taught me the raw, clean, universal good news of His love for everyone. He personally told me to go to the Gentiles. In 17 years of ministry I spent a total of 15 days in Jerusalem and spoke only with Peter and James. Other than that I have been living in the Gentile world. When I did finally go to Jerusalem to report what happened in Galatia and how the Spirit came on everyone, the leaders couldn't deny it. They accepted it. They added nothing to my message. Anyone who opposes the work that God is doing among the Gentiles -- a work that has nothing to do with following the Jewish way of life -- is denying the gospel of Jesus and is making His death on the cross a worthless and meaningless act. I'm sticking to my story because it is the truth that I received directly from Jesus."

To conclude today's thoughts, I'd like to encourage you. The message of Jesus is simple. God loves everyone. Everyone is welcome. Jesus taught us to love God and follow in the path of faith and love. There are no rules to bog it down...only the rule to love. There are many people in the world today who want to make it more complicated than that. They want to make being a "Christian" about a political philosophy or a moralistic legal system. They want to make it a cloning tool where everyone looks and acts exactly the same. In so doing, they heap guilt, shame, blame, fear, and hatred into the spiritual gene pool. Perhaps you feel attacked by these well-intentioned Christians. If you do, remember that Paul was too. It isn't easy to keep the message simple. Just remember, God does love you more than you can even imagine. Keep focused on the ministry of Jesus. *Be* the love of God, even to those who are trying to hurt you. I pray that Paul's words in this letter will be an ointment of healing for your battered soul.

Lesson 2

- Galatians 2

Study Questions

What conclusion did the church leaders come to regarding Paul's ministry to the Gentiles? Why?

What was the one practice they agreed to be united about? Why do you think that is true?

Why was Paul so angry with Peter?

Paraphrase vv. 14-21 in your own words in order to understand exactly what Paul is telling Peter.

Food for Thought

In chapter 2 Paul concludes the presentation of his personal credentials. By recounting his personal history he is emphasizing the fact that not only God, but also the founding leaders of the church in Jerusalem have validated his Gentile ministry.

For today, let's highlight three points from this chapter.

Two Ministries, One Faith

As we discussed in ch. 1, the "Judaizers" were convinced that a person must become fully engrained in the Jewish way of life – observing Sabbath, being circumcised, going to temple feasts, and following dietary law – in order to be a 'true Christian.' Paul is fighting, tooth and nail, against this form of ethnic exclusivism and cultural elitism/prejudice. In this passage we see that Paul's interaction with the leaders of the church in Jerusalem set a beautiful precedent for ministry that has valuable implications for life in our world. In vv. 1-10 Paul basically says, "We put our heads together and agreed that the Christian life in the Jewish culture looks and feels different than the Christian life in the Gentile world...and that's OK. It is OK for Christian Jews to follow the Jewish culture...really, it is. It is also OK for Gentile Christians to NOT follow the Jewish culture. We can shake hands in the 'right hand of fellowship' and agree to disagree on many, many practical areas of daily living. What unifies us is our faith in Jesus."

This debate is alive and well in the church today. Many people tend to look back to a place in history and, with a flourish of nostalgia and idealism claim that THAT way of life is how it should be NOW and ALWAYS. Some want to follow the laws of Moses. Some want to be like the Desert Fathers of the Middle Ages and be completely secluded from society and deny their bodies of physical pleasures like sex, drink, and good food. Some want to be like the pilgrims of the New England colonies and follow a strict Calvinist Confession. Some want to be like the Jesus People of the 60's and 'just love, man'. All of these people (and there are many more, to be sure) are looking backwards to a way of life and customs from another era and culture and say that Christians MUST look like that in order to be 'true Christians.'

On the other side of the debate there are those who don't want to look back to a past culture at all, but are looking forward and trying to understand our current culture and the path it is on, and the possible ways that it may unfold.

These future-thinking people are trying to find ways to make the timeless message of Jesus (not subsequent communities of Christians) relevant and accessible to the current and future cultures.

These two perspectives have great potential to clash when it comes to practical, everyday living. Just try to imagine a pot-luck where the following Christians have assembled for "fellowship."

Here is the cast of characters:

- A monk in a brown robe who believes that women in general and sexuality specifically are evil
- A Calvinist puritan man in a wide-brimmed hat with his submissive wife sitting in another room
- A 'green' vegetarian woman who believes that Christians should only shop at fair trade stores in order to fight economic injustice
- A 'kosher' Messianic Jewish couple that follows all the dietary laws of the Old Testament
- A pierced and tattooed, male, Hispanic, inner-city tagger (graffiti artist) who had never stepped foot in a church or read a Bible before the age of 17, but has been filled with the Spirit and speaks in tongues.

What would the kosher guy do when the tagger slapped a slice of pizza with ham and extra cheese on his plate? What would the puritan do when the female vegetarian wanted to open in prayer? You can imagine hundreds of ways in which these people could pass judgment on one another and privately think, "That person could not possibly be a Christian, they do _____!"

Who's right in this picture? Who's wrong? They all claim to love Jesus. They all claim to use the same Bible as their source of authority. How could these people live in unity?

This is a picture of the church in the world today. What should we do about it? We need to look to these 10 verses and follow the example of Paul and Peter. Let's shake hands and say, "I may not agree with the way you live, but I believe with all my heart that God's Kingdom is big enough for you to follow Jesus in the way you are doing it. You reach the people God has called you to reach, and I'll reach the people God called me to reach. Together, by being unified in faith, and diversified in practical fellowship, we can take the love of God to the whole world."

Old Habits Die Hard

In vv. 11-21 we see an intense confrontation between Paul and Peter. Peter had said with his words that he accepted this non-Jewish form of Christianity, but when push came to shove, and the heat was on from the Jewish Christians, Peter caved into the pressure and separated himself from the Gentile Christians. Paul was outraged and read Peter the riot act.

Looking at it from one perspective it would be easy for us to get discouraged by Peter's behavior and join Paul in pointing an accusing finger at him. However, we can also be encouraged by Peter's behavior. Good old Peter. He seems to be the poster child for what not to do as a Christian and church leader. He boasted about never leaving Jesus, and then he betrayed Him three times. Jesus forgave him and got him back on track by commissioning him to be a great leader of the church. In Galatians 2 Peter blows it with the Gentile believers. Yes, it was wrong, but I think we can cut Peter some slack and give him some grace. It is very difficult for people to cross over the kind of cultural bridges that Paul was asking the Jewish Christians to cross. Sometimes it takes a long time, and, in fact, it often never completely happens. Some people come a long way, but, truth be told, they are still a little uncomfortable with "those" kind of Christians.

As we move into the 21st century, let's be careful to give a lot of grace and understanding to each other. As we look across the field at the other camps of Christians, let's be careful not to throw stones at each other and remember that we are all on a journey that starts from very different places. They start different and take different paths, but, in the end, all lead into the heart of God. After all, if Peter struggled with this stuff, it will probably be hard for us to change and accept people that are different than us as well.

Dying to Live

In v. 20 Paul gives us one of the key principles to living life in the new world of freedom in the Spirit. He said, "I have been crucified with Christ and I no longer live, but Christ lives in me." If we want to live fully in the Kingdom of God and be the kind of people that Jesus wants us to be, then we need to get first things first. It's not about us. It's not about getting what we want. It's not about being "right" or having control over people, organizations, or situations. The first thing we should do when we wake up every day is to die. We must die to ourselves; die to our pride and our selfish desires. Not only that, we must also die to our addictions; our addictions to defeat, to despair, to self-hatred, to bitterness, to complaining, to negativity and a critical spirit. All of these things strive to control our lives and cause us to walk in the shadows of self. When we realize that all that stuff is meaningless and distracting from the love of God, then we can join Jesus in His death and die to those things.

For the Galatians, Paul was encouraging them to die to the Law. They did not need to slavishly follow Levitical regulations. Instead, if they identify themselves with the New Creation that comes through Jesus' resurrection from the dead, then the love of God could rule in their hearts and they would naturally obey God's fundamental law of love as the authentic overflow of their hearts.

Here is a daily prayer that we can use. Kill Me, Fill Me, Spill Me. Kill my pride and selfishness, Fill me with your Spirit and your purpose, overflow your love through me so that everyone I meet will see the freeing power of your Spirit through my life.

Lesson 3

- Galatians 3

Study Questions

Read Genesis 12:1-3ff

What promise did God make to Abraham?

What made Abraham "justified" in God's eyes? Why?

What point is Paul trying to make by bringing up Abraham in the letter to the Galatians?

According to Galatians 3, what was the purpose of the Law and its relationship between the Law and the present state of freedom in the Spirit?

What implications might v. 28 have on the church in our world today?

Food for Thought

Blessed to be a Blessing

Notice what Paul highlights in v. 8. He is recounting the covenant that God made with Abraham in Genesis 12, but he only highlights the phrase "All nations will be blessed through you." As we have already discussed, in the first century, the average Jew would have interpreted this verse to mean, "any nation that wants to abandon its culture and become Jewish will be blessed." Paul continues to deconstruct this distortion of truth by pointing out that the idea of "Jewish" wasn't even a reality when Abraham was alive. In fact, God had fully accepted Abraham and counted him as "righteous" in the law courts of God BEFORE he was circumcised. It wasn't any outward act or ethnic identity that made him special, it was simply his faith.

Notice how Paul very cleverly bypasses the entire Moses story and the Old Testament history and connects the faith of Abraham to the ministry of Jesus. By doing this he strips Israel of all potential ammunition to go back and say, "But Moses told us that we shouldn't do _____, or that we should do _____." Paul is saying, "It doesn't really matter what Moses says at this point. Moses helped to define you as a unique nation. He kept you safe. However, the purpose of your nation was to be a blessing to all nations. You were set aside to become the servant of all nations and a conduit of God's grace to the whole world. Instead, you took your gift and turned it into a curse, shutting the door of the Kingdom in the faces of everyone in the world, and, ironically, cutting yourself off from the Gracious Kingdom of God yourselves.

Now, Jesus stands before the whole world and makes the same offer that God made to Abraham. I will bless you to be a blessing to others. I will forgive you and empower you to forgive others and bring healing to the nations. That is grace and, if you believe it to be true (faith), you will walk in the love of God, no matter who you are or where you are from.

No Classes

There is one more key principle found in v. 27. When we are 'clothed with Christ' our class distinctions disappear. Paul said that there is "neither Jew nor Greek, slave nor free, male nor female." That list may not mean much to us, but perhaps something like this would ring a little louder: in Christ there is neither Republican nor Democrat, black or white, conservative or liberal, rich or poor. In v. 27 Paul was tearing down the social structure of his day. The Jews and Greeks hated each other and believed the other was worthless. Slaves were simply pawns in the hands of the authorities, principalities, and powers of the empire. Women were worth little more than cattle and were only 'saved in childbirth" – meaning they were good for nothing but giving sons to their husbands. Those were the oppressive systems that humans had constructed. Man's natural propensity is to be self-centered and to construct a social system that will profit the strongest and keep the weak and the opposition at bay. In the ancient world the male was physically stronger than the female so the majority of cultures developed one form of male domination or another. Conquering armies took the prisoners of war as slaves to demoralize the defeated nation. All of these things are evidences and consequences of a fallen and sinful human system. Jesus came to reverse all of these inequities. He came to set the captive free. He came to bring healing and freedom for the sick and imprisoned. In Jesus there are no class, race, ethnic, or gender differences. When we wear the clothes of Jesus we are judged only by our spirit – by the integrity of our character and the gifts that we have been given – and are called to contribute equally to the body of Christ so that we can be a blessing to the world.

Lesson 4

- Galatians 4

Study Questions

How does Paul use the images of a servant and a son in this passage? Why?

What brought Paul to the Galatians in the first place?

What did Hagar represent?

What did Sarah represent?

How does this allegory match up with the original story found in Genesis 16?

What is Paul's point in this allegory?

Galatians

Food for Thought

Paul uses a strange, yet common teaching method in chapter 4. It is called allegory and was used quite often by both Greek and Jewish teachers in the time of Paul. Allegory was a method of preserving the validity of the ancient, holy texts – Homer for the Greeks and the Torah for the Jews – while sidestepping the need to acknowledge a literal interpretation of the characters and/or events of the story.

Fortunately for us, Paul tells us very clearly that he is using the allegorical method to explain the relationship between the law and freedom in Christ.

For the purpose of this study, let's look at two lessons we can glean from this allegory:

No longer slaves

Paul's point in this analogy is very clear. The Law is a dead system that was good when it was established but has run its course. To continue following the Law (all the rituals and customs that created a Jewish self-perception) after the deliverance through Jesus would be to submit to a form of slavery and oppression.

Using the Old Testament

If you are familiar with the story of Genesis then Paul's allegory may have left you scratching your head. In the original story Hagar was the slave of Abraham and gave him a child through natural conception. Sarah was his wife and she conceived through a miracle in fulfillment of God's promise. So far, so good; Paul is tracking with the original story. If you were a Jew in Paul's day you would have stopped Paul right there and said, "Wait! I know what you're going to say. Hagar represents all of those awful Gentiles that God hates and Sarah represents us, the offspring of Isaac and Jacob, the inheritors of the holy city of Jerusalem. Right?"

Uh, no. Actually it's just the opposite. The offspring of Isaac and Jacob, the inheritors of the holy city of Jerusalem, are the children of the slave woman. Whoa! Them there's fightin' words, Paul!

Through his use of allegory Paul did a total reversal on the Jewish thinkers reinterpreted a passage of scripture that had been commonly accepted for centuries. As students of the Bible this must at least give us pause to wonder exactly what is going in here. How did the New Testament writers view the Old Testament and interpret it for the church? The irony for us is that if Paul had submitted this interpretation of Genesis to a modern Hermeneutics (the study of Bible Interpretation) professor, he would have failed the class because we are taught that you can't play with the original story that way.

So, what's going on here? Was Paul a bad Bible teacher? Of course not. He's one of the best that ever lived. There are two reasons why Paul was able to interpret the Old Testament in this way. First, he could do it because it was the commonly accepted method of teaching in his day. Secondly, Paul was able to do this because he had encountered Jesus and saw the Old Testament through new lenses.

Why am I spending so much time on this point? For students of the Bible in the 21st century and as inheritors of Modern Protestantism, we need to be aware of a couple things.

1. There are some Christian Doctrines that have been handed down to us through the centuries that appear to be "Biblical," and self-evident. In many ways the Christian community has fallen into the same trap that the Jewish community did in Paul's day. We can tend to think that we are the chosen ones and that everybody else is simply out of luck. We think that our cherished Christian practices of not doing this and doing that are what set us apart as "holy" and we try so hard to keep ourselves separated from the "sinners" and we remind the "sinners" of their status as often as possible. Yet, all the while we are actually living in the prison of pride and hatred as the offspring of the slave woman.

2. It was the Jesus event in Paul's life that helped him to see scripture in a new way. As Modern Protestants we have had a tendency to elevate the Bible to a god status. At times we have done this so much that we no longer have room for the Jesus event to take place in our own hearts, for the Holy Spirit to blow through us so that God's love can take root and grow. Each generation needs to have this happen. We need to ask God to show us what it means to be children of Promise, not of Law. How can we walk in faith and love that brings light, hope, and promise to the whole world?

Lesson 5

- Galatians 5-6

Study Questions

Why did Jesus set us free?

Why does Paul not want the Galatians to turn to Judaism and the Law? What is at stake?

How does Paul feel about his opponents? Why?

Compare and contrast the list of the "works of the flesh" with the "fruit of the Spirit." What do you observe?

Explain the idea, "a man reaps what he sows."

What does it mean to be a "new creation?"

Summarize the message of ch. 5-6 in your own words.

Food for Thought

Freedom. Paul's message can be summed up in that one word. Jesus came to set us free. This statement begs the question, "Free from what?" The Greek word that Paul uses is *eleutheria* and literally means to not be a slave. For the Greek culture it was only the "freeman" who could have any say or responsibility in government. A slave was nothing more than a beast of burden that possessed no level of right or privilege in society. As Americans, the idea of freedom is central to our self-identity. Our country was founded on the idea that no one person had the right to govern other human beings. We believe that there are certain inalienable rights that all humans possess. Isn't it interesting that it has taken over 200 years for a country that claims equal rights for all people to allow equality to all people.

In our day there are great battles raging over what freedom really means. If you were to take a "man-on-the-street" interview and ask people to define freedom you would probably hear things like, "I can do whatever I want," or "not having anybody on my back about anything." The lines of freedom and responsibility have become dangerously blurred. Where does my freedom to do anything I want end and my responsibility to the health and safety of the community begin?

Ironically, freedom is a very scary word for the religious establishment. One of the reasons that Paul's enemies were so afraid of his teaching is because they thought they he was teaching a doctrine of anarchy. "Without the Law," they would argue, "how can we know what God wants from us? If we follow your ways, Paul, and just 'let the Spirit lead' then aren't we opening ourselves up to all kinds of dangers? We know who we are by the laws we follow and if we step outside of that then we could lose everything, maybe even our salvation!"

In chapter 5 Paul responds to this challenge. "Yes, it is for freedom that we have been set free, but not the kind of freedom that you are talking about. You are talking about the recklessness that people mistakenly think is freedom. That is freedom according to the 'flesh.' I'm talking about true freedom; freedom in the Spirit."

He goes on to define true freedom by contrasting it to freedom in the flesh. Let's look at the lists that he presents in the original language.

Galatians

The works of the Flesh

porneia – extramarital intercourse; "to play the harlot"

akatharsis – the opposite of katharsis (to be clean), thus it means to be unclean.

aselgeia – license; the sense that you can do anything you want to do; usually refers to sexual excess.

eidolatreia – a compound word combining "eidol" (the image of a god) with "latreia" (service). It means the service or worship of a humanly constructed image.

pharmakeia – the use of drugs or potions in the magical arts.

ekthra -- "Hatred," "hostility" is a disposition, objective opposition, and actual conflict.

eris -- strife, quarrel, especially rivalry, contention, wrangling

zelos – "zeal;" the motivating energy behind actions; it can be well directed or misdirected; in conjunction with hatred and strife, it is a selfish motivation.

thumos – wrath; violent movement; to boil up

eritheia -- The idea is "base self-seeking," the "baseness" that cannot shift its gaze to higher things.[2]

dichostasia – division, dissension, objective disunity.

heresis – "sects;" small divisions of distinctive belief that exclude each other. We get the word "heresy" from it.

phthonos – envy; the feeling of displeasure produced by witnessing or hearing of the advantage or prosperity of others[3]

methe – to be drunk

komos - drinking parties involving unrestraing indulgence in alcoholic beverages and accompanying immoral behavior—'orgy, revelling, carousing.'[4]

The Fruit of the Spirit

agape -- love; God's kind of selfless love for the other.

chara -- joy; Joy expresses the whole person and aims at sharing, as in festal joy.[5]

eirene -- peace; the opposite of war

makrothumia - the combination of "makro" (long distance) and "thumia" (wrath; violent movement; to boil up); longsuffering; being willing to put up with each other for a very long time; distancing our wrath from one another. **contrast this with "thumos" listed in the fruit of the flesh.

chrestotes -- kindness; allowing space for repentance, even when punishment is deserved.

agathosune - the highest good possible; only God is good and He has demonstrated His goodness through His love and kindness in Jesus.

pistis -- faith; faithfulness; placing trust in something and then never giving up on it.

prautes - This word means "mild and gentle friendliness." ... Gentleness is a mark of culture and wisdom if it does not degenerate into self-abasement.[6]

enkrateia -- takes its sense from the stem *krat*- denoting power or lordship. *enkráteia* means "dominion over the self or something," with the nuances of "steadfastness" and "self-control"[7]

17

Here are two basic observations about the 'works of the flesh':

1. **They substitute the artificial for the real thing.** Instead of true intimacy between a husband and wife, it is cheap sex between two strangers. Instead of true healing through faith and submission to God's will, it's hocus pocus and magic potions to get what you want. Instead of the mysterious, infinite God, it's a hunk of wood or stone shaped into a beast. It's all about living to gratify the immediate desire instead of trusting in the bigger-picture plan of the Father. It's like being addicted to spiritual Twinkies when you should be eating a well-balanced diet.

2. **It's all about self-gratification.** The battle cry of the flesh is "look out for number one." The flesh is motivated by trying to figure out how to get out of other people what you need to make your life more comfortable and to get what you want.

3. **The byproduct is division.** Hatred, strife, anger boiling over, dividing into factions or 'sects' that are little spiritual ghettos of those who think they are "right" while everyone else is "wrong:" -- these are the character qualities of the flesh. When people function according to these "basic principles" then society will become a pressure cooker for death and destruction. Sin isolates. Isolation is Hell. People who live according to the flesh are creating Hell for themselves each day.

Now contrast the fruit of the Spirit. Everything is about the other. It is about placing the needs of others above the needs of self. It's about giving. It's about going the extra mile and not accusing or condemning but forgiving each other. It's about being controlled by the Spirit within you, not by a substance or a compulsion from outside you. It is the way of love. It is for this that we have been set free. In Jesus, in the Spirit, we are free to love.

There are three statements that summarize the letter to the Galatians. Paul is pleading with his people, "Don't get roped into a legalistic religious system...

The only thing that counts is faith expressing itself through love.

Do not use your freedom to indulge the sinful nature; rather, serve one another in love.

A man reaps what he sows.

Here's the bottom line. It doesn't matter what culture you live in. It doesn't matter what denomination your church belongs to. It doesn't matter what external rules you do or do not follow. What matters is if Jesus has grasped your heart and you are being changed from the inside out – a new creation. If you sow to anger, dissension, pride, etc. you will reap the Hell of your own design. If you sow to the Spirit then you will walk in the Spirit – in the Kingdom that Jesus brought to the Earth – both now and for eternity; ever growing in the love of God.

(Footnotes)

[1] For a good introduction to these forms of criticism please read Marshall. Exploring the New Testament. IVP

[2] Kittel, G., Friedrich, G., & Bromiley, G. W. (1995, c1985). *Theological dictionary of the New Testament.* Translation of: Theologisches Worterbuch zum Neuen Testament. Grand Rapids, Mich.: W.B. Eerdmans.

[3] Vine, W., & Bruce, F. (1981; Published in electronic form by Logos Research Systems, 1996). *Vine's Expository dictionary of Old and New Testament words.* Old Tappan NJ: Revell.

[4] Louw, J. P., & Nida, E. A. (1996, c1989). *Greek-English lexicon of the New Testament : Based on semantic domains.* New York: United Bible societies.

[5] Kittel, G., Friedrich, G., & Bromiley, G. W. (1995, c1985). *Theological dictionary of the New Testament.* Translation of: Theologisches Worterbuch zum Neuen Testament. Grand Rapids, Mich.: W.B. Eerdmans.

[6] ibid.

[7] ibid.

1 Thessalonians

As Paul embarked on his second journey (Acts 16-18), he had his sights set on Ephesus. This would have been a logical place to set up a mission outpost since Ephesus was the heart and soul of the Eastern side of the Aegean Sea. God had others plans for Paul. God called him to a Northern town called Troas. In this city Paul had a vision of a man from Macedonia, the province across the Aegean Sea, beckoning him to cross the water and preach to them. In obedience Paul set sail and worked his way across the Via Egnatia, the main trade route of the Roman Empire. In Philippi he was beaten, imprisoned, and asked to leave. After this he went to the city of Thessalonica. This city was the main seaport of Macedonia and had a large enough, and diverse enough, population to support a Jewish synagogue. Here Paul slipped into his normal routine. First he went to the synagogue and told them that Jesus was the Messiah that the Jewish scriptures had predicted. Some Jews and "God-fearing" Greeks believed Paul's message and a church was formed. Then, the second inevitable phase of his ministry began. The majority of Jews grew jealous and angry with Paul. They caused a riot and dragged Paul before the Roman magistrate accusing Paul of advocating a King other than Caesar. This was a treasonous offense and Paul's life was put in danger. In fear for his life, the new group of believers snuck Paul out of the city during the night and promised the government that he would never return. Thus, a newly formed church was prematurely deprived of its founder, teacher, and spiritual parent; they were ripe for confusion and sitting ducks for spiritual predators.

After his nocturnal escape Paul went to Berea, but was quickly chased out of that city by the Thessalonian mob. Eventually he landed in Athens to wait for the heat to die down and the political dust to settle. He wanted to get back to the Thessalonians but was blocked by adversarial forces. (Satan means "adversary") All the while he was deeply concerned for the wellbeing of his infant church in Thessalonica. "Timothy, please go back to Thessalonica and see how the church is doing. I'm so afraid that they will be beaten down under the persecution at the hand of our enemies and convinced to turn away from the message of Jesus. Go quickly and bring back news!"

Timothy did go to the Thessalonians, and with him he brought back some good news and a question. "Paul, you can relax a little bit. The good news is that the church has not caved into the pressure of the opposition. In fact, they have grown stronger in their faith under the heat. Their reputation for being faithful under pressure is so good that it is spreading throughout the whole region. There is a little issue of concern, though. They have a question. You know how you taught them that Jesus would return to establish his glorious Kingdom once and for all, and that they should place their hope in this return? Well, since you left some of the brothers have died (maybe they were killed, we're not sure). The people are very concerned about this. They thought Jesus was coming right back and that everyone would share in his Kingdom. Now that the brothers are dead, will they miss out on this glorious event? What should they think about this?"

This is the context for the First letter to the Thessalonians. In the first three lessons we will focus on this letter and listen in as Paul praises the church like a doting Father. He also instructs them with some practical issues that they need to work on. Finally, he encourages them to continue putting their hope in Jesus' return and to live as children of God. For us, we will benefit greatly as we listen to Paul's instructions on holy living. We will also be intrigued as we will peek into the larger topic of Jesus' return.

Lesson 1

- 1 Thessalonians 1-2

Study Questions

How does Paul feel about the Thessalonians? Why?

How does Paul describe their lifestyle?

Based upon Paul's self-defensive language, what accusations do you think are being made against him?

Why is Paul not with the Thessalonians in person?

Food for Thought

The simple message

The relief and pride is easy to detect in Paul's voice. He is so happy that his church is safe and is growing in light of all the difficulties that being a Jesus follower has caused them in society.

There is a golden nugget for us in vv. 9-10. Paul spells out the simple message of the gospel. This is probably an echo of the message that Paul presented to non-Jewish people in his evangelistic mission. As we look at it we can get a clue as to what to present to people that have no "Judeo/Christian baggage" to sift through. The message is clear:

> Turn from idols to serve the living and true God
>
> His Son was raised from the dead
>
> Wait for His Son from heaven
>
> He rescues us from the coming wrath.

Here's a project for you. Let's say you were sharing the good news of Jesus with a group of people who had no prior knowledge of the Bible (that group is increasing within the American urban scene, by the way). How would you communicate the above list in a way that they would understand? What are "idols" in our culture? What is the general concept of "god" in the culture? How would you communicate the idea of God's Son making a sacrifice, rising from the dead, and returning to bring Justice?

We are legit

In the majority of today's reading we find Paul having to defend himself once again. As you read the list of "nots" in vv. 3-9 you can just hear Paul's enemies firing off a list of accusations. That was their tactic. If they were to win the Thessalonian church back away from the message of Jesus then they had to commit character assassination on Paul. "How could you listen to Paul? He's just a rabble rouser. He's just another snake oil salesman coming through town looking for some gullible twits to believe his fairy tales and 'donate to his cause.' You've been manipulated and played like fools. Turn away from this charlatan before you get really hurt."

These constant accusations put Paul in a very difficult situation. If he says nothing then it sounds like he's guilty. Yet, as he defends himself he risks sounding arrogant or pompous. You can hear the tone of his voice change from chapter 1 to chapter 2. He says, "Please, guys. You can't honestly believe that our time together was a failure. I wasn't in it for the money. I worked hard to support myself so that you wouldn't have to. I wasn't using you, I love you. I've been like a mother and a father to you. I haven't abandoned you. I've been trying to get back to you, but Satan keeps stopping me. Please believe that I love you."

There are two points for today:

1. You have to either believe Paul or not. This may seem crass, but it's true. As it was in Paul's day, so it is in ours. It was Paul's word against his enemies. Paul's evidence for the validity of his ministry was this: he claimed that Jesus personally trained and sent him, people received the Holy Spirit through his ministry in the same way that the Holy Spirit came at Pentecost, and he never begged for money for himself but worked hard in order to not be a burden. His ministry was always other-oriented and Jesus-glorifying. If you are going to continue reading the letters and benefit from them, then you need to choose whether you believe Paul is legit or not. If you are not convinced, what further research would you need to do in order to make a decision one way or the other?

2. Presenting the message of Jesus is risky business. Ultimately, the call to follow Jesus is a call away from the status quo and the service of the cultural power structures. Whenever you reject the accepted "idols" – like money, fame, power, security, and imperial power – you will risk being ostracized, misunderstood, ridiculed, and persecuted by the status quo. The Thessalonians thrived under the pressure and placed their hope in the Jesus who would one day establish true Justice on the earth. Have you placed your full trust in him today, or are there still some areas of status quo lingering in your heart?

Lesson 2

- 1 Thessalonians 3-4

Study Questions

Why did Paul send Timothy back to the Thessalonians?

What did Timothy discover?

How does this news affect Paul?

What does Paul pray for the church?

List the specific instructions Paul gives the church? Are any of these problem areas in your life?

How does Paul encourage the church? Why?

Food for Thought

A Father's prayer

One of my favorite things about Paul's letters is the many prayers that he offers up for his people. As a matter of fact, here's a challenge. As we go through these letters together, pay special attention and watch for these prayers. Mark them down and make a collection. At the end of the study you'll have a wonderful little prayer book that will help you to be able to pray more effectively for the people in your life.

In 3:11-13 we find one of these prayers. Paul asks for three things

1. **May I be able to return to you**. This is a specific request that demonstrates his genuine love for the Thessalonian church.

2. **May your love increase and overflow**. Here, again, we see the idea of overflow. If we want to love the world, then we must first be filled up with the love of God. We need to believe that God loves us and that we are safe in His love. When we know this then we can love ourselves and be filled up with all that we need. Once we are set free and know the love of God, then we can overflow that love to everyone around us and be the conduit of God's blessing to everyone we meet.

3. **May He strengthen your heart so that you will be blameless and holy**. The heart is the center of who we are. This verse echoes Proverbs 4:23, "Above all else, guard your heart for it is the wellspring of life." If we want to live holy lives that reflect the glory of God, then it starts with the heart. We must have a strong resolve to not allow "enemy spies" to enter our mind and heart to distract us from Jesus. Part of the spiritual growth process is to learn practical ways to have a 'strong heart.' We need a spiritual calisthenics program for a strong spiritual/cardiovascular system.

Special Instructions

Paul give the Thessalonians four specific "work out routines" to strengthen their hearts. Remember, this is not an exhaustive list for everyone. Paul is like a personal trainer and these four areas are the areas that he knows the Thessalonians need to work on. We all need to work on these areas and watch out for them, but they may or may not be on the top of YOUR list right now.

Sexual Purity

The Greek word for this is *porneia* from which we get the word pornography. To the Greeks, *porneia* was sexual activity outside of marriage. Apparently this was a real problem among the Greek community. It happened on two levels. On one hand there was a common practice of prostitution with the "temple virgins." As a part of their religious experience the men would have sex with both women and men (depending upon the god) in order to get the gods aroused and willing to provide fertility to the crops. This was one of the main reasons that idol worship was so detestable to God. (Not to mention that the 'gods' were not true gods but cheap imposters.) On the other hand, there was a 'fast and loose' morality among the people. It was common practice to try to win another man's wife and extra-marital affairs were happening all the time.

Notice why Paul says porneia was so wrong. In v. 6 he says that we should exercise self-control so that we don't wrong our brother and take advantage of him. This issue is of extreme importance in our world since "free love" and "freedom of sexual expression" is one of the loudest voices in the crowd. How do you explain to a sexually promiscuous, non-Judeo/Christian society that *porneia* is destructive without sounding self-righteous, pompous, and condemning? Paul's argument in v. 6 is a good start. The purpose of sex is to be a physical expression of commitment and trust. True physical intimacy is the ultimate other-oriented act of submissive love. When the center of sex becomes the self and the gratifying of selfish desires, then the other person becomes an object to be used. Cheap sex is actually a form of abuse and is destructive to the other. When a person hops around from partner to partner they are not thinking about the other, but only about themselves. The more this happens the more difficult it becomes for them to trust others and to trust themselves. The more their physical urges are met, the deeper their true heart is buried behind a wall of calloused self-protection. Only through the commitment of marriage can the true purpose of sexuality be fully expressed and the heart set free to love fully.

Brotherly Love

Notice how brotherly love flowed right out of the warning against *porneia*. The Thessalonians were good at loving their brother, but perhaps they had not connected porneia with brotherly love. You can't love your brother if you are using him sexually.

Hard Work

Paul shoots off three quick rounds: lead a quiet life, mind your own business, and work with your hands. These are pretty straight forward instructions. I think we can all picture the person that is the opposite of these virtues. He's a freeloader who mooches off of others and sticks his nose where it doesn't belong. She's the housewife who has too much time on her hands and starts 'working the gossip circuit' with the other moms while waiting for the kids to get out of school. It's us, when we are tempted to make other people's business our business and the business of our friends.

Simply put, we need to strive for simplicity. It's that simple.

Hope in the Resurrection

4:13-18 most likely exposes the real purpose for Paul's writing of this letter. (**please note: remember that reading the letters is like trying to guess what is being said on the other end of someone's phone conversation) Apparently when Paul was in Thessalonica he placed a great emphasis on Jesus' immanent return. In other words, Paul probably believed, as so taught the Thessalonians, that Jesus was going to return within their lifetime and very soon indeed.

Stop and imagine this for a moment. The people of the Thessalonian church were of two kinds (at least). First there were the Jews. They had experienced oppression from various empires for the past 700 years. Here in Thessalonica they were the minority group within a Roman occupied Greek city. Their idea of the rulers, principalities, and authorities of empire and rule was one of oppression and suffering. The second group was the Greek who was also under the oppression of Rome. Centuries earlier Thessalonica had been the capital city of the Kingdom of Macedonia. It was the birthplace and launching pad of Alexander the Great and his conquest of the world. Now, it was an occupied city that had been subjugated by the Latin speaking Roman Emperor. The Greeks and Jews alike dreamed of a day when they could throw off the chains of Roman occupation and bask in a glorious Kingdom where they could be free.

The good news of Jesus was that He claimed to be the King of Kings and would someday return to establish His Kingdom. Imagine how you would feel and how you would live if you believed that within the year Jesus would return and wipe out the Romans, and you, being His disciple, would sit in a place of authority and see justice served on the oppressors.

This good news elicited two responses. In the oppressed it elicited hope and courage to change the status quo. In the oppressors it elicited alarm and forced the hand of authority to put down the rebellious rabble before things got out of control.

The people of Thessalonica were looking forward to being with Jesus when He set up His Kingdom, but they ran into a problem. Since the time that Paul had left the city some people had died in the church. The letter doesn't tell us how they died; perhaps they were old and it was their time, or perhaps they were executed as rebels by the government, we don't know. What we do know is that the theological understanding of Jesus' Kingdom was limited to the point that they did not know what to do with people who die. This gives us pause to wonder what it was that they did believe, exactly. For us, 2000 years later it seems so clear. Yet, the fact that they asked the question indicates that they had not yet understood the ideas of afterlife and what the "Kingdom of God" was really all about.

Paul had to assure them that death was not the end as was common belief among the Greeks and among certain sects of Jews. Our hope, as followers of Jesus, is in the resurrection. Jesus defeated death. He rose from the dead and ascended to heaven, promising that He would return. When He does return, the dead will rise first, and then all who are alive will be gathered together.

By the way, it is from this passage that the idea of "rapture" is drawn. The word "rapture" does not appear in the Bible. It is a Latin word that originally meant to be stolen away and came to mean any form of being transported. Often it meant to be transported emotionally into a state of great joy. Obviously, it was used to describe this passage in the sense of being caught up -- "stolen away" – with Jesus in the clouds on the day of His return.

The big question that Christians love to argue about is WHEN the rapture will take place. Well, you'll have to wait until lesson 5 to wrestle with that one. 2 Thessalonians deals with Jesus' return more explicitly so we will address it then. For now, it is important to note that the context of this passage is not to clearly articulate and map out the schema of the end times, but is simply to *encourage* the church in Thessalonica that those who had died will not miss out on the glory of Jesus' kingdom.

Lesson 3

- 1 Thessalonians 5

Study Questions

How will the Day of the Lord come?

What does that mean?

Describe how a "child of the day" should behave.

Which of these instructions is the biggest struggle for you? Why?

What can you do about it?

Food for Thought

In vv. 1-2 of chapter 5 Paul gives us one of the most important pieces of the 'end times' puzzle. He says that 'the day of the Lord' will come like a 'thief in the night.' What does this mean? It echoes Jesus' words in Matthew 24:26-27, "So if anyone tells you, 'There he is, out in the desert,' do not go out; or, 'Here he is, in the inner rooms,' do not believe it. For as lightning that comes from the east is visible even in the west, so will be the coming of the Son of Man."

In other words, "No one knows when it will happen, and, when it does happen, it will be quick, like a thief. No one expects the thief. So be ready!"

In Paul's concluding remarks, he draws upon a familiar metaphor. He very cleverly segues from his words about Jesus' return being like a thief in the night to talking about night vs. day; light vs. darkness; good vs. evil. From this metaphor there are three simple instructions:

Sons of the Day

It is important for the follower of Jesus to realize that he is a child of God. We are "Sons of the Day" not children of the Night. The good news of Jesus is the truth that He has brought us out of the darkness of fear, anger, self-hatred, selfishness, and self-destruction and has exposed to us that fact that the Creator of the universe is not a terrible ogre (like the Greek gods) who needs to be appeased, but is our loving Heavenly Father who has called us into a life of love, purity, and purpose. When we walk in the knowledge that we are children of the King, then we will walk in humble confidence that, no matter what anyone says or does, no one can remove us from the love of God.

Don't fear the "thief"

The great contrast in this passage is fear vs. hope. If you are living apart from the knowledge that God loves you, and if you are self-destructing in fear, anger, and self-absorption, then you live a life of fear. If death is the end and there is nothing more, then death is the enemy and is a fearful thought. If the gods are vindictive, selfish, self-absorbed entities that demand appeasement, then you live in fear for your life every moment. The idea of a god who will come "like a thief in the night" is one that, like a literal thief, would produce high levels of anxiety, fear, and self-protection.

Thessalonians

Jesus came to set us free from all that fear. As children of the day, with the lights turned on, we discover that the thief is not thief at all, but is our Daddy coming home from work. We look forward to that day with hope and joy, longing for the moment when we can scream in delight, "Daddy's home!" and run into His arms.

Live in the light

As is typical for Paul's letters, he concludes with a rapid-fire barrage of final thoughts for the church. It could be something like this, "Oh yes, I know I don't have much more time, and I'm running out of parchment, so, since you are children of the Light...live like it. Here's a list of things that you already know, but I want to remind you what God's children should look like so that you never forget to grow in these areas."

We could spend a long time on each one of these, but we don't have the space. I encourage you to use this list as a personal health checkup today. Meditate on each item and see how it is, or isn't, reflected in your life.

- Encourage one another
- Build each other up
- Respect your hard working leaders
- Live in peace with each other
- Warn the idle
- Encourage the timid
- Help the weak
- Be patient with everyone
- Be joyful always
- Pray continually
- Give thanks in all circumstances
- Don't put out the Spirit's fire (The Word of God is active through the Holy Spirit in the church, be open to that)
- Don't treat prophecies with contempt (God can still speak directly to your church)
- Test everything (just because someone says they have a word from the Lord doesn't mean they do...be wise)
- Hold onto the good (perhaps relating to the word of prophesy that is clearly from God)
- Avoid the evil (perhaps referring to the bogus 'word of prophecy' that comes from pretenders)

Supplemental note: the parenthetical notes in the last five points open up a huge discussion. Simply put, we need to be open to the idea that the Word of God is the dynamic interaction of God with humans through the Holy Spirit. Scripture is the inspired record of God's interaction with humanity. This has been a huge controversy in the church from its conception. Where is the balance between following the letter of the scripture vs. hearing the "Word of the Lord" through direct interaction with the Spirit?

Apparently this was an issue (albeit a side one in comparison) in the Thessalonian church. Paul's instructions are good for us today. Be open to the movement and instruction of the Spirit. Also, don't be stupid or gullible. Test everything against scripture and wisdom. Therein lies the fine balance. We need to be careful not to swing too far to one side or the other; we can't be too Bible focused or too Spirit focused. The two work hand in hand. Maturity and wisdom discovers where they blend. Hold to the good meat and throw out the bones!

2 Thessalonians

In between the writing of the First and Second letter Paul moved on to the city of Corinth and began an extended ministry there. Timothy brought back a response to the first letter and with it some shocking news. "Paul, you won't believe it. Someone has been circulating a crazy idea that Jesus has already returned! The Thessalonians are very worried that perhaps they misunderstood your teaching about Jesus' return and that they have missed out on the whole deal. Not only that, apparently many of the people have developed and attitude where they think that since Jesus is going to return so quickly (or that they have missed it altogether) that they don't have to work anymore. They think nothing matters since Jesus is going to change it all anyway. There is great confusion in the church, please write them back and shed some light on the subject."

In lessons 4 and 5 we will look at 2 Thessalonians. In the course of this entire study of Paul's letters this will be the only time we look at the topic of the "end times." When will Jesus return? What are the signs? It's been 2,000 years since Jesus and Paul's day, was Paul wrong about the second coming? Should we think about it at all, and, if so, in what way does it impact our lives today?

Lesson 4

- 2 Thessalonians 1-2

Study Questions

What will God's judgment do for the church? How?

What is Paul's prayer for the church?

What news alarmed the Thessalonians? Why?

What must happen before the Man of Lawlessness is revealed?

How does Paul describe the Thessalonians' relationship to the events related to the Man of Lawlessness?

How should they feel about these events? Why?

Food for Thought

Justice for the Oppressed

"We boast about your perseverance and faith in all the persecutions and trials you are enduring." Persecutions and trials. Think about that for a minute. The fact that you are reading this right now most likely indicates that you are a Christian within the privileged class of the world's population. (If you do not fall into the following description, please excuse yourself for a moment, but continue eavesdropping.) You probably live in the United States in which you enjoy freedom of speech. You probably enjoy the luxury of having running water on demand, a television set with either a VCR or DVD player. You have access to clean public transportation and sanitation and may even own your own vehicle. You have the freedom to publicly and openly attend the church of your personal preference with no fear of losing your house or employment as the result of that choice. You probably have at least one meal a day and feel hunger pains on an infrequent basis. If this describes you, then you fall into the privileged class of the world's population. You don't really know persecutions and trials.

Now, to further stir the pot, (please excuse any apparent racist or sexist language here, that is not my intent...just the opposite actually) if you are a white person, and especially if you are a male, and fall into the above categories, then you are even further up on the social pecking order of the world. I happen to fall into this category, so I can speak with confidence in this regard. We do not know persecutions and trials. The most we have probably suffered is a few heckles by the loudmouths at work calling us, "Bible-thumper" "Jesus-Freak" or something of the sort. Perhaps we have felt awkward because people change their language or quickly change the subject when we walk up to the group in the lunch room. Perhaps we are not invited to the "right" parties or are passed over for certain promotions that would move us from a really great job to an even better job. Well, (forgive my rudeness) boo-hoo for us. Can we really call that persecution? I think not.

The truth is that, on this side of history, we (the white Christian male) have been in the place of being the oppressor. We have done some pretty horrific things in the name of Jesus as we advanced the cause of "Christendom" across the New World. Why do I bring up our past sins during this study of 2 Thessalonians? I do so because we need to recognize how far removed we are from the perspective of the first churches that Paul planted. In order to truly grasp the meaning of Paul's words in this letter we have to shed the skin of "white man's religion" and our places of power and see the world from the other side of oppression. If you claimed that you were a follower of Jesus in the first century in Thessalonica, then you were proclaiming a death wish. We don't know if there were actual executions of Christians in that city, but we do know that life was miserable for the Christians. If you were previously Jewish then you were thrown out of the synagogue and cut off from your family. It was hard enough to be a Jew in that Gentile society, but without the support of the Jewish community you were probably completely lost. If you were a Greek you were thrown out of the social system and accused of angering the gods. Anything bad that happened in that city (storms, disease, wars, etc.) would now be blamed on you because of your insult to the gods of the city. You were probably cast out of your trade guild. Perhaps your home was burned. Your family imprisoned. You may even be dragged out of the city and stoned to death. If your accusers could prove to the Roman magistrate that your allegiance to Jesus directly attacked the worship of the emperor and claimed that there was a king higher than Caesar, then you would be charged of high treason and possibly sentenced to crucifixion. It all depended upon the temperament of the Roman official on duty.

How's that for persecution? If you are Paul, how do you preach the gospel in that hostile environment? What is the good news? In today's reading we catch a glimpse of one of the many facets of the good news of Jesus: Deliverance and Justice for the oppressed.

Before we explore that idea further there is one more piece of the puzzle that must be mentioned. In order to understand 1st century culture and the religious literature of the era you must be aware of a genre of literature called Apocalyptic. Simply defined, the Apocalyptic genre is one in which the author will write about great cosmic events in grandiose language, using wild and vivid metaphors to describe the end of the world. The purpose of the metaphors was to speak about actual contemporary, historical figures without committing blatant treason against the power structures of the empire. It was a kind of code. The purpose of apocalyptic literature was to encourage the oppressed and to remind them that in the end God will avenge those who have been abused by the power-hungry, self-serving, merciless tyrants who ignore the needs of the lower classes and use them to increase their own wealth. Apocalyptic language reminds the oppressed that they are not forgotten and that they are part of a bigger drama in which God's truth and justice will prevail in the end.

John's revelation is a good example of apocalyptic literature. There are many examples of this kind of writing from the Jewish culture flowing from the time between Testaments right through the first century. In other words, it was a commonly used way of writing religious material. There tends to be a flurry of apocalyptic literature during eras of massive cultural shifts. When the old culture feels that things are changing and that something new is emerging they tend to think that it is the end of the world and they begin writing apocalyptic literature. We have seen this to be true throughout Christian History as well, the least of which is our own past 20th century.

As we read this second letter to the Thessalonians we see Paul slip into a flourish of apocalyptic language of his own. It only makes sense. He had suffered greatly already in his ministry at the hands of the power structures of the cities in which he had ministered. And this was just the beginning of his sufferings. Here he was, having been ripped away prematurely from the Thessalonian church, hearing of their pain and suffering at the hands of the Jewish leaders, the Greek leaders, and the Roman magisterium. The reality of injustice boiled up in his heart and flowed over in a stream of "God will smite the oppressors! Justice will be served! Jesus will return on his great horse and bring those scoundrels to their just desserts! In this you can put your hope. Your suffering is not for nothing."

Now, that being said, there is one more aspect of this letter that must be addressed. Paul's message to the Thessalonians relied heavily on the hope placed in Jesus' triumphant return, so the Thessalonians were really setting their eyes on this event. However, someone had come into town and told them that Paul had sent them word and that Jesus had already returned and they missed it! Oh no.

You can just imagine the brilliant mind behind this scheme. Their enemy surmised, "If I want to neutralize this annoying new sect, and if I know that their whole hope and the fuel for their fervor is in the return of this Jesus character, then if I can convince them that he already returned then I will squelch their fire and the problem will fade away."

Paul responds to this lie with an emphatic "No!" In so doing he gives us one of the most confusing passages in all of his letters. He reminds the Thessalonians that they already had information that would let them know that Jesus could not have possibly returned. They already knew that before Jesus could return the rebellion had to take place and the man of lawlessness had to come and exalt himself as a god, and set himself up in the temple. And they already knew that the thing that was holding him back has to be taken out of the way before he can really do all these things. Don't you remember when I told you all that before?

At this point we, the 21st century reader, scream, "No, Paul, we don't remember. We have no idea what you are talking about! Who is the man of lawlessness? What is holding him back? When will it be removed? What does it mean?"

In this passage we run head first into the telephone game that we mentioned in the introduction and the allusive nature of the letters. Paul assumes that the Thessalonians know exactly what he is talking about. As they sit in Thessalonica and read the letter their heads start bobbing up and down in recollection of Paul's teaching about this. They think to themselves, "Oh yes, that's right. Paul told us that already." All the while we sit here scratching our heads thinking, "I have no idea what he's talking about."

Many, many Christians over the last 2,000 years have tried to make sense out of this. They tie this passage together with the prophecy of Daniel, Matthew 24, and the Revelation. They say that the man of lawlessness is equivalent to the Great Beast of the Revelation. At this point they are probably accurate. Of course, Revelation had not been written yet when Paul wrote the letter, but Daniel was burned into Paul's mind. There were doubtless many apocalyptic ideas floating through the early church. Everyone was trying to predict when Jesus would return and how it would interact with the Roman Empire.

It is most likely that the Man of Lawlessness and the Great Beast represent the same thing in both Paul and John's Apocalypse. The big question is, "what does it represent?" The honest answer is that no one really knows. Throughout the centuries there have been three basic types of interpretations:

1. **The Idealist view.** The Apocalyptic language did not represent any specific politic powers or literal historical figures. They simply represented the general idea of "Good vs. Evil" and presented the message that God will prevail in the end. The message to the Thessalonians was to not worry about their persecution, but to persevere because they will ultimately share glory with Jesus in Heaven.

2. **The Preterist view.** The Apocalyptic language referred to specific political figures in the day of the writer, and it predicted the overthrow of the Roman Empire. Many scholars believe that the Man of Lawlessness and the Beast was the Emperor Nero who

would come hard against the Church in the sixties. Nero had Paul and Peter executed in Rome. Perhaps Paul himself was the force that held him back. Paul's Gentile mission to "the ends of the Earth" had to be completed (he went to Spain) in order to fulfill Jesus' Great Commission. When that was finished then the Beast would be allowed to kill the great apostles and seem to be victorious for a season. Then, eventually the Roman Empire would be defeated and, ultimately would become a Christian state through the conversion of Emperor Constantine and the establishment of the Pope.

3. **The Futurist view.** The Apocalyptic language does refer to specific historical characters, but not of the Roman Empire. Paul was slightly off in his belief that Jesus would return in his lifetime. The Man of Lawlessness and the Beast are political figures that have not yet arrived on the scene of history in the 21st century. In order for these events to happen the temple in Jerusalem has to be rebuilt so that the Man of Lawlessness can establish himself in it. When He does so, then Jesus can return in a Great show of power and defeat him and bring final justice to the oppressed.

Do you see how there are strengths and weaknesses in each view? In each view it seems that Paul missed the mark somehow. Either he was talking about an overthrow in his day that happened, but Jesus didn't show up with a throng where the dead were raised, or it wasn't about his day and we're still waiting.

So, what do we do about it? What is right? Here are some simple suggestions.

1. **Take a deep breath.** In all of Paul's letters this is the only place he talks about it. It wasn't the major point of his theology. The bottom line of the letter to the Thessalonians was, "God will bring Justice, don't worry about your suffering."

2. **Acknowledge the unknowing.** As far back as Augustine the greatest scholars of the New Testament have said, "We dunno," in reference to this passage. There are too many holes in the letter, too much "allusive" language to be able to pin down a definitive interpretation. Let it go.

3. **Don't listen to dogmatic teaching on it.** If anyone tells you that they know and have it figured out...run away!! It's OK to speculate and talk about it for the purpose of honing your Bible study skills, but there are a lot of people who vest their whole identity in knowing the "End Times" and getting people

worked up about it. It is a subject that is not worth dividing the church over.

4. **Put your hope in what counts.** One way or the other, no matter what your interpretation of the Apocalypse is, the final answer is still the same: Jesus is the Victor over sin and death. He is the King of Kings and Lord of Lords. He is the one who loves us and sets us free from oppression and will bring Justice in the end. Put your hope in that and live like a child of the King. Love everyone, no matter their view of the end times!

Lesson 5

- 2 Thessalonians 3

Study Questions

What is Paul's prayer request for himself?

Summarize vv. 6-13 in your own words.

How should the church deal with the person who refuses to follow Paul's instruction?

Food for Thought

Living in the Light of His Return

Lesson 4 may have stirred you up a bit. Today, as we read the final chapter of 2 Thessalonians we can begin to gear down and bring some more balanced perspective to life. We have established that, one way or another, Jesus will return someday and, when He does, He will bring Justice to the earth. As followers of Jesus we can place our hope in this and draw confidence that God is in control, that God loves His creation, that God will not do anything that is cruel or vindictive, but will bring about true Justice according to His standard of Love and Justice.

Here are three things to keep in mind that Paul tells the Thessalonians (and us) in light of Jesus' return.

It hasn't happened yet

Don't let people tell you that Jesus has already come. People tried to fool the Thessalonians and throughout Church History different teachers have proclaimed at different times that Jesus has come and most of the "believers" missed it because of their apostasy. Don't believe it. When He comes, everyone will know it.

When it happens you don't have to worry

The point of the Revelation was to bring encouragement and comfort to the believers, not stress and anxiety. Paul said, "Encourage each other with these words," not, "scare everybody into behaving with these words." If you follow Jesus, then you are a child of the Day and you will not be "left behind" to suffer torture under God's wrath. Now, you may suffer torture under the cruelty of your fellow man, but not under God's wrath. Our hope is in the Love of God, remember that.

It's not an excuse for laziness

The final note from Paul is an exhortation to not be lazy. It seems that many believers in Thessalonica were freeloaders. We're not exactly sure why. Perhaps it was just their disposition and Paul was correcting them and reminding them that God's children aren't lazy bums. Get up and work! Or, perhaps, in light of the teaching about Jesus' immanent return, some of the believers developed the notion that since Jesus was coming right back they could leave their jobs, neglect their responsibilities, and simply wait on the mountain for Jesus to whisk them away into the glorious vacation in the sky. WRONG! Like it or not, we were created for work. Adam and Eve, before the fall, were given the charge to take care of the garden and name the animals. There was work in the Garden of Eden. Granted, it wasn't back-breaking, toil-and-sweat kind of work, but it was creative, productive, and purposeful work. As children of God we are called to continue this kind of work. We are still stewards of the planet. That probably will not stop in heaven. It will just be more like Adam's pre-fall version of work instead of the daily grind we experience today. Yet, it is still work. So, don't get lazy, get to work! Do something productive and honor God!

Let's conclude our study of 1 and 2 Thessalonians with a simple word of encouragement. Being a Christian isn't easy, but it's worth it. Whatever you do, don't stop loving each other, don't lose hope, and always stay purposeful. Live with passion like Jesus is returning tomorrow and work and plan with wisdom as if He will wait for another 1,000 years.

1 Corinthians

Welcome to Fabulous Corinth...Home of the Isthmian Games...the crossroads of the Roman Empire...the place where all your fantasies can come true...the home of hundreds of temples and thousands of prostitutes...the land of plenty... all are welcome, none will leave unsatisfied. This could have been a travel log for the city of Corinth in the days of Paul. In many ways ancient Corinth was like a cross between modern day Las Vegas and Los Angeles. Positioned on the small land bridge (the Isthmus) between northern and southern Greece, Corinth was a crossroads for commerce and cultural interchange. The city had developed a portage service where sea captains could pay to have their ships rolled across the Isthmus rather than sail around the treacherous southern cape of Greece. So, if you were traveling from the eastern part of the empire to Rome, or from Rome to the east...you went through Corinth. If you were traveling by land from the northern parts of Greece to the southern...you went through Corinth. Being at the crossroads meant that Corinth became a hustling, bustling melting pot of all the cultures of the Empire. It was a city known for its sexual immorality – even among the Greeks. And, as in many seaport towns that cater to the sailor, there was plenty of partying going on, day and night.

In order to set the stage for understanding Paul's first letter to the church that had been formed in Corinth we must identify four basic subcultures that were present.

1. **The Roman Government.** Rome controlled everything, so you can imagine how strategic this hub of commerce must have been to the Empire. The Roman law was present to settle disputes among the "restless natives" and to make sure that no insurrectionists would hamper the steady flow of economic prosperity that the Empire so lavishly enjoyed.

2. **The Greek Religions.** There were many temples upon the Acrocorinthian hilltop, yet all of them shared one thing in common... sexuality. Part of the ebb and flow of the ancient Greek religion was the process of appeasing and exciting the gods. The Greek gods and goddesses were scoundrels and schemers for the most part. They did not care for humans; they simply tolerated them and used them for their own pleasure. The humans' job was to approach the gods in such a way that they would evade their wrath and please them so that the gods would grant the human's request. The gods were appeased and pleased in two ways. First, the gods demanded the sacrifice of animals and agriculture. Second, the gods required entertainment and sexual stimulation. Therefore, the temples provided prostitutes, both male and female, to the men of the city to use sexually in order to arouse the gods and get them to be fertile and keep the crops coming. In short, if you were a worshipper of the Greek gods you lived in fear and in sexual addiction as a natural part of your religion.

3. **The Greek Philosophies.** Among the Greeks there were many "progressive thinkers" who found the sensuality and fear-based system of the ancient religions to be repulsive. In search of alternatives many schools of thought were developed over the centuries. While all of the schools had major differences, they all shared one basic idea. They believed that the physical world with all of its pain, suffering, addiction, fear, and strife was evil. Anything having to do with the physical pleasures – food, drink, sex, money, power – was seen as distractions from what is really important. To them, the only thing that was really real in the universe was purely spiritual. The philosophers sought ways to enlighten their minds and spirits in order to shed the bonds of the evil, physical world.

4. **The Jewish Culture.** As in any major metropolitan area in the Empire there was a substantial Jewish sub-culture. These Corinthian Jews abhorred the reprehensible ways of the "unclean" Corinthians and struggled to figure out how to live in this town while staying ceremonially clean according to the Laws of Moses. They looked forward to the day when Jehovah would send His Messiah, overthrow these pagan people and restore the glory of Israel.

A Church Caught Between Two Worlds

Try to imagine what it must have been like to be a member of this brand new grouping of people who claimed to follow Jesus as their Savior and Lord. By doing this they were offending everyone in the community. First of all, the only savior and lord that was to be acknowledged in the Empire was Caesar. He had saved the people from constant war and from economic devastation. Through the Pax Romana Caesar brought peace and salvation to the people through economic strength and judicial order. Because of this deliverance he had the right to declare himself their lord and to expect that they would gladly pay him homage through taxes and offerings of worship. This Jesus character was just a peasant Jew from Judea; how dare anyone exalt him as Lord over Caesar. Secondly, they offended their Jewish roots. Those who were emerging out of a Jewish culture to follow Jesus as their Messiah were heading into dangerous waters by listening to that trouble-maker Paul. He was advocating such nonsensical ideas like: you don't have to be circumcised to be in God's Kingdom, the dietary laws of Moses are not universal for all people, women have rights and are equal with men in God's Kingdom...the list goes on and on. To follow Jesus, under Paul's theology, is to risk bringing God's curse on your head. Finally, they were offending the Greeks. To claim that there is only one God in the entire universe was to deny the very foundation of civilization. Greek culture and identity was wrapped up in the codependency between the social life of the gods and goddesses and the worship and service of humanity to the gods. To deny the existence of these gods and follow one god would be a sure way to evoke the wrath of the gods and bring blight and pestilence on the land. Also, among the Greek philosophers it was an absurd idea to think that an almighty God, who is pure spirit, goodness, and truth, would even consider the idea of becoming a human and dwelling in the disgusting, filthy, sinful flesh-body that we are cursed to endure.

1 Corinthians

So, there they were, caught in the middle. Jesus was calling them into an entirely different way of life. No longer were they to hate each other. Instead, Greeks and Jews, men and women, slave and master were called to come to the Lord's Table and eat together as equals. How could they possibly do this? There were so many questions about the practical logistics of living this way in Corinth. There were so many cultural issues that were causing divisions among them:

What about the meat sacrificed to idols? Should we eat it or not? We know it's just meat, but there is so much baggage attached to it. What should we do?

What about the relationship between men and women? The Jews say women should always stay covered, silent, and out of the way. They are good for nothing but making babies and keeping house. The Greeks are torn. Some think women should stay out of the way, yet there is a growing, radical women's liberation movement where the women are trying to overthrow the authority of the men. Some Greeks even think women are pure evil and should be avoided altogether. Paul says we're equal and partners in the church. What does that look like? What should we do when we gather together? How does this impact our understanding of marriage and sexuality?

What about this idea of the Holy Spirit and the gifts that He gives to us? Some are saying that certain gifts are a sign of special favor and that God has exalted them above others. Is this true? How are we supposed to conduct ourselves when we gather together to worship God and share the Lord's Supper? Why is there so much tension over this?

What about the resurrection? There are certain Greek philosophers who say that Jesus never became human and that the resurrection and the second coming are purely spiritual events. They say that when we reach a certain level of enlightenment it takes us above the crude physical world, at that point we have been 'resurrected' and 'Jesus has returned' in our hearts. Is that right? What about our friends who have died and didn't hear that message? Are they eternally condemned?

There are so many teachers saying so many different things. Paul, we're confused. Please help us!

These were the cries for help that reached Paul as he was working across the sea in the city of Ephesus. Imagine Paul sitting in a tent-making shop with his friends Aquila and Priscilla. As they are working away a group of Corinthians barge into the shop with an obvious sense of urgency.

"Paul, we have news from Corinth. Things are not going well. Here is a letter that they have asked us to bring to you. They have so many questions. Please respond. But, Paul...we hate to bring this up because we don't want to be gossips, but there are other concerns that are not reflected in the letter. Paul, the people are beginning to break into factions. Some are starting to follow other teachers, like Apollos and Cephas. They are turning away from you and saying that you are teaching lies and heresy. It's getting ugly. Oh...and one more thing...they still haven't shaken the 'Corinthian' stigma. Sexual immorality is running rampant in the church, just like it does in the rest of town. It is so bad that one man is actually messing around with his step-mother...and to make it worse...nobody in the church sees this as a problem. Please, for our sakes, address these issues as well."

"Right. Thank you for the news. Please get me some parchment. Now, let's address this issue of factions first thing..."

And so the letter to the Corinthians was written. It is a combination of Paul's admonition of their sinful behavior and a direct response to their formal questions.

Over the next three sessions we will be looking at this important letter. Please be reminded that it is important to remember to keep the context of the letter always in the forefront of your mind. We must ask ourselves, "Was Paul making sweeping statements that applied to all churches for all time, or was he putting out specific brushfires within the context of a volatile cultural melting pot called Corinth?"

As we study together, let's ask the Holy Spirit to guide us and show us how we are to answer these questions in our own lives, within the context of our own culture, both inside our church and within our interaction with the culture at large.

Introduction to Part 1

This session our focus will be on chapters 1-5. Essentially we will be dealing with two issues. First, Paul addresses the issue of factions in the church. His argument spans across chapters 1-4 as he builds a case for how sad it is that the church has divided over the issue of human teachers. Each chapter will add a new layer to his reasoning.

Simply put, the argument could read like this:

Ch. 1 – "I can't believe you are arguing over who is the better teacher and who has the most wisdom. Men are fools, don't boast in them, boast in the Lord."

Ch. 2 – "I came to give you deep spiritual truth --the mind of Christ – that is for mature people."

Ch. 3 – "You aren't mature enough to hear my message and you still look to the human teacher. We are nothing; only servants planting fields and building houses.

Ch. 4 – In the end God will sort out all the judgments. Be careful that you do not become arrogant. I would hate to have to deal with you harshly when I get there!"

In chapter 5 Paul shifts gears and begins to deal with the subject of sexual immorality. Here he instructs the church in how to deal with a certain man that had crossed the lines of acceptability and needed to experience some church discipline.

Lesson 1

- 1 Corinthians 1

Study Questions

Paraphrase Paul's description of the church in Corinth in vv. 4-9.

From this prologue, what are the issues that you think Paul will be addressing?

What issue has caused division in the church?

How does Paul feel about people claiming his name? Why?

What are the two cultures that Paul identifies in this chapter? How does he describe the "wisdom" of those cultures?

Based on Paul's words in v. 26, what were most of the people like in the church of Corinth? How might this affect their ability to function in the city of Corinth?

How is the message of Jesus compared to the "wisdom" of the Jews and the Greeks?

What are some ways in which the contemporary church has divided in to "follower factions" like the Corinthians did? What affect, both negative and positive, does this division have on the church and the world?

Food for Thought

"I follow Paul," "I follow Cephas," "I follow Apollos," "I follow Jesus." It sounds like a political convention as each party screams for its favorite candidate.

What was going on in Corinth? It seems that there were competing theologies at play in the church at Corinth. This only makes sense given the nature of the church. In our introduction we highlighted the fact that the young church of Corinth was caught between four major cultural perspectives – Roman, Greek Religion, Greek Philosophy, and Judaism. What did it mean to be a follower of Jesus? What was the standard of truth for the new believer? Was it the Law of Moses? The wisdom of Rome? The Greek philosophers? The Holy Spirit? The teachings of Paul? The teachings of Apollos? What were the standards of conduct in this cultural milieu?

If you were a Jewish convert it would be easy for you to stay safely within the moral confines of Judaism and the traditional practices of everyday life. Yet, Paul called the believer to come out of that ethnically exclusive system and open up to the Gentile world. He said that the day of Moses' Law was past and we were now in the age of the Spirit and the Law of Christ.

If you were a Greek convert then the Law of Moses would be foreign gibberish to you and the free-thinking Greek philosophies about moral goodness and knowledge would be more appealing. Yet, Paul called the believer away from the sexual immorality, self-centeredness, and over-spiritualizing of things that was inherently present within the Greek system of thinking.

So, what was a believer to do? Who was right? Who held the truth?

Given this context it becomes easier to understand why a person would naturally lean toward the teacher that most resonated with his own way of thinking. As human beings we have an innate need to have things spelled out to us in concrete terms of black/white, right/wrong, do this/do that. Many teachers had moved into Corinth and began teaching various forms of the "Christian" message and the people of the church were beginning to migrate toward the teacher they most understood.

Some of the teachers were calling the believer to fully accept the Laws of Moses as the practical ethic for everyday life. This was similar to the "judaizers" that Paul addressed in the letter to the Galatians. Others were mixing the moral teachings of Jesus with the dualistic philosophies of Plato, the Epicureans, and the Stoics. These theologians tended to spiritualize the Gospel and

make it a mental game of enlightenment, rather than a holistic system that dealt with practical physical experiences.

This problem still exists in our world today. There are several "factions" within the church in the world. The major streams of Christian thought are: Roman Catholic, Eastern Orthodox, Mainstream Protestantism, Reformed Protestantism, Fundamentalism, Evangelicalism, Pentecostalism, Charismatic, Emerging...to name a few. Within these major categories there are hundreds of subdivisions that further carve up the body of Christ. Sadly, this portrait only depicts the Christian traditions within the "Westernized World." Among the 2/3 world and Eastern cultures there are many other variations of Christian Spirituality that have developed over the centuries.

How are we supposed to feel about all of these divisions? On the one hand we should mourn over it. Jesus prayed that His body would be one in spirit and purpose so that the world would know that He had come from the Father (John 17). Our factions and denominationalism is a sad testimony to the unity of the Body of Christ. Yet, on the other hand, we should dole out some grace for ourselves and realize that we are not much better than the Corinthians. We are human beings living in a cultural melting pot that is swirling with competing worldviews, all under the jurisdiction of the same Creator. In many ways we face the same situation that the Corinthians did. Paul called us away from the legalism of the Law into freedom in the Spirit, but he also warned us against the "wisdom" of the age and the immorality that inevitably comes with it. To quote Francis Schaeffer, "How should we then live?"

As we track with Paul's logic through chapters 1-4 we will begin to see some fundamental principles that will help us navigate these turbulent cultural waters. For today, there is one simple attitude that we glean from Paul. God uses the simple things in the world to confound the "profound." As soon as we think we are something special we have fallen into the trap. The simple truth is that we can never boast in a person – neither in ourselves nor in our favorite teacher – because we are simply simple humans. Our boast is in the Lord alone.

Stay tuned as we continue to unpack this issue over the next three lessons.

Lesson 2

- 1 Corinthians 2

Study Questions

In vv. 1-5, how does Paul characterize his original ministry in Corinth? Why?

To whom is the message of wisdom given?

How is this message of wisdom different from the wisdom of the Jews and the Greeks?

How is this deep wisdom accessed?

According to this passage, and the explanation of the Mind/Spirit connection in man, what do you think it means to have "the Mind of Christ?"

Food for Thought

Preach always, when necessary use words

This is a famous quote from Francis of Assisi, a medieval monk. In a sense, this is how Paul describes his initial ministry in Corinth. Paul knew that the people of Corinth had heard their fill of philosophical debates from the Greeks and great Rabbinical teaching from the Jews as to the nature of truth in the universe. What they didn't need was one more flowery teacher who was more full of himself and hot air than he was with real substantive truth. So, Paul entered into Corinth as a simple tentmaker who had a heart for God and for people. When he saw a hurting person he touched him with the healing power of God's love. He demonstrated God's law of love through action, not rhetoric. It was through the sleeves-rolled-up, roll-in-the-muck-of-humanity kind of ministry that Paul demonstrated the power of God's love to the Corinthians, and in so doing, won them over to follow the crucified and risen Jesus as Lord.

As I sit and write these words I am personally convicted by Paul's message. It is easy to sit in a comfortable Middle American coffee shop, typing on a laptop computer about the writings of Paul. Words. Words and more words. Blah, blah, blah. Is anyone reading them? You are, obviously, and I hope that they are being helpful to you. I hope they inspire you to allow Jesus to transform your heart and use you in purposeful ministry in the world. Yet, if the truth of Jesus remains in our head as mere philosophical concepts, but never moves through our hearts and into our hands and feet, then are we really doing anything other than puffing ourselves up with self-importance and empty rhetoric. Paul brought the Good News of Jesus first with a demonstration of God's loving, healing power.

But wait, there's more

In v. 6 Paul takes a sharp left turn from the previous ideas. Yes, the gospel of Jesus must come first with the simple demonstration of loving, healing power, but, it doesn't stop there. There *is* a deep wisdom. Paul came into Corinth prepared to share with them the deep mysteries of God. However, he knew that he must first establish an ethos of active, other-oriented love as the basis of the church so that no one would be confused about the "wisdom" he was offering. It was not the wisdom of the Rabbis or of the Greek Philosophers. Those "wisdoms" were humanly constructed systems that catered to the selfish nature and ultimately led toward self-protection and self-elevation at the expense of others. The wisdom of God was of a completely different nature.

God is the infinite Creator. He is the eternal mind that brought forth all matter with the mere power of thought. God exists in eternal trinity where love between Father, Son, and Holy Spirit is the foundational nature of existence. Humanity was brought forth as a loving and conscious act of the Trinity's will. God loves us and eternally desires for us to be known by Him, to be transformed by Him, to eternally grow deeper into the love of God. These are deep truths that are impossible for the tangled web of neurons in the human brain to grasp within the limited confines of our minds. The mind of God is the eternal force of the universe, the vehicle of which is the Spirit of God.

If you are scratching your head right now, good. So am I. That's the point. We don't understand God. How could we? Yet, God loves us and wants to be in relationship with Him and to grow in our knowledge of Him. That is why He has given us the Spirit. Through the Spirit of God we can know the mind of God; we have been given the mind of Christ.

Now, how does this help us in understanding how to deal with the competing worldviews we find ourselves in? After all, isn't that the real question Paul is dealing with? The answer to the question comes in chapter 3. I won't spoil the punch line until then.

For today, here is a thought to take with you. There is a deep and profound wisdom that God wants you to have. It is not a concept or a Law. It is His very self. God loves you deeply and wants you to grow in your knowledge of Him. He does not want you to grow in your theological prowess (although good theology is a necessary stepping stone in the process).

He wants you to grow in knowing Him and growing in the experience and assurance of His love. He gave you the Holy Spirit so that you could be connected to Him relationally and authentically. Go into the world today resting in the assurance that you are full in the love of God.

Lesson 3

- 1 Corinthians 3

Study Questions

What external behavior demonstrates to Paul that the Corinthians are not yet mature?

What are the two metaphors Paul uses to describe the kind of work he and Apollos have been doing? What is his point?

What will be judged in the last day? What will be saved? What is the criterion for this judgment?

Why should no one consider himself "wise" according to the standards of the age?

What promise, or statement of fact, does Paul declare about the Corinthians? How do you think this relates to the flow of his argument to this point?

Food for Thought

Some commentators have titled 1 Corinthians "Spanking the Saints." In this chapter we hear the first real whack of the paddle on the Corinthian backside. Paul says, "Yes, I did bring a deep spiritual wisdom for you, but you are too immature to grasp it. YOU ARE BABIES and are acting as such. GROW UP!"

The flow of his argument goes something like this (allow me to paraphrase)

You think that teachers are something important and that it really matters that you align yourself with the 'right' teacher. Don't you get it? The teachers you revere are nothing more than slaves out in the field. We are simply planting seeds on God's plantation. We are simply laying bricks on the master's house. We are nothing. We don't teach to exalt ourselves and get people to follow us. We are trying to build something wonderful for the Master. You are that something wonderful, not words and theologies. Someday the Master is going to look at what we have built and how we have built it. If we built it with our own fancy words and the power of our own personality, then it is like straw and paper. When He sets a match to it, POOF, it will be gone. All our work will be for nothing. But, if we build into your lives with the deep truth of God's love, then that will be like precious metals that will withstand His fire-test.

Don't be stupid by thinking you are smart. Stop focusing on the messenger and get your heart lined up with the message – Jesus. The truth is that all of these messengers have something good to say about God. They each present one facet of the multifaceted diamond that is the eternal truth of the infinite God. God wants to give you the whole diamond, so stop arguing over which side of it is the prettiest and embrace the whole thing with the love of Jesus.

Finally, we have some semblance of an answer to the question we have been entertaining this session. How do we deal with all of these Christian factions? Embrace them! God is truth. All truth is God's truth, regardless of who says it. If it's true, it's true. All human teachers have something good to say and all teachers tend to shroud the truth they do have in a big pile of petty baggage. Every theological tradition (like it or not) is a reaction to something else. Therefore, every theology has behind it some form of self-exaltation and self-protection that is trying to prove themselves to be right and the "other guy" to be wrong. That's just the way of the finite, fallen human. The deep truth of Jesus lies behind each of these theological caricatures of Him. Every brand of Christianity presents a truthful, but incomplete portrait of Jesus and the nature of the universe. It is OK to resonate with one more than the other, but it is a dead-end street to barricade yourself within a tradition and claim it to be the entire picture of the infinite God.

You may react to these thoughts and say that they open the door to (if not fully embrace) relativism. I do not espouse relativism because it is impossible for ALL things to be equally true. That is not what I am saying. I am simply acknowledging the fact that all of the denominations that read the same Bible and love the same Jesus tend to see different aspects of Him and follow different emphases within His teaching and ministry. We need to be aware of this and realize that the deep wisdom that Paul was offering to the Corinthian church was not an idea, but was a person. I do believe that much of our knowledge about the universe is relative to our place in life, but I don't believe that truth is relative. Truth is a person. His name is Jesus. He invites us to know Him. We, in our human frailty, continually struggle with His Spirit to grasp the infinite nature of His love and personality. May we struggle together and fall forward into this great mystery of life in God.

Lesson 4

- 1 Corinthians 4

Study Questions

Restate vv. 1-5 in your own words.

What negative attitude had many of the Corinthians slipped into? Why?

What choice does Paul give the Corinthians?

By what standard does Paul operate his life?

What must they do to determine their choice?

How does Paul contrast the apostles with the church in Corinth?

Why does he make this contrast?

What is Paul's warning?

Food for Thought

Who da Judge?

Paul gives us an invaluable principle to live by in vv. 1-5. He tells us not to judge each others motives. We can't know what is in a person's heart. The truth is that we can't even know what is truly in our own hearts. Only God knows, and only He can judge. So, take the pressure off yourself and let Him.

Notice what Paul says, "My conscience is clear, but that does not make me innocent." What a beautifully honest portrait he paints of the human condition. Basically, he is saying that we can only operate within the understanding, knowledge, and perspective we have. God does not judge us on the external, but on the condition of our heart. If we believe that something is wrong, but we do it anyway, that is sin that cuts us off from fellowship with God. But if we don't know it is wrong, our motive is pure. Paul is demonstrating for us, through this confessional, that we need to worry less about micromanaging each others' lives and get on with the business of making sure we have a clean conscience before God and simply living the life that we believe God wants us to live. It doesn't matter what people think of us, or what we think of others. As long as you are good with God, that is all that matters. If we all lived like that things would probably run much smoother.

Another Spanking

In the last part of chapter four Paul concludes his four-chapter long discussion regarding the factions that have arisen in the Corinthian church. This passage is dripping with sarcasm and irony. If you didn't catch it the first time, go back and read it through those lenses. Paul is mocking the church a little. He is saying, "Oh great and wise Corinthians. You are so smart. I wish we were as smart as you. Here we are, just lowly apostles. We're suffering for Jesus, but you must be living right because you are doing so well! GET A CLUE CORINTHIANS!!! Don't you see that it is arrogance that lies at the base of everything you do? You follow after these different teachers (me included) in order to prove yourself to be "right" to everyone else. You get caught up in words and split theological hairs. Don't you see that your lack of humility and love is destroying the church? We, the great teachers you are following, are out in the mud pits, serving Jesus in humility and obscurity. We aren't like the great orators who use their wealth and power to validate their words. We are servants of the one true Lord, Jesus. Please stop this pettiness and get your heart in the game. I want to come see you, but if I find that you are still fighting about who's "right" and whose "wrong" I'm going to have to take out my paddle in person and, believe me, it won't be pretty. Please let me come to find you living in peace with each other.

What is our word for today? It is the opposite of arrogance. Our word is humility. As followers of Jesus we are called to be humble in everything we do. We should never get caught up in power struggle debates over theological minutia. One of Paul's repeated messages to his churches was that he came to preach Jesus alone. All of the other stuff is important, but it really has more to do with preference than it does with ABSOLUTE TRUTH. Jesus was the truth, He was the only one who had the right to tell everyone to go to Hell, and yet He bowed His head and let them send Him there instead. He was willing to die rather than fight to prove Himself right. If you have the truth, then you don't need to defend it, simply live it. If you are wrong, then you need to simply adjust. Let's walk in humility today and let the love of Christ be demonstrated by our actions to others.

Lesson 5

- 1 Corinthians 5

Study Questions

What blatant sin had been reported in the church?

Aside from the obvious sinful act, what was really getting Paul upset with the church as a whole in regard to this situation?

How does Paul use the imagery of yeast in this

passage?

v.9 indicates that there had already been a letter written to the church prior to this one. What was Paul's specific instruction in that letter?

How might Paul's instruction to separate from sin be misinterpreted? What impact would that distorted interpretation have on the world?

How did Paul instruct the church to deal with the sinful man?

Read 2 Corinthians 2:1-11. Did the Corinthians obey Paul's instructions?

How does Paul follow up on these instructions? Why?

Food for Thought

Stating the Obvious

Let's begin today's study by stating the obvious... this is unbelievable. The church not only had a member present who was sleeping with his mother-in-law, but the church openly accepted it and condoned it. They were proud of it!

How could this have happened? We can't know the exact answer to that question, but we can speculate. There are two possibilities that we'll mention here (there are more, of course, but two for this discussion). The first could be that the Corinthians had a distorted interpretation of Paul's teaching on Freedom in Christ. Notice on the illustration it says, "Freedom run amuck." It is possible that one of the major problems within the Corinthian church is that they took Paul's proclamation that we are no longer under the Law to mean that they could do anything they wanted to do. Remember in the letter to the Galatians Paul defended against the accusation that the Freedom he was espousing was a sense of license. Perhaps the Corinthians took it that way so that even a gross sexual sin like this was applauded as "Freedom in Christ."

The second possibility is that some of the Corinthians had blended their belief in Jesus with some of the Greek philosophies. Many of the Greek schools believed that there was a separation between the body and the mind/spirit. The only thing that mattered was what happened in the mind/spirit, so what happened with the body made little difference. In other words, if you believe the right things then you can do whatever you want with your body and it won't affect the destiny of your soul. This "freedom" led some Greeks to indulge in every form of physical indulgence with no hesitation.

Whichever the reason, the result was the same. The church had embraced a very distorted view of the gospel that had allowed them to harbor a deadly and destructive practice within the community. What were they to do about it? Bottom line...expel the brother. Why? Paul uses bread as a metaphor to explain. Here we see Paul drawing from his roots as a Pharisee, for this was a favorite of that group. Sin had always been seen as a form of spiritual yeast. If a little bit is allowed to remain in the dough, in an environment that fosters it, then it will spread throughout the dough and transform the whole thing into "leavened" bread. For the Jews, one of the strongest symbols of purity was the unleavened bread that came out of the Passover tradition. To be the people of God you must eat unleavened bread, bread with no yeast, and have no yeast in your home. Here Paul agrees and pleads with the church to get rid of this dangerous element. This is called church discipline.

At this point you may be confused and a bit concerned that this passage may give license to the self-righteous in the community to go on witch-hunts and stick their hypocritical fingers in everyone's faces shouting "Sinner!" Didn't Jesus say to not judge your neighbor? What right do we have to throw someone out of the community? "He who is without sin cast the first stone." Didn't Jesus say that? Isn't Paul going a little too far here? To address this very valid concern, let's look at two things

What Judgment is not

In v. 10 Paul makes a very important disclaimer. He says that the church is not called to disassociate with the world because they are sinners. That is silly since you can't remove yourself from the world, plus it would be counterproductive to Jesus' commission to go into all the world to make disciples. We shouldn't judge the world for their sin...they're sinners. Sin is what sinners do. Our job is not to condemn them, but to lovingly demonstrate for them that there is a better way.

Many Christians need to hear this message in our culture. America is not a Christian nation. It is a democratically free nation that allows for freedom of speech and freedom of religion. God did not ordain the United States to be His blessed nation to bless all nations. That was Abraham and the nation of Israel. Currently, the church is carrying the torch to be a blessing to all nations. America is not the church. The church lives within America and, as American citizens, we have the right to believe what we believe, to publicly gather, and to say what we want to say. So, how are we using that freedom? Are we condemning sinners for being sinners, or are we demonstrating God's love for the World? Are we using our freedom to make a difference in the world by being conduits of God's unconditional love to people who are caught in cycles of self-destruction, or are we beating them over the head with their own sin and slamming the door of the Kingdom in their faces with the message, "God hates you! Boycott you!" Yes our culture is riddled with immorality and anti-god propaganda, but what else should we expect? As ambassadors for Jesus, we need to make sure that we are internally inoculated against temptation and externally motivated to penetrate culture to bring the life-giving message of God's love to people who have been wounded by Christianity and desperately need to see the power of God's transforming love at work in their lives.

What Judgment Is

The kind of judgment that Paul is advocating is an act of love, not hatred. It is for the purpose of restoration and reconciliation, not self-righteous condemnation. Look what he says in v. 5. The reason you "hand him over to Satan" is "so that the sinful nature may be destroyed and his spirit saved." You aren't trying to destroy the man; you are trying to destroy the sin within the man. To "hand him over to Satan" means to give him what he thinks he really desires and see if he really likes it. You see, this man thought he could have his cake and eat it too. He thought that he could gratify his sexual desires and still experience the joy of intimate fellowship with God and His people. You can't do that. Jesus said you can't serve two masters. It is not possible to openly cherish sin, with no remorse, and openly cherish the Spirit. Selfishness and self-gratification automatically turn your eyes away from God and onto yourself, thereby severing fellowship with God. Paul's instructions brought clarity to this truth and encouraged the church to help the man see the destructive power of his choices by living fully in their truth. Hopefully, when he wakes up with Satan and no one else, he will see the destructive nature of his actions and come running back home to a loving community.

We need to be very clear about something. This level of "church discipline" has to do with people who are blatantly cherishing sin and still trying to be in fellowship. This is not about people who are honestly fighting against their sin addictions, or people who occasionally slip into a trap here and there. Once again, this is about the motivation and condition of the heart. If a person struggles with sin, then we are instructed to "carry one another's burdens" (Galatians 6:1-2) If a person is openly playing fast and loose with the freedom of Jesus and arrogantly and openly participating in destructive behavior, with no intention of repenting from it, then the most loving thing we can do is cut them off from fellowship. Think about it, can you really be in fellowship with them anyway? If your heart wants to sow to the Spirit and walk in purity, then is it possible to be an intimate soul mate with someone who is pulling in the opposite direction? No.

Intimacy. That is what this is really all about. God does not call us into a system of rules and regulations. He calls us to intimacy with Him. Intimacy with Him is fostered within the intimate fellowship that is the church. Intimacy is built upon vulnerability and the ability to trust that everyone else involved in the community is looking out for your best interest and not their own self-preservation. Sin is all about self-gratification and the using of others to make you feel good. Sin and intimacy cannot coincide.

Jesus didn't call us to go and be intimate with the world, He called us to go and make disciples. That is why we don't "expel" the world. He did call us to be intimate with Him, and He called His church to be a place of intimacy that reflects the very heart of God on Earth. That is the dance we all dance together. Deep in our hearts we long for that safe place where we can trust another human being enough to be ourselves without fear of rejection or condemnation. In that space we can open up, we can crawl out of our hard shell of self-protection and become the person that God originally designed us to be. Yet, that type of relationship is the hardest thing on the planet to foster. So we dance. One step toward intimacy, step on a toe, one step back. Yet, we must dance until we get it right and enjoy the beautiful music of God's love.

If you read 2 Corinthians 2:1-11 you'll see that the Corinthians did follow Paul's instructions to the letter. Unfortunately they followed it to the letter and not to the spirit. They kicked the "sinner" out and made him suffer dearly for his sin. Paul had to correct them and remind them that the point of the expulsion was repentance and reconciliation, not righteous vindication.

The purpose of the church is to be a place of loving intimacy where people hold each other in authentic accountability. Perhaps if this is the environment we foster within our community then we won't have to get to the place where a person is so enamored with self-destructive behavior that we would have to turn him over to Satan. If we do have to do that, let's make sure that we do it in love and not self-righteous condemnation.

Reading Paul's Mail

1 Corinthians part 2

This session we continue our study of Paul's response to the reports and the questions he received from the church in Corinth. Over the 5 lessons of this session's study we will look at three major issues that Paul addresses.

Chapter 6 – This chapter is actually part 2 of Paul's reaction to the reports of sexual immorality. In chapter 5 he instructed the church to expel the immoral brother. In chapter six he continues to explain his reasoning behind this line of action.

Chapter 7 – In this chapter Paul begins to directly respond to the questions that the Corinthian church had sent to him. As you read, watch out for the phrase, "now about..." This is an indicator that Paul is addressing another one of the questions. In this chapter he speaks about the issues of sexuality and marriage.

Chapter 8-10 – The next question that the Corinthians ask is such a big one that it takes Paul the span of 3 chapters to adequately address it. They were perplexed over the issue of meat that had been sacrificed to idols; should they eat it or not? To our minds this may seem like an

irrelevant issue, but you will see that there are some wonderful transferable principles that are vitally necessary to be able to live out the Kingdom of God on Earth.

While we will look at one chapter a lesson and make some application from it, please keep in mind that this is an extended logical argument that can only be understood in its entirety. We'll do our best to keep the forest in view in spite of the trees.

An overall theme

At this point it would be good for us to be reminded that the Corinthians were living in the battle between worlds. As we highlighted in the introduction to last session, the church in Corinth was being pulled by conflicting cultural perspectives. On the one hand there were the free-wheeling Greeks who had very little moral law, and on the other hand there was the tradition-laden Jewish culture that had sanctioned itself off from the world and hid behind its moral superiority. Standing in another corner was the pervasive Greek philosophy that separated the spiritual from the physical and, in so doing, allowed for both an overactive repulsion of physical pleasure on the one hand and an over indulgence of physical pleasure on the other.

All of the questions that the church raises for Paul flow from the pressure and tension that they were feeling as they were caught between these conflicting world views. Who's right? How should we be living in light of the message of Jesus, the risen Savior and Lord of the world?

Lesson 1

- 1 Corinthians 6

Study Questions

Why should the Christians not take each other before the Roman court to settle disputes?

Who should be settling the disputes?

What does the presence of lawsuits within the church indicate to Paul regarding the condition of the Corinthian church?

How should they be behaving toward one another?

What kind of people were they acting like?

How does Paul feel about that?

Why is porneia (sexual intercourse outside of marriage) wrong?

What is Paul's attitude toward (or, better, theology concerning) the human body?

Food for Thought

A Higher Standard

There are two ways that we can read chapters 5-6. If you were to outline them, the flow would go something like this:

- You are proud about the sexual immorality of your brother. Don't be proud; expel him before he ruins the whole group.
- Don't drag each other to the Roman courts like the wicked do. Behave like the children of God that you are. The wicked won't inherit the Kingdom, so don't slip back into those old ways.
- Sexual immorality is a sin that destroys your body, and your body is a good thing that God really values...He even lives in it!

The first way we could read it is:

Subject 1: expel the immoral brother

Subject 2: don't take each other to court

Subject 3: don't be sexually immoral

In this view we have three disjointed, isolated topics. Each has something very important to say to us both then and now.

However, there is another way it could be read. It doesn't seem like there is a distinct break between these topics. Rather, it seems that Paul flows seamlessly through all three sections and thus sandwiches the issue of disputes between his introduction and his conclusion regarding the topic of immorality. The question is, "Why?"

It is possible that Paul is dealing with an issue here that is much larger than sexual immorality alone. Now, of course, he is violently opposed to the open acceptance of porneia within the fellowship of the church. Yet, perhaps he sees this as a symptom of something much deeper going on. It may be that the church was actually divided about this issue and, instead of resolving it within their own community, they brought it before the Roman judicial system.

Here we see the heart of their problem. The church had not yet realized that they were no longer part of the world system from which they had emerged. The answers to their questions were not in the law courts of Rome, or at the schools of the Greek philosophers, or even at the foot of the Rabbi who taught the Torah. Through their vow of allegiance to Jesus, the King of the whole world, they were now part of a system that was above all those systems. It was a system that did not call for vengeance or retaliation or self-indulgence. It was a system that lives with the ethic of loving one another and placing the needs of the other ahead of one's own. The answers to their questions were found in the Word of God – Jesus Himself -- as His Spirit dwelt within their own body/temples.

Freedom vs. Responsibility

In this chapter we see a phrase that is repeated twice in this letter and elsewhere in key passages within all of Paul's letters. It is found in verse 12, "Everything is permissible for me, but not everything is beneficial." Here is the Law of Paul. Yes, Paul was advocating an ethical system that was free from the ethnic exclusivity and bondage that came from the Jewish distortion of Moses' Law Code. In that sense, everything IS permissible...technically. For that Paul was deemed a heretic and a flaming liberal by the Jewish culture. He was accused of advocating a "libertine" lifestyle in which the individual was free to pursue any activity that would fulfill his own needs and desires. This kind of moral relativism was a threat to God's covenant people and was a slippery slope that would lead the deceived into the fires of Hell.

Ironically, Paul was not only accused of being libertine, but, to his dismay, many of his followers had distorted his teaching and began to practice a lifestyle that reflected this idea. Many of the new believers had attached themselves to the Greek philosophy that believed the body and all things physical were meaningless and therefore had no impact on one's spiritual life. Thus people were indulging their bodily desires for food, relaxation, and sex in a self-centered, uncaring frenzy.

Paul's response to this was, "STOP IT! The freedom that we have by being citizens of Jesus' Kingdom is not freedom to stuff our face and get our cheap thrills. It is the freedom that only comes when we die to our self and rise to a new life that is God-centered and other-oriented. We are not free to serve ourselves; we are free to serve others. When people approach our physical bodies, they are not encountering some meaningless flesh-suit that can be used and abused because it will be ultimately discarded in the end. No, they are approaching a beautiful creation of God that was designed to be the temple, the dwelling place of the Spirit of God and the vehicle of God's healing love to the whole world. Yes we have physical desires and needs for food, rest, and sex, but those desires and needs have purpose. Food fuels the Spirit vehicle, rest keeps it refreshed and long-lasting, and sex both procreates it for future generations as well as reflects the intimate bond of love that can only be experienced through selfless covenant. This is the freedom that I am advocating and that Jesus brought to us when He died on the cross and rose from the dead."

We need to ask ourselves today, "How is my temple being used?" Am I taking care of it well by eating right, getting proper sleep, and exercising? Am I keeping it sexually pure, both in my thought life as well as my physical activities? Or, am I devaluing God's creation and simply using it and abusing it to feed my own selfish cravings? We live in a society, much like Corinth, that caters to the self-centered indulgences. Let's be sure to keep our eyes focused on God and others, while properly taking care of our temples.

Lesson 2

- 1 Corinthians 7

Study Questions

How should a husband and wife view each other's bodies?

What is Paul's instruction to the unmarried or widowed?

What is his instruction to those who are married? Whose words are these?

What do you think Paul means by "the rest" in verse 12? What is his instruction to them? Whose words are these?

What is the governing principle for these instructions? (verse 15)

Summarize verses 17-24 in your own words. What does he mean when he says "retain your place in life?"

Why should they remain where they are? (verses 25-35)

In light of this passage, how would you describe Paul's view of sexuality and marriage?

Food for Thought

Setting the Stage

Chapter 7 is one of those passages that has been a hotbed of controversy in the church ever since the day it was written. What is Paul talking about? What is he actually saying? At times it seems that he is contradicting himself.

If we are going to understand the heart of Paul's message we need to start by correctly translating verse 1. There are two issues that need clarity at this point. First, please understand that the word "marry" is not a good translation. In the Greek language the verse literally reads, "good to the man the woman not to touch." A smoother translation would be, "it is good for a man to not touch a woman." The Greek word translated 'touch' is the word *hapto* and it means, literally, "to light a fire." In the Old Testament it had the sense of touching something that would make you unclean according to the Law of Moses. When it is used in the context of a man touching a woman it meant touching sexually and carried with it a negative, unclean attitude toward the sexual touching: thus being used in the sense of fornication. So, the issue is in this chapter is not about marriage, but is about sexual intercourse between a man and woman. There is a big difference and this clarity will change the lenses that we wear when we try to interpret this passage.

The second point is to understand exactly what Paul is saying. Paul is not saying that marriage is bad, or that sex is bad. In fact, he is saying just the opposite. We must read verse 1 carefully and properly. Remember that Paul is responding to a question that had been written in a letter by the Corinthians and sent to Paul. Imagine Paul sitting at a desk with their letter sprawled out in front of him. He thinks to himself, "Now, what was their first question? Ah, yes, here it is: 'Someone in the church has proposed that it is good for a man not to touch a woman (it is good to not have sex)...how do you feel about that, Paul?' Hmmm...let me see. Considering all of the careless and destructive sexual activity taking place in Corinth, that is a valid question. Here's what I think..."

Now, before we try to interpret this chapter, let's set one more piece of context in place. Remember we said that the Corinthian church was caught in the crossfire of a war between clashing cultures. The area of sexuality was one of the biggest issues that pitted these cultures against each other. To put it simply, there were four basic ideologies that were vying for the Corinthian's allegiance in regard to sexuality.

1. **The Ancient Greek Religions.** The worshippers of the ancient Greek gods viewed sex as a part of their worship. The men would have sex with the temple prostitutes, both male and female, in order to arouse the gods. Their bodies were hunks of meat used sexually in the temple of the gods.

2. **The Greek Philosophers, camp "A."** All Greek philosophies were based on the premise that there was a separation between the physical and the spiritual realms. This is called Platonic Dualism. Platonic because it was popularized by the philosopher named Plato who lived a few centuries earlier, and Dualism because it saw the universe divided into two separate compartments –Good/ Spirit vs. Bad/Physical. The practical application of this philosophy took on two forms. The first form is found in camp "A." This camp saw all physical things – desires for food, rest, sex, power, etc. – to be repulsive and evil; they were to be avoided at all cost. Therefore, they would propose that "it is good for a man to never have sex with a woman." Why? Because sex was the lowest form of human filthiness. Women were disgusting, sexual desire was a sign of a weak mind, and the truly enlightened would never stoop to such degradation.

3. **The Greek Philosopher, camp "B."** Another group of philosophical schools applied Platonic Dualism in an entirely different fashion. They reasoned that, since the flesh and all matter were really illusion in the first place, it didn't really matter what I did with my body. Why not party like it's 1999! Eat, drink, and be merry, for tomorrow we die. Throw caution to the wind! Party hardy! Indulge yourself, because all that matters is that you have correct belief and ideas in your mind and your spirit will transcend the physical world and none of this partying will matter.

4. **The Jewish culture.** Of these four camps, the Jewish ethic was closest to the heart of God. That only makes sense since it was based on the Torah that God had given the people. However, over the centuries the Torah had become distorted. By the time Jesus and Paul were alive it had come to be understood that men basically owned their wives. Women were little more than slaves and good for nothing other than making babies and keeping house. A man could do

what he wanted with his wife, both sexually and otherwise, and the woman had very little, if anything, to say about it. You can imagine the types of physical and sexual abuse that kind of system had the potential to foster.

With that context in mind, we can summarize this chapter with three basic messages.

Being Single is Good

Paul was a single man who felt called by God to be single so that he could devote himself to serve the Lord. Something that we don't understand about this is that, for a Pharisee, this was a shameful thing. In the Jewish culture it was considered dishonorable for a man to not have a wife. The core unit of the covenant people of God was the family, and the man was the priest of his household. God instructed the man to instruct his children in the ways of the Torah and to pass on the traditions of his people to the next generation and the generations to come. A man's quiver was supposed to be full, and if he had no arrows, how could he obey God? If a man didn't marry and have as many children as he possibly could then he was snubbing God's grace and his gift of procreation, and actually violating his purpose in the world. Even further, it was a pagan practice to castrate the priest (called a eunuch) so that he could be celibate and devoted to the worship of the gods. Therefore, the shepherds of God's people, above all else had to be married and procreate. Thus, it was required for a Rabbi to have a wife, otherwise he could not teach. So, just imagine how the Jews must have felt about this single, celibate, rabbi who proposed a Kingdom of God apart from circumcision and the Law of Moses. That's just pure blasphemy from the pit of Hell.

Paul is saying to the church, "yes, it is OK to be single and sexually celibate. Actually I personally prefer it. I would recommend it to everyone, because it keeps your mind focused on God and not on the inevitable complexities that come with a wife, children, and the duties of maintaining a household. Yet, I realize that singleness is a gift that is not given to everyone. Still, it is NOT a sin to be single. It is a privilege."

Here's the message for our world. If you are single, don't listen to the Christians who make you feel like you are not complete because you aren't married. Don't you hate it when people make you feel like you have terminal cancer when you tell them that you aren't married? You aren't sick! You don't have to be married to be complete. You don't have to have children to be honoring to God. You are valid just the way you are. If you desire to be married and have children, then that's fine, but don't desire it because you think it is what a 'good Christian' is supposed to do. You do what God is asking you to do. The truth is that the freedom you have in your singleness is a gift that married people can only fantasize about. Use it for God's glory. Get out there and set the world on fire with the love of God!

Being Married is Good

Now comes the flip side of Paul's argument. In response to the statement that 'it is good for a man not to touch a woman,' he says, "WRONG!" God created sex. It is good. It is natural. Don't you remember that God created Adam, then created Eve from Adam's body, then said that it was not good for Adam to be alone, and then said that they should become one flesh? The act of sexual intercourse between a man and a woman that are united in an eternal covenant before God is about the closest physical image to the intimacy that we share with God.

Paul is saying to the Jewish culture, "The man does not dominate the woman. His body belongs to her and her body belongs to him. This shows equality in marriage. Sex is not about getting what I want; sex is about giving to the other. In the covenant bond of marriage a man and woman can take all the time necessary to discover the needs of their spouse and learn to serve one another in every way – emotionally and physically."

To the Greek culture, Paul says, "The universe is not divided into the spiritual and the physical. The spiritual and the physical are intermixed. God is in all things and loves all of His creation, even sex. Sex is good. It is not a filthy act that only those bound to their animal-like instincts succumb. It is a gift of God for the bond of marriage. Sex outside of marriage is self-focused and destructive, that's true. We need to run away from that like the plague, but that does not mean that sex itself is filthy. "

Here's the message for our world. If you are married, then rejoice in that. If you have children, then raise them well and in the rule of Jesus' love. Don't use sex as a tool to manipulate your spouse or as a vehicle to meet your own needs. Talk to each other. Talk about your sexual issues. Don't be afraid to say what you like and what you don't like. Seek to meet each others needs and, in so doing, you will be reflecting the Kingdom of God on Earth.

Being Undistracted is Best

For the majority of this chapter Paul instructs the people to "remain as you are." What is he talking about, and why? Once again, we must remember that the Corinthians were being pulled in multiple directions. Some people were saying, "If you want to be a true Christian you have to come over to our camp and be like us." Others were saying, "No, you need to come over here and be like us." Paul was responding by saying, "NO! You don't have to go anywhere and be anything other than what you are. Being a follower of Jesus has nothing to do with being in a particular culture. One culture looks and feels this way, another looks and feels that way. Some think you can't be single and be a good Christian. Others say you can do whatever you want sexually as a Christian. Still others say you shouldn't have sex at all, even if you're married. All extremes are wrong. If you are married, stay married and enjoy sex. If you are single, stay single and enjoy your freedom. If you want to have sex, then get married because porneia will kill you."

"But," Paul continues, "you are all missing the point. The Kingdom of God isn't about marrying and giving in marriage. It isn't about being single or not being single. The Kingdom of God is about having a heart that is devoted to God and devoted to the love and respect of the other.

If you are a single person and Jesus' Kingdom rules in your heart, then you will not have sex with another person, male or female, because you love that person and do not want to steal anything from them in order to fulfill your own selfish desire. And, you know that you can't give to them sexually if you have not given everything to them in a covenant of marriage. Therefore, if your eyes are on Jesus you will be free from porneia.

If you are married and the Kingdom of God rules in your heart then you will love your spouse more than yourself and will not use or abuse them. That is what this is really all about, so stop your bickering and arguing over whose culturally based sex and marriage ethic is "right" and start focusing on Jesus' plan for the Kingdom of God on Earth."

The message is the same for us. The key to this whole passage is found in verse 35, "that you may live in a right way in undivided devotion to the Lord." The world we live in is a distraction. Does that mean it is evil? No. God created the world and called it good. We were meant to live in the physical world, to enjoy nature, to care for the planet, to love and touch and hold each other, to eat and drink, to dance, to paint, to sleep, to play, to work. All of these things are good. And, in the same space, all of these things can become distractions that can take our focus off of God. Isn't it ironic that the very good gifts that God has given us to point us to Him can become distracting idols that can consume our hearts, minds, pocketbooks, and schedules and steal our relationship with Him?

Let's remember that we are not in control of the things in our lives. We do not own our home, or our spouse, or our children, or our destiny. These things are gifts from God, given to us to use for His glory in order to be conduits of His blessing to the world. We can either let them distract us from Him, or be the tools that He uses to draw us close to Him. How will you use your beautiful, physical world for God today?

Lesson 3

- 1 Corinthians 8

Study Questions

What is the contrast between knowledge and love?

How is God described in verses 4-7?

How does this knowledge affect one's view on eating idol meat?

How does one's theology (understanding about the nature of God) affect one's daily practice (in this case, the eating of meat)?

Restate verses 9-13 in your own words.

What might be some possible "idol meat" issues in our current culture?

Food for Thought

Setting the Stage

As 21st century readers it could be very easy to gloss right over these 13 verses and think that the issue of meat sacrificed to idols is so foreign to our culture that there is no relevance to our lives. Please don't make that mistake. There are some precious gems in this chapter, and the two that follow, that, when the practical issue of meat is knocked off the sides, will shine brightly on the topic of living in Jesus' Kingdom in the 21st century.

Keep in mind the theme that has been running through our study. The Corinthian church was being torn apart by conflicting cultures. How was it possible for a Jew to be in unity, the bond of peace, and the intimacy of being one body with a Greek? If there was any one issue that divided the church right down the middle and made it impossible a) for the church to interact with the broader culture of Corinth and be a missional presence, and b) for Jewish Christians and Greek Christians to sit down at a meal together, it was the issue of meat that had been sacrificed to Greek and Roman gods.

Allow me to let a couple of scholars set the stage for us on this issue.

> *Sacrifice to the gods was an integral part of ancient life. It might be of two kinds, **private** or **public**. In **private sacrifice** the animal was divided into three parts. A token part was burned on the altar...' the priests received their rightful portion...' the worshipper himself received the rest of the meat. With the meat he gave a banquet. Sometimes these feasts were in the house of the hosts; sometimes they were even in the temple of the god to whom the sacrifice had been made.... The problem which confronted the Christian was, 'Could he take part in such a feast at all? Could he possibly take upon his lips meat that had been offered to an idol, to a heathen god?' If he could not, then he was going to cut himself off almost entirely from all social occasions.... In **public sacrifice**..., after the requisite symbolic amount had been burned and after the priests had received their share, the rest of the meat fell to the magistrates and others. What they did not use they sold to the shops and to the markets; and therefore, even when the meat was bought in the shops, it might well have already been offered to some*

idol and to some heathen god....

What complicated matters still further was this – that age believed strongly and fearfully in demons and evils....they were always lurking to gain an entry into a man's body and, if they did get in, they would injure his body and unhinge his mind....These spirits settled on the food as a man ate and so got inside him. One of the ways to avoid that was to dedicate the meat to some good god.... It therefore followed that a man could hardly eat meat at all which was not in some way connected with a heathen god. Could the Christian eat it? ....To the Christian in Corinth, or any other great city, it was a problem which pervaded all life, and which has to be settled one way or the other." [1]

From that description you can see the theological dilemma that the new believer would have. Now, read this next piece and see how it impacted the practical life of the church as it gathered together.

The early believers met in houses (cf. 1 Cor 16:19; Rom 16:5; Philem 2; Col 4:15) not strictly by default (i.e., because there was nowhere else to meet) but deliberately, because the house setting provided the facilities which accommodated the practices of the early communities.... The one feature of the assembly that necessitated a house setting was the common meal, including the Lord's Supper. Based on the tradition of the Last Supper (Mk 14:17; cf. 1 Cor 11:17–34), which was held in an "upper room," the early Christian meal was an important aspect of the life of the community. The house, in addition to being at the immediate disposal of the community, furnished the facilities for the preparation of common meals. It is no coincidence that when the meals no longer featured in the gatherings, the house setting was no longer necessary. When food preparation and dining facilities were no longer required, a large hall (and later the basilica) was found to be more appropriate for the growing number of Christians. [My insertion: note the implications for house church!!!]

The nature of the early Christian gatherings—especially for meals—took on added significance when the Gentile converts were included. For a devout Jew to associate with a Gentile, or "sinner," was perilous, as is readily observed in the Gospels when the Pharisees criticize Jesus for having table fellowship with "sinners." Although Law abiding Jews allowed the possibility of restricted table fellowship between a Jew and a non-Jew (i.e., with proselytes, resident aliens and God-fearers), the rules and regulations were so stringent that they did not promote broad associations.... [2]

This issue has impact in two arenas. First it impacted the gathering together and intimacy of the local church. Here you have a group of people who are supposed to be a family, and their primary form of gathering and worshipping God was to gather in a home around a meal, yet the very thing (food) that was supposed to unite them was dividing them. What did you eat?

Secondly, it impacted evangelism. If a Christian was forbidden to eat meat, then that basically meant they could never go to the home of a non-Christian for a meal, because the chances were that what was set before them had idol meat in it. That meant that children could not visit their parents and share a meal. That meant that when your neighbor invited you over for a friendly barbeque you had to decline. A strict rule of NO IDOL MEAT automatically cut you off from the world. What were they to do?

Knowledge vs. love

In this passage it seems that Paul is talking to two groups of people who possess 'knowledge.' The first was the Jewish crowd. Jews knew that idols were nothing because they knew that there was only one God. The Shema (Deuteronomy 6:4-6) was the core of their theology and it declared, "Hear, O Israel, the Lord our God, the Lord is one." For the Jewish crowd, the idea that not eating meat might cut them off from the pagan world was a good idea. That was the point, after all, wasn't it? Even more than circumcision, the Jewish dietary laws set the Jewish family apart from the "world" and by default, made it impossible for them to interact with Gentiles on a heart-felt, "table fellowship" level.

The second crowd that possessed knowledge was the Greek philosophy crowd. The word translated "knowledge" is the Greek word *gnosis* from which the later philosophical system called Gnosticism derived its name. True Gnosticism didn't emerge until the second century, but the seeds of that philosophy were very present in Corinth as Greek converts to Jesus tried to reconcile his message with their dualistic ideas. The Gnostics believed that being a Christian was all about having the right ideas about God in your mind; special knowledge. Spirituality was an internal affair, a private matter, that had little impact on daily life and behavior. Those with "weaker minds" were the ones who were caught up in childish issues about meat and diet and sexual behavior and the like. The ones with "knowledge" were above all that and were able to do whatever they wanted because they knew that there was one God, who was pure spirit, who didn't care about those trivial issues.

Look at how Paul addresses both groups and turns their theology inside out. In verse 6 he heads straight for the beloved Shema and redefines it. There is one God, yes, and there is one Lord. That Lord is Jesus. What was Jesus all about? He was about love. Did Jesus care about being considered unclean because of interacting with unclean people? No. Jesus was the one who went to the Samaritan woman and gave her living water. He was the one who interacted with "sinners" and "tax-collectors." He was the one who said to the Pharisees that it is not what goes into a man's mouth that makes him unclean, but it is what comes out of his mouth that makes him clean or unclean. In other words, it is the condition of the heart that is the issue here, not the eating or not eating of meat. Jesus didn't come to isolate His people from the world; He did not come to condemn the world, but to rescue the world. The kind of 'knowledge' that the Jewish and the Greek crowds had was the kind of knowledge that fills you with pompous, self-righteous hot air. It makes you float above the crowd in an aloof and disconnected condemnation of the ignorant masses below you. The love that Jesus brought to the world, and expects His followers to emulate, is the kind of love that gets down in the mud with people and becomes a bedrock of truth upon which people can stand and begin to see the true nature of the God who created them, loves them, and calls them home to sit at His table and eat with Him. Knowledge puffs up, but love builds up.

The power of belief

Notice what makes something sinful for someone. Is it the meat that is sinful? Is the meat actually infected with demons, so that if you eat it you will become possessed? No. Meat is meat. Idols are nothing. However, if a person believes that the meat is infected with demons, then it will be and they will be infected. Did the meat do it? No, it was their disobedience that did it. For many of the new believers the idol meat was tainted and they could not bring themselves to eat it. For the Jew, it was breaking the dietary laws that were so ingrained in their mind that they would feel like they were betraying God by eating. For the Greek convert the idol meat brought back so many memories of former behaviors that it would feel dirty to eat the meat. If they were convinced that it was wrong, then, for them it was wrong.

This has two implications for us. First, it demonstrates the importance of the continued pursuit of God's heart and knowledge about who He really is and what He really wants from us. Our beliefs are dictated by our knowledge of God, not just cognitive information, but our being known by God relationally. The battle is in the mind, because what we believe will impact how we behave.

Secondly, it helps us to have empathy and love for others who seem to be fixated on a certain sin or a code of behavior. Many Christians in our world are struggling through these issues. True, we don't have meat that has been sacrificed to idols in our culture that is as obvious as it was in Corinth, but that doesn't mean that there isn't tons of idolatry going on all around us. As Americans, our culture worships the god of power, money, individuality, personal rights, freedom, convenience, self-fulfillment, etc. Nearly every, if not all, power structures in our society – government, schools, corporations, even churches – bow down to the god of efficiency and the bottom line. Ethical shortcuts are taken at every turn. Our airwaves are saturated with escapist, lust-gratifying, marketing and entertainment that caters to our desire to numb out and take care of self. In light of this, most of the things we purchase and consume are tainted with idolatry.

As one example among thousands, many Christians view the issue of fair trade is a huge area of idolatry and corruption. They observe that the mega corporations use and abuse poor countries and exploit their situation so that Americans can save a few cents on their latte or DVD player. They are appalled by this, and rightly so, and can't believe that a Christian would advocate such a practice by purchasing certain items or shopping at certain establishments. Are these products meat that has been sacrificed to idols? In many ways, yes, they are. It would be easy to make a case that almost everything we do in our society is, in some way tainted by the idolatry of American consumerism.

There are many other examples of idol meat in our culture. Should Christians drink alcohol? Should Christians watch movies and support Hollywood? Should Christians boycott companies who support issues like abortion, gay marriage, etc.? Should Christians go to Disneyland? Have women wear pants? Allow children to go to public schools? Participate in government? Go to war? Dance?

Listen to 'secular' music? The list goes on and on, depending upon which flavor of Christianity you are discussing.

What do we do with all these issues? Do we run away? Do we isolate? Do we condemn those who flaunt their freedom around, or conversely, condemn those who make a big deal out of everything? The answer lies here, in this passage. The person who thinks it is defiled, to him it is defiled and if he partakes in it, he is actually sinning and opening up his heart to the enemy to sow the seeds of blame, shame, doubt, fear, bitterness, anger, and such.

Freedom to love

Once again, Paul comes back to defend and further define his message of freedom in Christ. To be free is not to do whatever one wants. To have knowledge about the silliness of meat and idols is not the freedom to condemn and trivialize the issues and ridicule those who are wrestling with it. We have been set free to love others. We have been set free from the need to be "right," to stroke our own ego, and to indulge in whatever we want at the expense of others. We are dead to ourselves and alive in Christ to come along side every human being, meet them where they are, respect them in that space, and draw them into the love of God so that they can grow in it and thrive in the Kingdom of God.

In lesson 4 Paul will expound further on what this kind of freedom looks like. For now the simple message is this, "Be careful that the exercise of your freedom does not become a stumbling block to the weak."

Lesson 4

• 1 Corinthians 9

Study Questions

What rights does Paul claim to have?

How did he gain these rights?

What analogies does Paul use to defend his claim to these rights?

Did Paul exercise his rights? Why or why not?

What social strata did Paul voluntarily associate himself with? Why?

What seems to be Paul's motivating force behind his explanation in verses 19-27?

Food for Thought

In Paul's world social status was everything. The social strata in the Roman Empire went something like this: Caesar was the image of God and the savior of the world, his governors were the principalities and rulers of the various regions in the empire and their word was law. Within each local city the pecking order went down the chain:

1. Roman magistrate
2. Local government of the city; comprised of wealthy, landowning men. These were the only people who had the right to vote
3. Dignitaries such as philosophers, scientists, and artists (these were a special sub-class of #2; therefore they had the right to vote and participate in state affairs.)
4. Guild workers who earned their living by a craft
5. Wives of wealthy land owners who managed the affairs and commerce of the estate
6. Non-Roman Citizens who worked or farmed to simply survive, but had no rights
7. Freedmen – former slaves who had earned their freedom through paying back a debt or were given their freedom as a reward from their master.
8. Women
9. Children
10. The poor and sick that were not slaves but outcast by society
11. Slaves – humans who were owned by others and had no rights whatsoever. (ironically this class made up about 2/3 of the population)

Unlike some cultures, like India, where a person is born into a caste and has no chance for upward mobility, the Greek culture did allow for people to better themselves and move up the social scale. This mobility-possibility fostered a spirit of competition, self-exaltation, and the exhibition of ones own credentials in order to ensure ones place in the social pecking order. It was common practice for a great teacher to come into town, flaunt his great eloquence in the public square, boast about his vast achievements and high connections, and expect that the people will throw their money at him in order to further his great work of deep thinking and educating. Dignitaries of this sort were always invited to the best feasts and seated in the place of honor at the banquet.

According to the cultural standard, Paul fit into the third category. He was born a Roman citizen which gave him the right to participate in state affairs and protected him from mob law. He was also a highly trained rabbi who had studied under one of the most respected rabbis of his generation. So, when Paul entered into a new city he had the right to enter both the public forum where he could debate his ideas with the philosophers as well as the synagogue where he would be invited to teach from the Torah. Beyond those unique and special rights, he had the additional unique standing to have been hand-picked by Jesus Himself and given the authority of an apostle – a special ambassador that had the right to speak on behalf of Jesus. When it came to rights and privileged place in society, Paul was in the upper echelon.

So, why are we talking about this? Why does Paul spend much of chapter 9 articulating his special rights to the people who obviously knew that he had them? Is chapter 9 a new topic that changes from the topic of idol meat in chapter 8?

The key to understanding this passage and how it relates to chapter 8 is the word *freedom*. In 8:9 Paul instructs the Corinthians to "be careful that the exercise of your freedom does not become a stumbling block to the weak." In 9:1 he continues the flow of thought by using himself as the prime illustration for his point. "Am I not free?" Allow me to paraphrase,

> "You Corinthians are still concerned with social status. You worry yourself over who is 'in' and who is 'out'; who is important and who is a loser. You worry about cultural issues that divide you and social status that divides you. If there was ever a person who had the right to look down his nose at all of you and exercise his rights to force you to serve him hand and foot, it was me. I have the right to tell you what to do. I have the right to flaunt my education and my fancy words in front of you so that you will bow in awed reverence of my eloquence, knowledge, and social status. You should be supporting my ministry and pampering me like all those other schools treat their teachers. I have the right according to both Greek standards, Roman standards, and Jewish standards.

> But do I exercise those rights? NO I DON'T. Now, don't take this the wrong way. I'm not using reverse psychology to guilt you into supporting me. I'm not boasting in myself. I'm simply showing you the kind of ethic that Jesus has introduced to the world. The Kingdom of God is an inverted system from the Roman Empire and all other human systems. In the Kingdom of

> God, the greatest leaders become slaves. The actual image of God and Savior of the world did not strut His stuff across the heavens and force everyone to bow down to Him like Caesar, the imposter, does. Just the opposite. Jesus emptied Himself of all His glory and His rights and made Himself the lowest of the low. Then He asked His followers to do the same. I have come to you in humility and in a spirit of servanthood so that I could demonstrate God's love to you.

> Laws about food mean nothing to me. What matters to me is people's hearts and lives. I want to reach everyone with the good news that Jesus is the true Lord and Savior of the world. I want to bridge cultural gaps, mend broken fences, and bring unity to the body of Christ so that we can demonstrate the Kingdom of God in the world. If that means that I have to submit to Jewish laws in order to fellowship with Jews, then I will. Who cares? If it means that I have to eat at a meal in a pagan home and eat meat that has been offered to an idol, then I will. Who cares? I'll do whatever it takes to demonstrate the love of God to as many people as possible.

> I know I've been accused of being a libertine and a moral relativist and that I promote wild freedom. Well, if this kind of slave-identity is the kind of freedom that they mean, then so be it. Just let the record show that I am not serving myself. I am serving Jesus by serving you."

The challenge to us today is easy to say and extremely difficult to live. How much of our arguing in church is about the gospel, and how much of it is about defending ourselves and our personal rights and social standing? Are we afraid to look stupid? Are we afraid to lose power within our social structure, at whatever level? Are we afraid of being misunderstood and falsely accused, and thereby wrongly prosecuted and persecuted? According to Paul's example, we are called to rise above all of those ideas. Better stated, we are called to sink below all of those ideas, take off the trappings of self and status, put on the towel of the slave, and wash whoever's feet God shoves in our face, regardless of who or what they are.

Lesson 5

- 1 Corinthians 10

Study Questions

What kinds of things caused God to be displeased with the Israelites when they were wandering in the desert with Moses? Why?

What promise does Paul make to the church in verses 11-13?

How does Paul feel about idolatry? Why?

Restate verses 23-24 in your own words.

What should be the motivation behind all of our actions?

Food for Thought

In 10:1-11:1 Paul concludes his line of reasoning regarding the issue of meat sacrificed to idols. (It is important to include 11:1 in this. It isn't the intro to the next chapter; it's the punch line to chapters 8-10)

As you read chapter 10, and listen for the voice on the other side of the phone, you can hear two arguments that have been launched at Paul regarding his teaching about freedom and how it relates to the issue of idol meat. Let's analyze it by constructing a dialogue between Paul and his accusers:

A = Accuser
P = Paul

A: Paul, isn't true that by allowing Christians to eat meat that has been sacrificed to idols you are opening them up to idolatry. Isn't that the very thing that God warned Moses and the Israelites to avoid during the time of the Exodus?

P (verses 1-22):

Short answer: Of course I'm not promoting idolatry, I'm promoting unity in the body of Christ!

Long answer: You make a very good point. Yes, it is true that the Israelites got into a lot of trouble when they messed around with idols and sexual immorality. God was very displeased by this and many of them cut themselves off from fellowship with Him as a result.

However, notice what the problem was. They began as a unified group, eating the spiritual food. When they were unified they were actually eating the food of Jesus. It was when they started chasing after their own desires and meeting their own needs, rather than relying on Jesus to care for them, that they got into trouble.

Those stories are a great example for us. You're right; we should never worship idols or participate in sexual immorality. However, we are the ones who are responsible for those things. God has provided an escape hatch from temptation and He is always there to give us the strength to say no to it.

66

1 Corinthians

Here's the deal. We aren't in the Old Testament any more. We don't need to make sacrifices at Solomon's temple, nor do we need to make sacrifices at Zeus's temple either. We are all one in Jesus. We come to the Lord's Table where we are all one, regardless of culture, races, gender, or social status, and we eat the meat of His body and the drink offering of His blood. Anything that gets in the way of that unity threatens to divide the church and is a tool of Satan.

Of course we don't want anything to do with demons and idolatry. That is why we are promoting freedom from the laws and cultural barriers that divide and conquer us.

A: Paul, isn't true that you are promoting a libertine philosophy that say you can do whatever you want? Isn't that dangerous?

P (verse 23-30):

Short answer: Of course that's dangerous. If I were preaching that, then we'd all be lost.

Long answer: Yes, technically, by being free from the Laws of Moses we have the freedom to eat anything and do anything. Yet, as I have already said in this letter, doing anything I want anytime I want would be idiotic. It would not be very beneficial to the body of Christ if we lived that way. It would not build up the body of Christ, it would actually destroy it. You see, the whole point of freedom is to look out for the good of others.

What I am proposing is that it is possible for a follower of Jesus to go into a Greek home and enjoy a meal with that family without even batting an eye over the nature of the meat. Don't bring it up. Just smile, eat it, and get on to the real issue which is bridging the cultural gap and sharing the authentic love of Jesus with a neighbor. If the issue does come up, then submit to whatever the rule of the other man's conscience is. If you are going to offend somebody, then skip it. It's not worth offending somebody just to uphold your right to eat a pork chop! Be sensitive to others and put their needs before your rights.

(verses 31-33)

Let me conclude all of this with one simple phrase: IT'S NOT ABOUT YOU. Everything you do is for God's glory. He's the one we serve, and He's the one we answer to. Don't let anyone play God in your life. You do the things, or don't do the things, that you believe God has instructed you to do, or not do. Do it with conviction, and do it to demonstrate love for God and love for others.

(11:1)

If none of this makes sense, reread chapter 9, and just do what I'm doing. Put your pride in your pocket, risk being misunderstood, stoned, ridiculed, and attacked theologically and philosophically. Do it all so that you can simply live out the love of Jesus and so bring in the Kingdom of God in the Earth.

We've covered a lot of ground this lesson. We've probably also sparked a lot of controversial issues within your mind and your spiritual group. The question we need to ask ourselves, as ambassadors for Jesus in the 21st century, is how can we come to a place of selfless love in which we can serve each other and demonstrate the love of God to all people without falling into the trap of idolatry ourselves. Jesus did it. Paul did it. I know we can do it to.

67

Reading Paul's Mail

68

1 Corinthians

1 Corinthians part 3

This session we conclude Paul's response to the questions that had been presented to him from the church in Corinth. There are two questions left:

#1 - "What about spiritual gifts? What are they? How are we supposed to use them?"

Couched inside this question are two of the most controversial questions that the church faced in the 20th century:

What about speaking in tongues?

And

What about the role of women in the church?

We'll have fun trying to sort those out.

#2 – "Someone told us that the resurrection of the dead was not literally a physical resurrection. Is this true? If so, then how are we supposed to understand Jesus' resurrection and life after death?"

In chapter 16 Paul places a P.S. on the letter and reminds the church that he will be coming to take a collection for the church in Jerusalem that had recently come across some hard times. In that we will discuss giving and the subject of generosity.

69

Lesson 1

- 1 Corinthians 11

Study Questions

How is the relationship between a man and a woman described in verses 1-10?

How is the relationship between a man and a woman described, being "in the Lord" in verses 11-16?

In what way were the Corinthians abusing and misusing the Lord's Supper?

What is the purpose of the Lord's Supper?

What warning and instruction does Paul give the Corinthians regarding the Lord's Supper?

Food for Thought

At first glance it seems that chapter 11 is the beginning of a new section in the letter. In chapters 8-10 Paul addressed the issue of idol meat. Now, in chapter 11, he moves on to two seemingly unrelated items. The first item is regarding the role of women in worship and the second is about the observance of the Lord's Supper.

I would like to propose that this is not how we should read chapter 11. Having two unrelated "miscellaneous" items in between the issue of idol meat in 8-10 and the issue of spiritual gifts in 11-14 isn't logical. It makes more sense to read chapter 11 as a continuation of the previous section and interpret its content within that context. This makes sense when we observe the pattern in the letter. Throughout the letter Paul is addressing specific questions that had been presented by the Corinthians. We can detect the place where Paul ends one discussion and begins to address the next question with the phrase, "Now concerning..." In 8:1 Paul says, "Now concerning food sacrificed to idols..." Then he proceeds to build a theological perspective for the next few chapters. The next time we see that phrase is in 12:1 where he says "Now concerning spiritual gifts..." In chapter 11 Paul does not abruptly change gears, but continues a stream of thought from the end of chapter 10 right through chapter 11.

With this in mind, let's rewind the tape a bit and start with chapter 10 to see how the logical flow moves through to the end of chapter 11:

Chapter 10

- Don't be like the Israelites in the desert and be tempted into idolatry.
- Don't follow idols or worship demons, because when we sit at the Lord's table, we are coming together as a unified family – one loaf, one body; undivided.
- Everything is permissible, but not everything is beneficial, so don't needlessly offend anyone in the name of exercising your rights. Instead, do everything for God's glory and look out for the good of others so that they may be saved.

Chapter 11

- Now, let's talk about examples of doing things for God's glory and looking out for others:
  * *Example one: women in worship. OK ladies. Yes, it is true that in Christ you have been liberated from the oppression that culture has set on you. Yes, it's true that you technically have no law*

governing you, but let's be reasonable. You know that the *Greek prophetesses* utter their prophecies in a wild frenzy with their hair flying everywhere. You also know that only the prostitutes flaunt their long hair in order to entice the men to come in with them. You also know that only slaves and convicted adulteresses have their heads shaved. It is like that everywhere in the Empire, no matter what culture you visit. So, think about it. When people visit your gatherings, do you really want them to mistake you for one of the wild prophetesses of the Greeks, or the hookers, or the adulteresses? That would be counterproductive, wouldn't it? The purpose for your liberation is for you to be able to pray and prophesy along with the men in public, not like it was in the Jewish synagogue when you were kept silent. That is groundbreaking stuff. Yet, if you push this freedom and go wild with your hair flying around, uncovered, then you are circumventing the purpose of your freedom by bringing glory to yourself instead of God, and bringing disgrace to the community. Out of love for others and respect for God, please just follow the social customs and keep your head covered.

* *Example two: eating the meal.* Now we come to the conclusion of the issue regarding eating meat. When you come together as the family of God to share the common meal together, it seems that some of you have forgotten what the Lord's Supper is really all about. You think this meal is like all the other feasts that go on in Corinth. What are those feasts for? They are like the Who's Who of society. You can tell where a man falls on the social pecking order by the seat he has at the table. The rich eat first and eat a lot while the poor and the slaves just stand around drooling and wishing they were as special as those who are gorging themselves. That kind of stuff is totally inappropriate at the true Lord's Table. At this table there are no divisions. At this table everyone comes together as equals. We come together to remember that there is one Lord who, being God, humbled Himself by becoming human, voluntarily gave up His rights, allowed Himself to be

executed as a criminal, then rose bodily from the grave to establish His true governance over the Kingdom of God. We are His children and the Father has invited us to His table. This is not a place to jockey for position and grab all the goods. This is a place to become humbled in the presence of the Lord and sit side by side with your brothers and sisters. Out there, in the streets of Corinth, that guy sitting next to you may be considered your inferior, but here, at the Lord's Table, he is your brother and you are to respect him, love him, and treat him like the child of God that he truly is.

You see, regarding the question of meat sacrifice to idols, the issue isn't really meat at all. The issue is ***focus***. Are you focused on the cultural divisions that lie between Greeks and Jews, men and women, slaves and freemen, rich and poor, the 'ins' and the 'outs?' Or, are you focused on the fact that Jesus abolished all that stuff when He died and rose from the dead and He calls you to live above all that stuff. We are called to do everything we do for the glory and honor of God, nothing else. If your actions are needlessly causing someone to be confused and to stumble into a pit of self-destruction, then abdicate your rights and do what's best for the community. Serve one another and bring God glory.

What about the Woman thing?

At this point it would be easy to happily glide along and skirt the issue of women in the church of the 21st century. The big question that has been, once again, dividing the church for the last 50 years, has been how to interpret this passage in contemporary life. Should women have their head covered in church? Should women be subjugated under the authority of the man?

I do not presume to have the definitive answer on this topic. Much more learned scholars than I will debate this until the Lord returns. Here are some simple thoughts, humbly submitted for your appraisal:

Men and women are different. One of the things that Paul was trying to uphold was the uniqueness of the genders. In his proclamation that, in Christ, there is not male or female (Gal 3:28) there was the built-in possibility that his idea could be distorted and become a "unisex" theology. This couldn't be further from the truth. Men and women are extremely different from one another, and that is good. Paul supercedes the Law of Moses and the cultural mores of the Greeks and goes back to the creation story to demonstrate this truth. God created male and female in His image. Notice what that says; the image of God is both male and female. Within the dynamic, contrasting, diverse unity of the man and the woman lays the very image of God. God is community and relationship, and, ultimately love.

Look at this rich theology that Paul presents. He compares the relationship between the Father and the Son to the relationship between the man and the woman. The Son is the glory of the Father. The woman is the glory of the man. We believe that the Son and the Father are co-equal and co-eternal. Yet we also believe that the Father is not the Son and the Son is not the Father. It is a deep, deep mystery. So it is with the relationship between a woman and a man. They are co-equal and co-bearers of God's image. Yet, the man is not a woman and the woman is not a man.

What's the point of this? Simply this: No matter what the culture says, there are differences between men and women. Many of those differences are obvious, some are more subtle. As followers of Jesus we should celebrate the differences in the genders and not mush them together in a strange idea that the differences don't exist.

Culture plays heavily on the issue. The real difficulty in this issue is to know how much our understanding of gender roles are dictated to us by our host culture and how much is intrinsic in the original creation of man and woman. It is possible that Paul himself may have struggled with this issue (I know I may be stepping on some theological toes with that statement). Look at verse 14. He says, "Does not the very nature of things teach you that if a man has long hair, it is a disgrace to him, but that if a woman has long hair, it is her glory?" Well...um...no, not really, Paul. Where in nature does it demonstrate that? I think Paul was arguing that this cultural norm was so prevalent in the world of the Roman Empire that no one would argue against it. Everyone -- Roman, Greek, and Jew -- practiced the tradition of men having short hair and women having long hair. The men did not cover their heads in public, while the women did. That was just the way of things.

That isn't the way of things in the 21st century. Nobody covers their heads as a rule in our society. In fact, it is just the opposite. Let's do a quick experiment. Think back to old photographs that you've seen or old movies from America in the late 19th century and early 20th century. What was a common theme among the dress of men in society? Men wore hats everywhere; all the time. Why is that? Where did that tradition start? The only people who seem to cover their heads now are either cowboys, good-ole boys with baseball caps, or skater-dudes with knit caps. Of course, that will change with culture.

So, where does the issue of women keeping their head covered in church play into that when women don't cover their head anywhere in our culture? The cultural equivalent for today may have to do with modest dress and a seductive or rebellious air. It probably wouldn't be a good idea for a devoted follower of Jesus to come bouncing into worship, braless, with a tight tube top, a G-string and fish-net stockings. Somehow that might send the wrong message to the men (and other women) of the family and be a bit distracting. Things would get even more complicated if this woman were to get up in front of everyone and say, "Yesterday, while I was working the street corner, God gave me a word for you all." Imagine what that would communicate to the first time visitor? It is one thing to openly welcome the truly seeking prostitute into your church and meet her where she is, regardless of her attire. It is another thing to allow a leading woman in the church to project this kind of image as a representative of Jesus to the world.

It's all about the heart. As was the case in our discussion of idol meat, so it is in the discussion of head coverings. The specific issue of meat and head shawls is a dead point. It is irrelevant to life in the 21st century. However, the deep principle behind it is still alive and well. The truth about Paul's instruction was that women had been liberated in the church. The part we often overlook in these debates is the fact that Paul was acknowledging the fact that women were prophesying and praying publicly in their worship gatherings. That was unheard of in Jewish tradition. The message of Paul to these liberated women was, "enjoy your freedom, but don't be jerks about it. Respect the traditions, don't be needlessly misunderstood as a pagan prophet, and do everything out of love for others and for the glory of God."

Lesson 2

- 1 Corinthians 12

Study Questions

What is the test of the Holy Spirit in verse 3?

How many Spirits are there?

How many gifts are there?

What is the purpose behind each manifestation of the Spirit?

What is the point in Paul's analogy of the human body?

Does everyone get every gift?

Is one gift given to everyone? Why or why not?

Food for Thought

If you have any background in Evangelical churches, then chapters 12-14 are very familiar to you. Perhaps you have even taken spiritual gift inventories to determine where to best plug into the body of Christ so that you can begin active ministry. That is all well and good, but often times when a passage becomes so familiar to us we can lose its original context. Remember, the Corinthians have proposed the question to Paul regarding spiritual gifts. Our question should be, "what was their question?" Once again, we are sitting in the room while Paul is on the phone with the Corinthians, trying to guess what they are saying on the other end.

It seems that there was confusion in the church regarding the nature of the Holy Spirit and how the Spirit was manifest in the church. The part that we tend to lose sight of as modern readers is the fact that, in Greek culture, the ideas of people uttering prophesies and speaking in tongues, and doing miracles was not a new concept. In fact, the "wise" people of the Greek religion were doing it all the time. Within the hundreds of temples there were active prophets and prophetesses who were mystically connected to the gods and goddesses. The common person would seek out these people, often called "oracles," for wisdom and advice in their lives. Many would practice divination where they would do things like read the patterns in the entrails of a slaughtered animal, or the droppings of oil on water, or the alignment of the stars, or the patterns of the clouds to determine the will of the gods. Often these visions would be accompanied by mystical utterances and trancelike convulsions of the body.

So, when the Holy Spirit of the one true God showed up in Corinth, the people were trying to figure out what made this kind of filling with the Spirit different from the other. Paul proceeds to answer this question by pointing out some key distinctives:

The Spirit serves Jesus as Lord. Herein lays the heart of Paul's gospel.

Allow me to jump to our current society for a moment to demonstrate that when it comes to the role of the Holy Spirit we are wrestling with similar issues in our churches. As Eastern philosophy floods into the mainstream of Western American life, and as Pentecostalism and the Charismatic movement continue to sweep through the Christian denominations, the Western, Modern, Scientifically oriented, Evangelical Christian scratches his head and says, "What is from the Holy Spirit and what is not?"

You see, throughout history, all across the world, 'wise' people have tapped into the power of God's creation and discovered how to do amazing things like heal the sick, control the mind, gain universal knowledge, predict the future, control the elements, even raise the dead. This is true even today. In Eastern traditions they have found many ways to heal the body through herbs, meditation, and tapping into the life-energy-source of the universe. Are they fakes? Some are, but most aren't. They have actually tapped into something very real. They have been able to discover this power because God created the universe and His power resonates within it. The universe is a vast place and the mysteries of how it functions are infinite. As humans, created in the image of God, we have the insatiable desire to discover the power of God and understand how the power works. When we discover those powers and forces and figure out how to harness them, then we can do amazing, even miraculous things. For example, electricity was not invented in the 18th century; it was simply discovered and harnessed. If an ancient person were to see what we could do with electricity, they would think we were magicians. To the Westernized, Modern, Scientific mind, the Eastern healers look like freaks and charlatans, but the truth is that they have just discovered another source of power and learned how to harness it.

Now, back to Corinth. The Corinthian Christians were asking similar questions. In the time of Paul many cultures had discovered powerful ways to tap into God's natural healing power that is resident in the universe. If you were a resident in Corinth and you became ill you would probably go to the local healer who would do some form of ritual over you, tap into the healing power of the universe, and you would be healed. As we already mentioned, those "wise" people would probably speak in tongues and do many wonders.

Notice Paul's first distinctive about the Spirit. The Spirit of God is in submission to Jesus as Lord. The problem with the prophetesses and wise men were that they were operating outside of the will and authority of God. They were using their powers for their own glory. Isn't that what power does to us. If you had the ability to heal people with a touch, what would you do with it? If you didn't believe that there was a God who was ultimately in control of everything, and if you believed that life was essentially meaningless, and that the highest value was to do good for yourself, then wouldn't you be tempted to use your power to dominate others and get them to serve you. Be honest. You could have people eating out of the palm of your hand if you knew how to heal them, or predict their future, or cast a spell to make someone love them. That kind of power, under the authority of nothing but the self would be the ultimate addiction that would consume your soul, eat you up, and leave you for dead in a heap of self-absorbed futility.

Paul says, "Oh no. That is not what the Holy Spirit is all about. The Holy Spirit is about one thing; service to Jesus Christ as Lord and Master of the universe. Anything that is done outside of the will of God, in service to His Son Jesus is a tool for the enemy."

There is one Spirit. The Greeks believed in multiple gods. Those gods were in constant battle against each other. Humans were caught in the crossfire of cosmic ego rivalry and lived in constant fear wondering which prophet of which god they should go to for advice. Paul said, "Stop it! There is only one God. Those idols are 'mute.' They aren't real. There is only one Spirit. All power belongs to God and comes from God. There is no cosmic struggle. There is peace and harmony within the Kingdom of God. God loves you and He gives you one voice to listen to and calls you to be part of one body."

There is one purpose. Here is a very important distinctive. The purpose of the Spirit is to bring about the common good of the community. Those Greek freelancers who were tapping into God's power outside of His authority were in it for themselves. They wanted to be rich and famous and exert power over others. Paul says, "Hold on. Being a part of God's Kingdom is not about exalting yourself. The Spirit moves in you and you have access to His power for the benefit of others. As soon as you use that power for your own glory or for your own gain or to position yourself as more important than others, then you have moved out from under the authority of Jesus and the purpose of the Spirit."

There are many parts. In the same breath that Paul calls for one body he denounces the tyranny of spiritual cloning. There are many parts in the body of Christ. There are many kinds of people that serve many different functions. In order for a community to work you need to have people in every place in life. Think about what life would be like in your neighborhood if we didn't have a sanitation department. Garbage and human refuse would pile up and we would become infested with vermin and disease. We desperately need the men and women that faithfully collect our trash from the curbside. Now the tendency in the look-out-for-myself society is to look down on the sanitation workers and see them as the lower end of the socio economic strata. Be honest. How many young parents hold their children in their arms and wish that someday she will grow up to be a garbage collector? And yet, Paul says, "In the Kingdom of God the socio-economic strata are flattened out. There is no better/worse, more important/less important dichotomy here. In the body of Christ we all have a function and all of those functions serve to bring honor and glory to Jesus, because He is the head."

For life in the church of the 21st century, there are three questions we need to ask ourselves.

1. What is your spiritual gift?

2. How do I view the other spiritual gifts? (Do I think I'm superior, or do I think I'm inferior to the person who has the gift of _____?)

3. (most importantly) Have I submitted the use of my spiritual gift to the authority of Jesus and for the purpose of the common good of the body, not my own glory?

Lesson 3

- 1 Corinthians 13

Study Questions

What part does love play in the spiritual gifts? Why?

How is love described?

What part does love play in God's grand, eternal scheme of things?

Food for Thought

Ahh.... Today we come to the eye of the storm. Nestled in the middle of the constant correctives to chaotic Corinthians comes a beautiful gem that radiates the deep truth of God's Kingdom. Paul tells us about love; the most excellent way.

This short section has poetic form that can be divided into three sections.

Without Love You are Nothing

Here is a truth that we often forget. Just because you have a spiritual gift it doesn't mean you are spiritual. You could write tons of books about God, heal thousands of people, feed and house millions of homeless people, and do great and wonderful things, but if love is not the central driving force behind it, then Jesus will look at you and say, "Depart from me, I never knew you." Don't be easily impressed by "super-spiritual" people. God isn't. Love is all that matters.

What's Love Got to Do With It?

The previous section begs the question, "Yes, but what is love?" We throw that word around all the time. "I love ice cream" "I loved that movie" "I love this new lipstick color" "I love you." What are we really saying when we use the word love? More importantly, what is Paul saying when he uses the word love?

First of all, in Greek there are four words that we translate "love." The first is "Storge." It means the kind of love you can have for an inanimate object or a pet. The second is "eros." It deals with the sexual passions exchanged between a man and a woman. The third is "phileo." It means brotherly love; the kind of love exchanged between friends. The fourth is "agape." It is the kind of love that God has for His creation. God's love is agape love and it is agape that Paul is talking about in this chapter.

So, what is agape? Let's do a quick word study and explore the list of adjectives that Paul uses to define agape.

LOVE IS...

Makrothymeô - longsuffering, patient

God has a really long fuse and a really high boiling point. It takes a lot to stir Him up to anger. That doesn't mean He lets sin slide, it just means He gives us lots of chances to make mistakes, get up, make things right, and do it again before He finally brings judgment.

Chresteuomai – Good, excellent, kind.

In Rom. 2:4 Paul has tó chrçstón as a noun to describe the divine kindness which allows space for repentance, but which the impenitent disdain and hence store up wrath for themselves. What is meant is God's gracious restraint in face of His people's sins prior to Christ. chrçstótçs is used interchangeably in Rom. 2:4, and it occurs again in 11:22 with reference to God's gracious act in Christ. As Paul sees it, kindness constantly characterizes God, but this kindness finds particular expression and completion in His saving work in and through Christ. The continuity of God's kindness may also be seen in 1 Pet. 2:3, which applies Ps. 34:8 to Christ: "You have tasted the kindness of the Lord."[1]

LOVE IS NOT...

Zeleuô – to be zealous

The usual translation of this term is "zeal": a. as the capacity or state of passionate commitment; b. comprehensively for the forces that motivate personality (e.g., interest, taste, imitative zeal, rivalry, fame, enthusiasm); c. in the bad sense jealousy, envy, competition, contention.[2]

Love does not get overly emotional or worked up when the other gets out of line.

Perpereuomai – boast or brag.

Of contested origin, perpereuìomai relates to arrogance in speech, being associated with such concepts as loquacity, bluster, bragging, etc. It suggests a literary or rhetorical form of boasting. In 1 Cor. 13:4 it carries such varied nuances as arrogance, pretension, and impotent chatter. Antiquity in general opposes such boasting, but Paul bases its renunciation on the love that makes possible the eschatological life disclosed in faith and hope. Since God has opened up this possibility in Christ, the action of love is presented in personal terms. We do not set aside perpereuìesthai by practice etc., as in Stoicism; love itself sets it aside in us when we take this more excellent way.[3]

Physioô –puff up

"to puff up, blow up, inflate" (from phusa, "bellows"), is used metaphorically in the NT, in the sense of being "puffed" up with pride[4]

aschemoneô – a schemer, act unseemly toward another

"to be unseemly" (a, negative, and schema, "a form"), is used in 1 Cor. 7:36, "behave (himself) unseemly," i.e., so as to run the risk of bringing the virgin daughter into danger or disgrace, and in 13:5, "does (not) behave itself unseemly."[5]

Love doesn't take advantage of others or force itself upon another.

Zeteo ou heauto – seek after herself

1. Religiously this term denotes first the seeking of what is lost by the Son of Man with a view to saving it (Lk. 19:10; Mt. 18:12; Lk. 15:8). But it can also refer to God's requiring much from those to whom much is given (Lk. 12:48), or fruit from the tree (Lk. 13:6-7), or faithfulness from the steward (1 Cor. 4:2), or true worship from the righteous (Jn. 4:23). From this twofold use we see that the divine seeking involves at the same time a divine claiming. In John 8:50 the point seems to be that the Father looks after the glory of the Son and will judge those who refuse him recognition.

2. In many instances human seeking is the point. The basis here is the Greek use of zeteìo for philosophical inquiry (cf. 1 Cor. 1:22; Acts 17:27) and the LXX use for seeking God (cf. Rom. 10:20). The seeking of God in prayer in Mt. 7:7ff. follows LXX usage. Seeking covers the broader orientation of will: the seeking of God's kingdom and righteousness (Mt. 6:32-33), the seeking of things above (Col. 3:1), the seeking of the great goal of life (Mt. 13:45), the seeking of justification (Gal. 2:17). Such seeking can be perverted into the request for a sign whereby the demand of the gospel may be evaded (Mk. 8:11-12).[6]

Love makes its hearts desire to be for the other, not for herself.

(note: LXX is the Septuagent, the Greek translation of the Old Testament)

paroxynô – be provoked

The verb means "to spur," "to stir to anger," passive "to be provoked, incensed." ... In the NT the verb occurs in Acts 17:16, where the meaning is not that Paul is stimulated to preach but that he is honestly angered by the idolatry. Similarly in 1 Cor. 13:5 love does not let itself be provoked- there were many provoking things at Corinth.[7]

Ou logizomai to kakon – does not think about the bad, or keep a log book of the bad

Love does not keep a record of wrongs. It doesn't keep score of all the bad things you've done and then bring them up against you in a fight. Love forgets the bad.

Ou chaire epi te adikia – does not rejoice in what is not right

As the opposite of *dikaiosyìne*, it denotes "violation of the divine law," heading the list of vices in Rom. 1:29. It also means "legal injustice" (Rom. 9:14). It can have, too, the nuance of "unfaithfulness" (Rom. 3:5). In Rom. 6:13 it is a controlling force.[8]

INSTEAD. LOVE...

Synchairô aletheia – rejoices in truth

Chairo is the word for joy and is one of the fruit of the Spirit. With syn in front of it the meaning is "has joy together with" What does love rejoice with? Truth.

IN ALL THINGS, LOVE...

Stegô – covers ... all things

This verb comes from a stem meaning "to cover," "to conceal." It is a rare term but persists in both prose and common speech. Its basic meaning is "to keep covered," but this gives it such senses as "to protect," "to ward off," "to hold back," "to resist," "to support." It can also mean "to keep secret," "to keep silent," "to keep a confidence."[9]

Pisteuô – believes...all things

pisteuìo means "to trust" (also "to obey"), "to believe" (words), and in the passive "to enjoy confidence" (cf. the later sense "to confide in").[10]

elpizô – hopes...all things

The OT element of trust is strong when the relation is to persons, as in 2 Cor. 1:3; 5:11; 13:6. Trust in persons is the point in 1 Cor. 13:7, though it rests on trust in God (v. 13).[11]

Hypomenô – hyperwaits; waits for you until the bitter end

hypomeìno has the senses a. "to stay behind," "to stay alive," b. "to expect," c. "to stand firm," and d. "to endure," "to bear," "to suffer." hypomoneì means a. "standing fast" and b. "'expectation," "waiting." While hypomeìno is at first ethically neutral, hypomoneì becomes a prominent virtue in the sense of courageous endurance. As distinct from patience, it has the active significance of energetic if not necessarily successful resistance,

e.g., the bearing of pain by the wounded, the calm acceptance of strokes of destiny, heroism in face of bodily chastisement, or the firm refusal of bribes. True hypomoneì is not motivated outwardly by public opinion or hope of reward but inwardly by love of honor.[12]

Oudepote Ekpiptô – never fails

This word means "to fall out of or down from," "to make a sortie," "to go forth," "to deviate or digress," "to be cast ashore," "to be expelled," "to be omitted,'" "to stretch," and "to let slip." It is mostly literal in the LXX for various Hebrew terms; thus it denotes an ax flying from the shaft, a chopper slipping from the hand, a star falling from heaven, trees or horns that fall, flowers that fade[13]

Love never falls or ends.

Putting it all together... (a paraphrase)

> Love puts up with us even when we blow it, it is the most excellent way of goodness and kindness that gives us a chance, because it has a low boiling point.
>
> It doesn't toot its own horn or puff itself up. It doesn't force itself on others, it doesn't seek after its own desires. It is other-oriented.
>
> It doesn't get all riled up over silly things or keep a list of offenses to use against you. It doesn't get excited about the wrongs we've done, instead gets very excited when we dwell in the truth.
>
> In all things love protects us, believes in us, has hope that we will make it to the end, and always waits up for us, no matter how long it takes us to get there.
>
> In the end, love will never let us down or give up on us.

Love is All You Need

Paul concludes this love poem by reminding us that we are in the middle of the story. Right now we are on a journey in which we are being formed into the people that God made us to be. We are there, but not completely. In this in-between state we need the spiritual gifts to guide us and keep us on track. When we arrive fully in God's presence then the gifts will be useless for us.

When you boil it all down, the purpose for the gifts is to produce faith, hope, and love in us. Think about it. We continue on the journey because we believe that the journey is real. That is faith. We press on because we believe that the destination will be better than our current state and will be worth the effort. That is hope. As we travel we are called to do it all in love. When we arrive in the presence of God we will no longer need faith or hope because we will be there. The only thing we will need in that place is love. God is love. When we finish the journey we will be fully engulfed in the richness and infinite depth of God's unfailing love. Only love remains, now and forever. Live in its way.

That is the love of God for His people. That is the promise in which you can rest as a child of God. That is the example that Jesus set for us and the way of the gospel that He sends His Spirit to empower us to practice. That is why there are spiritual gifts.

Lesson 4

- 1 Corinthians 14

Study Questions

How does Paul feel about tongues?

How does Paul feel about prophecy?

Create a compare/contrast chart between tongues and prophecy.

Why should women be silent in the church?

What is the purpose of the public gathering?

How were the Corinthians violating that purpose?

Food for Thought

If ever there was a chapter in the Bible that held the hottest pot of controversy in the church it is probably 1 Corinthians 14. In the 20th century the two topics raised in this chapter divided almost every church in America. If a church wasn't being ripped apart by people debating over the role of tongues and prophecy then it was dividing over the role of women in the public arena of church life.

This is a very difficult section to write because we don't have enough time to deal with it adequately. The truth is that volumes have been written on each topic...and the controversy still rages on.

I will try to simply highlight the debates for you so that you can be more informed about what is going on. At the end I'll try to synthesize Paul's message in the context of the letter.

Tongues and Prophecy

The church in the Westernized, Modern world can be divided into two basic categories when it comes to this topic: Word Centered and Spirit Centered. In the sections below we will define tongues and prophecy from each perspective.

Word Centered

The spiritual gift of tongues and prophecy were present only in the era of the original apostles. These gifts served as God's vehicle to bring His authoritative word to the newly forming churches. Once the Apostles had written their gospels and letters to the churches, and had died off, then the church no longer needed tongues and prophecy because God's Authoritative Word had been captured in writing and preserved for the ages. Today the Holy Spirit still gives practical gifts such as teaching and administration, but the "manifestation" gifts like tongues, prophecy, healing, etc. are no longer necessary. The way the Holy Spirit speaks to us is by helping us understand the message of the Bible and applying it to our lives today.

Spirit Centered

The spiritual gifts of tongues and prophecy were given to people throughout the body of Christ, not just to the apostles. All of the gifts that were given to the early church are still present and active in the church today because the Holy Spirit has not changed. The Word of God is not limited to the Bible. Technically, the Word of God is the interaction God has directly with people through His spirit. The Bible is inspired and authoritative, and governs the Holy Spirit interaction of today, but it is not the only way to hear God's message.

A Continuum

As with all theological debates, there is a continuum of perspectives on this issue.

Word-Centered Extreme

Tongues and prophecy in the modern world are from the devil and are to be avoided. They are too subjective and open to personal agendas and manipulation. They challenge the authority of the Bible and lead people into deception and heresy. People who practice tongues are either channeling demons or are self-deluded and seeking an emotional high that makes them feel important.

Word-Centered Moderate

Tongues and prophecy are not evil, but they are unnecessary for the Modern Age. All we need is a correct interpretation of the scripture. We ask the Holy Spirit to guide us in this pursuit and empower us to serve Him well in the world. We can be open to tongues-speaking believers and agree to disagree, but we do reserve some skepticism toward their motives and behavior.

Word-Spirit Balance

Tongues and prophecy are alive and well today as they were in the ancient world. However, they are simply two of the many spiritual gifts mentioned in the letters and are not the definitive marks of the Spirit's presence. The definitive mark of the presence of God's Spirit in a person's life is the fruit of the Spirit as listed in Galatians 5, not a specific gift of the Spirit. There are many gifts given, tongues and prophecy among them; some people receive one, others receive another. There is not one gift that all people receive.

Also, the Bible is the authoritative Word of God for objective discernment, but the Word of God is still active through the personal interaction of the Spirit with His people. God speaks directly to His people, but He will never contradict His character as it is demonstrated in the Bible.

Spirit-Centered Moderate

A person does not need to have the gift of tongues to be saved. However, it is a sign of the second baptism of the Holy Spirit through which a person receives deeper connection with God. We can be open to non-tongue speaking believers, but we reserve some skepticism as to whether they really are functioning under the leadership and guidance of the Holy Spirit.

Spirit-Centered Extreme

Tongues and prophecy are the signifying marks that determine whether a person is actually saved and has the Holy Spirit dwelling within. People who don't have tongues have been deceived by the Modern, scientific mindset of intellectualism, have squelched the Spirit of God, and thereby are committing the unforgivable sin.

So, who's right? How do we know which camp to align with? I'll not say whose right, but I will show my cards and tell you where I stand at this point. I fall in the "Word-Spirit Balanced" camp. I tell you that so you know that the rest of this teaching flows from that perspective.

Paul's Words

Let's look to see what Paul actually says about these topics. In Paul's letter he is not denying the existence of these gifts within the general body of the church. He's actually encouraging them. Ironically, Paul does not lump them together as we do in the modern world. Paul's controversy is actually between the use of tongues in public worship versus the use of prophecy in public worship. Look at how Paul creates a compare/contrast chart between tongues and prophecy.

Comparison Chart

Tongues	Prophecy
Speaks to God in mysteries	Speaks to men for edification, exhortation, and consolation
Edifies himself	Edifies the church
Unintelligible sound	Distinct, intelligible words
A foreign language	An understandable language
Unfruitful for the mind	Edifying for the mind
Recommended by Paul	More highly recommended by Paul
A sign to the unbeliever	A sign for the believer
People will think you're insane	People will be convicted and repent
Allowed in public only when there is an interpreter	Allowed in public, but must be done in an orderly fashion

The real question for us, before we can decide which camp we fall in on the issue in the Modern World, is to determine what tongues and prophecy really were in the ancient world.

What is "tongues?"

The Greek word that we translate "tongues" is *glossa*. Literally the phrase Paul uses is "speaks in a tongue." There are basically two theories about what "tongues" means.

An ecstatic, spiritual language.

This theory acknowledges the fact that many religions in the ancient world recognized the practice of ecstatic, unintelligible speech as a sign that a person had contacted the spiritual realm of the gods. In light of this, a tongue is understood to be the process in which the human being makes a connection with the Holy Spirit and is taken into a higher realm of understanding. In a sense he is speaking in the language of God and the angels. The person speaking in tongues is not consciously aware of the objective meaning of the words, but is somehow mystically transformed through the process of making contact with the Spirit and being overtaken by Him. When the Spirit moves in a person the human mind is being transported into a realm that is beyond human words.

If this theory is true, then Paul is saying, "Hey, tongues is a private prayer language. It's good for you, but it does nothing for everyone around you. Save it for your prayer closet and don't flaunt it in the public gathering."

A supernatural ability to communicate cross-culturally.

The second theory understands "tongues" to literally mean a foreign language. In the ancient world of the Empire there were thousands of language groups living in very close proximity. Everyone spoke Greek as a trade language, but if a person wanted to communicate deep truths they spoke in their native tongue. In the story of the tower of Babel, God divided the nations by confusing their tongues. As a symbol of Jesus' mission to unify the world and bring all nations into the blessing of God, the Holy Spirit gave people the ability to speak in the hearer's native tongue. This accomplished two things. First, it demonstrated a miracle to the listener that this foreigner could speak his language

fluently. Second, it allowed the messenger to communicate the truth of God deeply and quickly, bypassing the painstaking process of learning a new language. Imagine how long it would have taken Paul to complete his missionary travels if he had to learn each language he encountered. Thus, tongues is a sign for the unbeliever, but does no good for a local congregation that all speak the same language.

If this theory is true, then Paul is saying, "Hey, tongues is for other people that you are trying to evangelize. If you use it in your local gathering then you are just showing off. Keep quiet and listen to the teaching that speaks to everyone in the group."

You can see that these two definitions are very different and the one you hold to will dramatically impact your stance in the larger debate. So, what's the answer? Honestly, I think its both. I think it is a deep mystery that we, in the modernized, Western world have lost sight of. One thing I do know, it was very real in the Corinthian Church and was causing all kinds of problems for them.

What is "prophecy?"

Now we must ask the same question regarding prophecy. It is important that we remember that all the religions of the ancient world had prophets. This was not only a Jewish or a Christian concept. That is why the Old Testament is full of so many warnings against false prophets. So, how was the role of the prophet understood in Corinthian culture? Kittel says,

> prophets in the Greek world are people who declare things imparted by the gods in direct inspiration or through signs, their task being one of interpretation. Oracle prophets proclaim the will or counsel of the gods in answer to direct questions that cover the whole range of private, political, and cultic life. Human criteria control the selection of oracle prophets, who usually come from higher social classes, and even their inspiration tends to be induced by human initiative. Oracle prophets enjoy high esteem and have official positions, so that they may often be asked to lead delegations etc. In some cases the verb *propheteuio* may include stating and presenting the question.[14]

Simply put, prophets were spokesmen for the gods. When a prophet spoke, he or she spoke in clear, intelligible words and delivered the message that the god wanted the people to hear. A Christian prophet was a person that spoke the words of the one true God, under the authority of Jesus, and in the power of the Holy Spirit.

What about women?

Before we pull it all together, let's fold the issue of women into the mix. At first read it sounds like Paul is prohibiting women from talking in church. Wow! That is a hard pill for the 21st century woman to swallow. Is that what Paul meant? What is he talking about? The first thing we must acknowledge is that Paul has a seeming contradiction in this letter regarding women in the church gathering. In chapter 11 he acknowledges that women do pray and prophecy in public. Here in chapter 14 he says that women should keep silent. Well, which is it? Whenever you encounter an apparent contradiction like this, there are basically three options for dealing with it. Either a) Paul is contradicting himself and he is conflicted, b) a later scribe inserted this passage because of cultural issues unrelated to Paul himself, or c) Paul is not contradicting himself but is actually addressing two different issues altogether. Options "a" and "b" leave us with some real problems of integrity in the scripture, so it is always best to explore "c" as far as possible in situations like this.

Read the following commentaries for some good insight:

> While addressing the topic of church order, Paul briefly digresses from his contrast of prophecy and tongues and regulations concerning them to address the interruptions of some women occurring during the teaching period of the church service. Unless Paul changes the subject from women's universal silence (v. 34) to asking questions (v. 35a) and back to universal silence again (v. 35b), his general statement about women's silence in church addresses only the specific issue of their challenges in verse 34a. The issue here is thus their weakness in Scripture, not their gender.

> **14:34.** Biblical law includes no specific text that enjoins silence or submission on women, although Paul could refer back to his creation argument in 11:8–9 or to the effects of the curse in Genesis 3:16. But he can also use "law" generally (1 Cor 14:21); thus here he could be referring only to the generally subordinate position of women

in Old Testament times. (On this reading, Paul counters an objection of Corinthian prophetesses, who do not think they should be in subjection; although Paul may not believe they should be subjected in all cultures, that they were in the Old Testament period suggests that it is not wrong for them to be submissive in some cultural settings. According to another view, Paul cites the Corinthians' view in 14:34–35 and refutes it in 14:36; cf. comment on 14:22. Others object that 14:36 is too weak to supply a refutation for 14:34–35.)

> **14:35.** Informed listeners customarily asked questions during lectures, but it was considered rude for the ignorant to do so. Although by modern standards literacy was generally low in antiquity (less so in the cities), women were far less trained in the Scriptures and public reasoning than men were. Paul does not expect these uneducated women to refrain from learning (indeed, that most of their culture had kept them from learning was the problem). Instead he provides the most progressive model of his day: their husbands are to respect their intellectual capabilities and give them private instruction. He wants them to stop interrupting the teaching period of the church service, however, because until they know more, they are distracting everyone and disrupting church order.[15]

> Obviously, this must be interpreted in light of 11:5 where it is clear that Paul understood that women were permitted to prophesy and to pray in public. The expression possibly has reference to what is alluded to in verse 35. They were not allowed to interrupt the service by speaking in tongues.[16]

Bringing it together

So what was Paul's issue with the Corinthians in this chapter? The issue was not that they were speaking in tongues, the issue was how they were speaking in tongues and how they were handling their public gatherings. Truly, it is the exact same issue that was at the heart of the idol meat controversy. The issue was arrogance. When the Corinthians got together they were continually trying to jockey for position and demonstrate how important they were. Can't you just see it now. 20-30 people gather together in a home for the purpose of sharing in the Lord's Supper together and having fellowship. As soon as they begin entering the house the fashion show begins. The wealthy members strut in pompously, flipping their gold embroidered tunic in the face of the carpenter. They brush past him and set their huge basket of choice meat, cheese, bread and fruit that they brought for the pot luck. "Oh yes, I had my servant run down to the market this morning, just so that I could bring the finest food to the feast." The carpenter and the slave girl only had some day-old loaves to bring.

After everyone has arrived you can see the rich people gathering to talk to the rich people and the poorer people standing over on the wall and hoping not to upset anyone.

The leader of the fellowship calls everyone together to begin their time of teaching, prayer, and encouragement. As soon as he opens his mouth, one of the poor people with the gift of tongues starts spouting off a stream of unintelligible sounds. This makes him feel really important because in normal Greek culture it was only the high class oracles that could do things like that. He spouts off for quite a while as everyone looks at him in uncomfortable disbelief.

Not to be outdone by a commoner, the rich woman with the gift of tongues starts spewing forth over the top of the poor guy's sounds. Before you know it there is a cacophony of spiritual one-upsmanship going on and the whole meeting is in total chaos.

When the man who is responsible to lead this meeting finally gets the people settled down he begins to teach from the Old Testament and remind the people about what Paul had taught them regarding Jesus and how he was the fulfillment of the coming Messiah. Just as he starts getting into a rhythm of teaching, one of the uneducated women pipes up with a question that displays her ignorance and really derails the teaching. Then another woman, who really enjoys this freedom and the attention it gives her, asks another inappropriate question. The poor teacher, out of politeness, has to stop every other sentence and answer basic questions.

So here's the church service: Arrogant tongues-speakers are trying to outdo each other to show that they are more loved and honored by God; the rich are bringing huge spreads of food to the feast and leaving the poor out; the women are prophesying with their heads uncovered and their hair flying around like a hooker; and the other women are pestering the teacher with irrelevant and childish questions. Now picture a visitor coming into that home to witness this mess. He thinks, "You guys are nuts! I definitely don't want anything to do with a God who produces this kind of chaos. I'm outta here!"

So Paul writes to the Corinthians and says, "STOP IT! Listen, the purpose of the gathering is for bringing glory to God and for mutual edification. God is not the God of chaos, He's the God of order. He brings order out of Chaos, don't you remember? So, here's what I want you to do. No more tongues in the public arena. That gift is for private prayer and for cross-cultural communication. If it happens at all, then it must be interpreted, otherwise it is meaningless and chaotic. When you come together, make sure everyone has something to contribute that is edifying for everybody. Take turns and let everyone speak, or sing, or bring whatever they are bringing. When someone is teaching, don't let the women keep interrupting. Let them go home and have their husbands bring them up to speed in the Torah and the proper behavior for public teaching. That way the group time won't be wasted on simple questions. When they're ready, then they can contribute to the mutual edification of the group. Remember, prophecy is the truth telling about God. It builds you up. Let that be the guiding principle for your meetings."

So What?

I realize this lesson has had a lot of reading. Hopefully it has been helpful. For the church in the 21st century the message remains the same. When we gather together we are coming for two reasons. First we come to honor and glorify our Risen Savior, Jesus Christ. We come together in equal humility in a spirit of service to Him. Secondly, we come together for mutual edification. That means we are to build each other up. We are there for the good of the other, not to get out of it what we want. God's love is selfless and other-oriented. May that be the spirit of our gatherings.

Lesson 5

- 1 Corinthians 15-16

Study Questions

Chapter 15

What are the essential points of the message of Jesus that Paul presented to the Corinthians?

Why is belief in the resurrection essential?

What will happen when Jesus brings about the final resurrection?

What effect would there be on our lives if the resurrection were not real? Why?

What is the nature of the resurrection body?

Chapter 16
Why was Paul taking up a collection?

What advice did he give the church about taking up the collection?

Identify all the places that are mentioned. What does this tell you about the church?

Food for Thought

Today we look at the last two issues that Paul addresses. In chapter 15 we see the last question that was presented to Paul. In chapter 16 Paul tells them about his plans.

The Resurrection

The heart of chapter 15 is found in verse 12, "how can some of you say that there is no resurrection of the dead?" Apparently a theology had taken root in the church that denied the physical resurrection. We cannot be positive about the exact nature of the teaching, but it is likely that it was some form of Greek Dualism that had been blended with the teachings of Jesus. Remember that the dualists believed that the physical world was evil and the spiritual world was good. It was inconceivable to this worldview that the God of the universe would take on a human form and die the death of a criminal. Instead, they proposed that Jesus simply *appeared* as if He were human, but was not really so. They denied that He was physically killed, and therefore did not believe that He rose from the dead. They acknowledged the truth of His moral teaching and blended them into their own theological perspective. For them, the resurrection was a metaphor referring to enlightenment of the mind and the transcendence of the Spirit from the shackles of the physical world.

This was outrageous to Paul. He couldn't believe people that had heard the message of Jesus from his lips had been sucked into this esoteric philosophy.

"Don't you remember the message I gave you?!? Let's review:

- Jesus actually died. He died to make the sacrifice for your sins.
- He was physically buried. That means He was really dead.
- He was raised from the dead. To prove it He appeared to many people and ate and drank with them, like a real person.
- Then He appeared to me and told me to tell you this message.

To believe in the physical resurrection of Jesus is so central to the Good News of His Kingdom that without it we might as well pack it in. If there is no resurrection then we're all a bunch of blubbering idiots who might as well go get blasted and go out with a bang!"

"OK, Paul. Let's say we believe you and there is a resurrection. We've seen decayed bodies before. How can that be raised to life? What about bodies that are burned up, or eaten by sharks, or some kind of mutilation? How can those be resurrected?"

"That's a good question, but a misinformed one. Don't you get it? The resurrection process is one of transformation. We will not be the same as we are now. We will be physical, but in a spiritual/physical form that goes beyond our comprehension. Unless a seed dies and is buried, it can't become a plant. Unless a caterpillar goes into the cocoon, it can't become a butterfly. Unless the physical body dies and is buried, it can't become the physical, glorious thing that it was designed to be.

With that in mind we have a solid hope to latch onto that will give our lives meaning and purpose. If the resurrection isn't real, then we are hopelessly lost. But, praise God, it is real and we have a glorious hope that will give us the courage to stand strong through any kind of trial. Keep hope alive!"

Here are some practical challenges for us.

1. **Don't get duped by an esoteric philosophy.** Our culture is full of "New Age" thinking that denies the existence of the physical world. They deny the uniqueness of Jesus as the suffering Son of God who died to pay for sin and rose to conquer death. The true test of any belief system is centered on the Resurrection. If it is not acknowledged, then run away from that system.

2. **Be encouraged.** There are plenty of things in life that can wear you down. Many times it can seem that the battle just isn't worth it. Don't forget that there is a glorious finish to the story. Jesus did rise from the dead and He is going to bring you into that glorious state of resurrection. Allow that truth to fill you with hope.

3. **Live in the resurrection power.** The power that raised Jesus from the dead is the same power that He offers to you right now through the Holy Spirit. Not only do we look forward to the hope of an eternal state of resurrection glory, we also live in the power and the promise of resurrection power in daily living. We aren't just waiting around until Jesus takes us home. This world and this life, in all of its physical reality, is a good and wonderful thing that we are called to

redeem in the here and now by using it for God's glory. Go out and live the life today!

The Collection

In chapter 16 Paul gives a P.S. at the end of the letter. After he had finished answering the Corinthians' questions he adds one more item to the list. He reminds them that he will be coming to them soon in order to take up a collection for the church in Jerusalem. Jerusalem had suffered from a famine and the people were in dire need of assistance. In an act of charity and unity in the body of Christ, Paul was collecting money from the Greek churches and taking it back to the church that had so bitterly critiqued his ministry. This was an incredible gesture that demonstrated the love of Jesus and the unity of His body.

What this is not

This passage is not a command for all churches on tithing. When Paul says to give money on the first day of every week, he was not telling every church everywhere to give ten percent to the local congregation when the church doors open on Sunday morning.

What this was

This was a practical way for the church to give a great deal of money to Jerusalem without it feeling like a huge gouge to their pocketbooks. By giving a little bit each week, over time it would add up. Then when he arrived there would be a huge amount ready to go and Paul would not have to brow-beat anyone to cough up more money.

Now, does that mean that we shouldn't give a tithe to the local church each week? I didn't say that. I'm just making sure that greedy pastors who need to pay the mortgage don't misuse this verse and guilt their congregations into giving.

The real message for us from this passage is to remember that a huge part of the practical demonstration of Jesus' love is to have a generous heart. When people are hurting it should be our knee-jerk response to give to them whatever it is that they need. The people of God are not stingy. We are givers. We think of the needs of others more than our own needs. That is why we give to the local church. We give to a collective pot so that when needs arise they can be met without hesitation or delay. So give away!

Final Thoughts

We have spent the last three sessions burning our way through this first letter to the Corinthians. In this letter Paul was spanking the saints. The Corinthian Christians were a wily bunch that were trying to figure out how to live in unity when they were surrounded by and emerging from radically contrasting worldviews. They struggled with arrogance and a need to establish a social pecking order in the church. They struggled with knowing which aspects of their old culture were good and which needed to be laid aside. They struggled with knowing how far they could go with freedom, and how to use it wisely. They questioned the issues of sexuality, marriage, idol meat, gender roles, spiritual gifts, the public gathering, and the resurrection. All in all, they were a lot like us.

Paul sums up the answer to each and every question in 16:14, "Do everything in love." May we be a community that is filled with the Love of God and overflowing that love to everyone we meet.

Endnotes

[2]Kittel, G. (1995, c1985). *Theological dictionary of the New Testament*. Translation of: Theologisches Worterbuch zum Neuen Testament. (Page 297). Grand Rapids, Mich.: W.B. Eerdmans.

[3]ibid (Pages 833-834).

[4] Vine, W. E. (1996). *Vine's complete expository dictionary of Old and New Testament words* (Vol. 2, Page 497). Nashville: T. Nelson.

[5] Vine, W. E. (1996). *Vine's complete expository dictionary of Old and New Testament words* (Vol. 2, Page 59). Nashville: T. Nelson.

[6] Kittel, G. (1995, c1985). *Theological dictionary of the New Testament*. Translation of: Theologisches Worterbuch zum Neuen Testament. (Page 300). Grand Rapids, Mich.: W.B. Eerdmans.

[7]ibid. (Page 791).

[8]ibid. (Page 23).

[9]ibid. (Page 1073).

[10]ibid. (Page 849).

[11]ibid. (Page 231).

[12]ibid. (Page 582).

[13]ibid. (Page 847).

[14]ibid. (Page 953).

[15] The IVP Bible Background Commentary : New Testament

[16]*King James Version study Bible*. 1997, c1988 (electronic ed.) (1 Co 14:32). Nashville: Thomas Nelson.

Reading Paul's Mail

2 Corinthians

Introduction

An Apostle in Pain

It is always important for us to remember that Paul's letters are not abstract theological textbooks, or a sterile encyclopedia of quick and easy answers to questions of life in all ages. These letters are real-life personal correspondences between a man and the churches that he had planted. This truth is especially important when approaching 2 Corinthians. In this letter we plunge the depths of human pain and climb the heights of euphoric hope as we listen to Paul's interaction with a very troubled group of people.

Since the writing of 1 Corinthians much had happened to Paul. He had been working in Ephesus for two years (The story is found in Acts 19). During the first portion of this ministry things had been going very well. Many people were choosing to follow Jesus and were being set free from their lives of idolatry and sorcery. Many churches were being planted in the surrounding region through the teaching ministry of Paul.

Then something terrible happened. Paul was being attacked on two fronts. On the one side the people of Ephesus turned on him. We know

from the book of Acts that a riot took place, but the way Paul talks in 2 Corinthians it sounds like something even worse happened that marked him on a much deeper level. We don't know what happened, but we know that he was troubled by it. On the second front the reports about and the correspondence between Paul and the church in Corinth were going from bad to worse. The church was being overrun by teachers that were bad-mouthing Paul, trying to discredit him, and attempting to convert the believers into a legalistic religious system that was destructive to their souls. Paul felt that he was being abandoned, betrayed, and defeated.

As you read this letter try to go to that place of mixed emotions with Paul. On the one hand he was frustrated with the ignorance and arrogance of the Corinthians. He was angered and jealous toward the antagonistic ministries that were undermining his work. Yet, he was deeply concerned with a parental compassion for his spiritual children in Corinth that were being pulled back and forth by confusing messages.

89

He was hurt by their harsh attack against him, but longed to see their relationship healed and restored. He was worried that all would be lost and his ministry would be a complete failure.

How many Letters?

When we look closely at Paul's letters to the church at Corinth we discover that 1st and 2nd Corinthians are actually 2nd and 4th Corinthians. In 1 Corinthians 5:9 Paul refers to a letter that he had previously written to them. We'll call that letter A. That means 1 Corinthians is letter B. In 2 Corinthians Paul refers to a previous letter that was very severe and caused great sorrow at Corinth. He also says that his next visit to them will be his third visit. Acts only records 2 visits to Corinth. Apparently, while Paul was in Ephesus for two years he wrote a painful letter to the Corinthians and made a very painful visit to them that was not recorded in Acts. Thus, 2 Corinthians is letter D and the missing letter is letter C.

Here is the timeline:

Acts 18:1-17 – Paul works in Corinth for 18 months with Aquila and Priscilla and plants the church in that city.

Acts 19 – Paul works in Ephesus for two years

- Letter A written to warn against sexual immorality

- Corinthians respond to letter A with a written list of questions

- Letter B (1 Corinthians) written in response to a negative report and the list of questions

- Paul visits Corinth and apparently has a very troubling time with them. Things do not go well.

- Paul promised to visit Corinth first on his trip to collect relief funds for the starving church in Jerusalem.

- Paul writes Letter C and sends Titus to deliver it. In the letter he very harshly reprimands the Corinthians, causing them extreme sorrow. Paul planned to meet Titus in Troas to find out how the Corinthians responded to letter C. He was very worried that all may be lost in that city.

Acts 20:1 -- Paul sets out for Macedonia.

- He does not find Titus in Troas as planned and becomes even more worried. He continues on into Macedonia.

- He finally finds Titus and, to his great relief, discovers that the Corinthians had actually received letter C well and repented. Paul then planned to go to Corinth.

- Paul writes letter D (2 Corinthians) in preparation for his visit.

Acts 20:2 – Paul arrives in Greece (probably Corinth) and stays for three months.

2 Corinthians

Making Sense of the Illustration

Let's take a moment to examine the illustration. On the left you'll see the Corinthian church being persuaded that Paul was a fraud. Many teachers had entered the city and began presenting a gospel message that was very different from that of Paul's. We aren't exactly sure what their theological position was, but from the evidence in 2 Corinthians it appears that they were a hybrid of Judaism and a Greek philosophy called Sophism. Basically they believed that Christians should follow the Law of Moses and maintain their Jewish heritage. They acknowledged that Jesus was the Messiah, but denied that He was an actual human who came in the flesh, died on the cross, and rose again. In this way they had adopted Platonic Dualism and reinterpreted the Old Testament and the story of Jesus through this grid. Jesus was a manifestation of God that was sent to teach us a moral code of ethics and nothing more. In addition, these teachers practiced the common method of teaching in the Greco-Roman world in which they "tooted their own horn" boldly for all to see. Since they were great orators and respectable men who dispensed great wisdom it was expected that their followers would support them financially. Paul sarcastically calls them "super-apostles" as they hoist themselves up on a pedestal and flaunt their "letters of recommendation" for all to see and be amazed.

As we follow the word balloons you'll see the basic flow of the dialogue between Paul and the Corinthians. The first problem the Corinthians had with Paul was that he had told them one thing and done another. This alleged hypocrisy was great fuel for Paul's enemies to sow further seeds of doubt regarding Paul's integrity and credibility.

Next you'll see Paul defending himself against the accusations that were being hurled against him. The Corinthians were wondering where Paul's letters of recommendations were and why he didn't strut into Corinth flaunting all of his power like these other men did. Paul responds by giving a "resume of a loser for Jesus." In a very sarcastic tone Paul lists all of the ways that he was a "loser" in the world's eyes. Yet, these "failures" were actually the marks of a true apostle of Jesus and servant of the Kingdom of God.

Notice the arrow that swings in the background from the left to the right and points towards Titus. This shows that Titus finally met up with Paul to set his mind at ease regarding the Corinthians. Paul was worried that his last letter had upset them so badly that they had finally abandoned him, and Jesus, altogether. Titus brought him great relief as he reported that the Corinthians had not abandoned the faith, but were eager to continue cultivating their relationship with Paul.

Given his relief at this news, Paul is encouraged to continue his planned trip to collect money to help the suffering church in Jerusalem. He spends two chapters preparing the Corinthians for his arrival to receive their generous gift.

Finally, in chapters 10-13, Paul turns an emotional corner and begins severely scolding the church again. These three chapters have been a puzzle to scholars for centuries. It is very difficult to understand why Paul would shift gears so abruptly in midstream in this letter. The shift is so severe that some commentators have suggested that this section was actually a separate letter altogether that was fused with the prior letter during the copying process. It is difficult to know exactly what is going on here. The one thing we do know is that Paul's final words to the church in Corinth are harsh as he, once again, defends his ministry against the accusations of his opponents. In this section he speaks more intensely about his own personal weakness and how God can only work through weak people, not strong, successful, self-aggrandized, "winners."

91

Lesson 1

- 2 Corinthians 1:1-2:11

Study Questions

In 1:1-11, how is God described and what does He provide?

What kind of circumstances has Paul recently experienced? How has this affected him?

Against what accusation is Paul apparently defending himself?

Why did Paul not go to Corinth?

In 2:1-11, how does Paul describe his previous visit and letter to the Corinthians? What was the purpose of his last letter?

How should the Corinthians treat the brother they disciplined? Why?

Food for Thought

God of Comfort (1:1-11)

Peppered throughout this passage is the word comfort. This translates the Greek word *parakaleo* which literally means *to come alongside*. This language takes us back to the upper room in John 16 when Jesus described the role of the Holy Spirit to be the Paraclete; *the come alongside*. If ever there was a time in Paul's life when he needed a "come alongside" it was now. He was suffering. In Ephesus he had been arrested, possibly imprisoned, and beaten. After a good run of fruitful ministry everything had turned sour and he was forced to leave. Then, to further his pain, the church in Corinth was teetering on the brink of disaster. They were about ready to betray Paul and follow a false message. Then, to even further his suffering, Paul's journey was leading him into hostile territory; Macedonia. The last time he was there he had been imprisoned and run out of every town in which he had tried to start a church. The Thessalonians had to promise that Paul would never return. Now that he was heading that way to collect money for the starving church in Jerusalem he had to have at least a slight tinge of anxiety about the welcome he would receive.

He was physically beaten, emotionally exhausted, and very anxious about the final outcome of his dealings with Corinth. If ever a man needed comfort, it was Paul. So how does Paul deal with these hardships? He finds comfort in them through Jesus. Look at what he says in verse 9, "this happened that we might not rely on ourselves but on God." His statement reminds me of the story of Joseph found in Genesis. Joseph was sold into slavery by his own brothers, but instead of being bitter and vengeful he said, "You intended to harm me, but God intended it for good" (Genesis 50:20)

In our lives there are many opportunities for us to become bitter and resentful. People are people and they tend to do nasty things to each other. If we want to, we could easily find a reason to be upset with just about everyone we know for some reason or another. Be careful. Bitterness and resentment are a lot like potato chips...you can't eat just one. Once you latch on to those attitudes they tend to move their whole family into your heart and make a mess of things. The antidote to that is to take the attitude of Paul. He found the comfort in it all. The comfort is in taking a bigger perspective and realizing that God has everything under control. No matter how bad things may seem to be we can always rest assured that we can "set our hope that he will continue to deliver us." Be encouraged and rest in God's "come alongside of you."

Simple and True 1:12-24

Throughout this letter Paul is defending himself against several accusations. The first of these accusations was that of being a two-faced liar. At one point in his interaction with the Corinthians he had promised that he would visit them first after he left Ephesus. Things changed, however, and Paul headed north toward Troas. The Corinthians were upset and called him a liar.

We can identify with this situation from both sides. We can sympathize with the Corinthians on this point. Don't you hate it when someone says they are going to do something and they don't do it? It really makes it difficult to trust that person in the future because their integrity has come into question. Does their "yes" really mean "yes?"

We can also feel for Paul. The poor guy had such a difficult time with the Corinthians the last time he went there that he didn't want to run back into that hornet's nest. His plans had changed and he didn't have the chance to tell the Corinthians. Things happen. That doesn't make him a liar. Don't you hate it when you do something with pure motives and you are still perceived as being a bad guy?

There are many lessons we can learn from this exchange, but we will just focus on one. Here we are reminded of Jesus' words in Matthew 5:37, "let your 'yes' be 'yes' and your 'no' be 'no'". There is no room for double speak in the Kingdom of God. Paul sums this lesson up nicely with two words; holiness and sincerity. In 1:12 Paul says that he has always dealt with the Corinthians in 'holiness and sincerity'. The literal Greek translation is *haplotes* (simplicity) and *heilikrinea* (sun tested)

Let's look at each of these words.

haplotes -- a. "Simplicity," b. "noble simplicity," as of heroes, c. "purity," "singleness of heart," and d. "generosity."[1]

A singleness of heart. This means that we should have no ulterior motives when we speak with people.

Heilikrineia – *Heilos* = sun; *krineia* = judge. It literally means to be tested by the sun. In the ancient world certain potters would try to cheat their customers by sealing up cracks in their pottery with wax. At first glance the pot looked whole and having integrity. But, when you held it up to the sun you would see the sunlight shining through the wax and realize that you were being conned. In the Latin language this word was sanceres, meaning sans (or "no") wax. From this word we get the English word "sincere."

To be *heilikrineia*, to be sincere, is to have complete integrity and to not cover up anything in your life.

In computer language there is a display called a WYSIWYG (pronounced "Whiz-ee-whig") **W**hat **Y**ou **S**ee **I**s **W**hat **Y**ou **G**et. That is how followers of Jesus should be. We should be WYSIWYGs. Because our hearts are under the authority of Jesus we should have nothing but pure motives and plain speech come out of our mouths. Never should there be flattery for the purpose of promotion or perks. Never should there be polite brush-offs with sarcastic after conversations. Never should there be gossiping or backbiting. We should be characterized by being the kind of people that, when people look us in the eye and hear our words, they get the real deal every time.

Paul knew that he was a WYSIWIG, and, with the gospel of Jesus – the author of truth – as his witness, he had not lied to the Corinthians.

Restore the Repentant Brother (2:1-11)

In 1 Corinthians Paul had instructed the church to expel the immoral brother that was sleeping with his father's wife. They obeyed; and obeyed with a vengeance. Apparently, they not only expelled him, but they made him suffer for his sin. In this current letter Paul says, "Whoa! Ease off a little. I see that you were willing to obey, but you've gone overboard. Bring him back and restore fellowship before you swing to the other side of the danger zone and be rigid and unforgiving."

There is a certain amount of irony in this situation. In 1 Corinthians 5 Paul instructed the church to turn the man over to Satan in order to save the man's soul. Now the Corinthians were in danger of being devoured by Satan if they don't forgive him. Here we need to learn this lesson and take caution. As Paul says, the Devil's schemes are tricky. If he doesn't get us through being tolerant of sin, he'll get us by being intolerant of sinners. The truth lies in the middle of these extremes on the path of love. True love for God and others loves people enough to not allow them to wallow in self-destructive behavior, but to equip them and come along side them to be able to overcome it. It doesn't shun and abandon people who are struggling with sin; it walks with them and empowers them to be victorious.

Lesson 2

- 2 Corinthians 2:12-3:18

Study Questions

Why was Paul upset?

What impact does Paul's ministry have on a region as he passes through it?

How are some teachers handling their teaching ministry? How does Paul compare himself to this philosophy of teaching?

Why does Paul talk about "letters of recommendation" in this passage?

What is Paul's letter of recommendation? What does that mean?

Why did Moses veil his face?

Describe the comparison that Paul is making between himself and Moses and Paul's teaching and the Law. What is his message with this analogy?

What effect does the Lord's glory have on his followers? How does that promise affect you emotionally, intellectually, and spiritually?

Food for Thought

In this section Paul defends himself against the second accusation brought against him. The false teachers in Corinth were making a big issue over the idea of needing "letters of recommendation" in order to be taken seriously as a teacher. In our culture an equivalent to this language would be having the right degrees from the right schools. The false teachers were trying to convince the Corinthians that they shouldn't listen to a teacher like Paul unless he has the right credentials and the right connections. They claimed that Paul was a renegade that did not have the proper backing of the "true church" or of any Philosophical school and that Paul's claim to being an apostle was bogus.

Paul responds, "You want credentials? You want a letter? YOU are my letter. The evidence of the Holy Spirit transforming your lives under the authority of Jesus is all the 'proof' you need."

Then Paul launches into a beautiful analogy that compares his ministry with that of Moses'. Allow me to paraphrase what Paul said:

In the story of Exodus, Moses was called by God into his presence where He came in contact with God's glory. In this glorious place God gave him the Law in order to govern the Israelites as they traveled through the desert and moved into the dangerous land of Canaan. The glory that Moses experienced was real, but it was temporary. In the same way, the Law was real, but it was temporary. When Moses came into God's glory it transformed him and his face shone brilliantly, but the transformation was temporary. It didn't last. In fact it began to fade as soon as he left God's presence. Moses was embarrassed by the fading glory so he hid it from the people behind a mask. Today many who follow the law are still blinded by that mask. They can't see the true glory of God that shines through Jesus. My ministry, however, is different than Moses'. Because of Jesus we have access to the presence of God on a continual basis. I don't have to be embarrassed and wear a mask because the glory doesn't fade. I don't have to hide behind credentials and an air of importance because the glory of Jesus shines through my face to all who want to honestly look at it. I'm not the only one privy to this glory; all of us have access to God's glory, and when we bask in that glory we are transformed by it. Unlike Moses, our transformation is not

temporary. It doesn't fade. In fact it increases with each day that we walk in the light of that glory. Each of us is like the caterpillar that is metamorphosizing from one state to the next. Each day we become more like Jesus through the power of his Spirit.

Now, if that is not "proof" or a valid "letter of recommendation" then I don't know what is!

Today's message is simple, yet deeply profound. If you are a follower of Jesus then you are being transformed. The word being translated as *transformed* is the Greek word *metamorphao* from which we get the word metamorphosis. In the same way that a caterpillar morphs into a butterfly, so are we changing into the people that God designed us to be. In the same way that a seed morphs into a mature plant, so are we fulfilling the potential that God has invited us to fulfill.

Here is a thought for you today. You are no longer a seed; you are growing. Turn your face to the Son and let His light excite the process within you. You are no longer called a caterpillar; embrace the transformation.

Lesson 3

- 2 Corinthians 4:1-5:10

Study Questions

What attitude has God's mercy produced in Paul? Why?

Describe the kind of ministry that Paul opposes.

Why does Paul say people don't understand his message?

What is Paul's message?

What does Paul mean when he says that the treasure is held in a jar of clay? What does the clay jar represent? What is the jar's purpose?

How does Paul explain his extreme suffering? Why is it happening?

What is Paul's attitude toward his current state of existence? Why?

What is the purpose of the Holy Spirit?

Restate 5:10 in your own words. What implications does this verse have for daily living?

Food for Thought

Today there are four basic ideas to think about...

Don't Give in to the Bad

This section has a repeated phrase that states the main theme. It is found in 4:2 and 4:16. Paul says, "We do not lose heart." The Greek is a phrase that is difficult to translate. It is the word *enkakos*. *En* = into *Kakos* = evil or bad things. Literally the phrase reads, "we not into bad things." Every English translation takes a different approach to translating this phrase. Some various translations are; "we faint not," "we never give up," "we're not about to throw up our hands and walk off the job," "we are not discouraged."

Paul's circumstances help us understand his meaning. He is surrounded by bad things. He's being attacked on every front; theologically, ethically, physically, relationally. Yet, because of his strong belief that God has graciously called him into this ministry to the Gentiles, he does not cave in under the pressure of all these bad things.

So it should be for us. As we read this section we will see further reasons for the hope that Paul has and the hope that we can cling to when times get difficult.

A Counter Attack

Before we explore the beautiful hope that Paul describes, we must take a moment and observe the counter-offensive that Paul launches against his accusers. By claiming the things that he denounces he is, in fact, accusing his opponents of behaving according to these standards. As we read this list it would do us well to create a filter for our own lives so that we can fend off any teachings that might try to distract us from the simple message of the risen Jesus.

We can tie this accusation back to 2:17 where Paul says,

> Unlike so many, we do not peddle the word of God for profit. On the contrary, in Christ we speak before God with sincerity, like men sent from God.

In this passage he further expounds on that thought by saying,

> we have renounced
>> secret and shameful ways;
>>> One translator puts this phrase as follows: *"we have renounced the things that one hides from a sense of shame."*[2]

A true messenger of Jesus has nothing to hide. They have no hidden agendas or ulterior motives. They don't have skeletons in their closet. That doesn't mean they are perfect. It means they are honest about who they are and what they are trying to accomplish. They are an open book for all to read.

we do not use deception,

Also translated, "we do not walk around in cunning and craftiness"

A true messenger of Jesus does not need to use flowery words or misleading jargon to coax people into believing. As Paul said in 2 Timothy 4:3,

> *For the time will come when they will not endure sound doctrine; but wanting to have their ears tickled, they will accumulate for themselves teachers in accordance to their own desires*

Paul's message was simple and clear: Jesus is the risen Messiah and the Lord of all things...believe and follow.

nor do we distort the word of God.

Also translated "adulterate," "falsify," "twist God's Word to suit ourselves," "handle the Word deceitfully."

The "word of God" is, first and foremost, Jesus himself. John told us "in the beginning was the Word and the Word was with God and the Word was God... and the Word became flesh and dwelt among us." Secondly, the word of God is the message of the Gospel that Jesus presented to his apostles and commissioned to be spread to the world. The word is the good news that Jesus is the Lord and Savior of the world, the one who has conquered sin and death and opened the way to know the Father fully and forever. Thirdly, the word of God is the written record of the apostles' words that we have collected in the New Testament documents.

A true messenger of the Gospel respects all forms of the word of God and does not twist or distort it in order to fit his own scheme. Paul's opponents were denying the first word of God, and thus all the others, by claiming that Jesus did not become human and die for our sins. Paul didn't necessarily claim to understand the gospel message, he simply laid it out there in all of its wonderful, mysterious glory for people to either grasp or deny.

As we navigate the postmodern era, we need to be careful to use this filter to carefully discern everything we hear. Just because someone is highly educated doesn't mean they have a corner on the truth of the word of God. If a teacher does not acknowledge the physical death and resurrection of Jesus, and even more importantly, the authority of Jesus as Lord of all things under which all things must come into submission, then we need to walk away from that teaching.

Jars of Clay

Now we continue the picture of hope that Paul paints for us and the reason that he does not cave in under the pressure of the bad. The secret to "success" in the ministry of the good news of Jesus is to realize that we are nothing. We are simply jars of clay. We are a simple vessel that has no intrinsic value in and of itself. The teachers that were tempting the Corinthians considered themselves to be "golden vessels" that were special and important. They believed that they deserved to drive a BMW and live in a mansion because God had anointed them and given them an esteemed place. They believed that their wealth and social status was an evidence of God's blessing in their lives, and that the people of the church should bow to them in deference and give money to their cause.

Paul shakes his head in disbelief at this line of thinking. He reminds the Corinthians that he (and we) are simply common, ordinary clay jars. We are the generic brand. We are the thrift store special. We are the everyday flatware for the kids to use.

Why are we this? We are jars of clay for two reasons. First, we have died to all that glittery stuff. It's meaningless to us. We see it to be the shiny lure of the fisherman and nothing more. It's eye candy that robs your soul. When we bought into the death of Jesus we crucified our need to be validated by the social trappings of status and prestige. Secondly, we are simple because if we are shiny, golden vessels then the glint off of our surface may compete for attention with the true shine of Jesus' glory. We are simply vessels. When people see us they should not say, "Wow! Now there's an awesome vessel." Instead, they should say, "Wow, I'm not sure how it got there, but all I can see is the glory of Jesus' love shining into my life." To switch metaphors, we need to be transparent glass that lets the light of Jesus shine directly through us instead of stained glass that looks pretty because of Jesus' light shining behind us.

A Future of Glory

You may be thinking, "That last section sounds nice, but how can we possibly live that way in our culture. Image is everything. How can we be nothing without being totally obliterated?" That is a valid and complex question. The practical living out of that truth will look different in every person's life, and must be under the authentic leading of the Spirit. However, there is one underlying principal and promise that Paul gives to us that should be the primal force behind the ability to die to the "stuff" of life. Paul says we fix our eyes not on what is seen but what is unseen. We deny the temporal – the stuff that will decay and rust in a hundred years – and fix our attention and intention on what is eternal. Paul's internal motivation to withstand the garbage and the pain was his deep-seated conviction that this life is not all there is. He believed that there was more to come. He believed that the mortal would be swallowed up by the immortal.

You see, our relationship with God is like a marriage. Right now we are only engaged to God. He gave us an engagement ring; it's called the Holy Spirit. The Spirit is our deposit guaranteeing what is to come. We have a valid and authentic relationship with the Father, under the authority of Jesus, and in the powerful promise of the Spirit, but we have not yet consummated that relationship. We are like the bride eagerly awaiting the day when our groom will sweep us off our feet and take us into his wedding chamber. Then we will know the fullness of intimacy with God for which we were created. Until then we practice His presence. We rehearse, through the spiritual disciplines, the intimacy we will someday know fully. If we believe this to be true, deep at the core of who we are; if it is more than wishful thinking; more than a mental aspiration; if it is a core belief in the depths of our being, then we will be able to die a thousand deaths to this world and love others with all of our heart.

Naked and Unashamed

Before we leave today's rich passage of hope, we need to deal with a very real and very sobering verse. In 5:10 Paul says, "we must all appear before the judgment seat of Christ, that each one may receive what is due him for the things done while in the body, whether good or bad." Let's tie this image with our previous metaphor of being engaged to God. (Please be advised; this next idea may not be totally appropriate for children) If an engaged couple has been sexually pure throughout their premarried life, what is one of the greatest anxieties for them? On their wedding night they will stand naked before each

other. Think about that. To stand naked before someone takes a great deal of trust. What are our greatest fears? They will laugh at us. They will not find us attractive or desirable. They will reject us. They will abuse us and take advantage of our vulnerability. I will be inadequate. The list goes on and on. When we finally come before God, to consummate our marriage, we will stand naked before Him. The question is, will we stand naked and unashamed, or will we cower in fear before him? This goes back to 4:2 when Paul renounced the false teacher's method of working in "secret and shameful ways." When we come before God on that day, will we be trying to hide our nakedness in shame, or will we run into the arms of the lover of our soul?

How can we know that we will be able to stand naked and unashamed on that day? Many people have a myriad of answers to that question. To keep true to what I believe is the heart of the Word of God in Jesus' ministry and Paul's ministry, I believe that the way to stand unashamed before God on *that* day is to operate in an authentic way in *this* day. The great deception of humanity that began in the Garden of Eden and persists until this day is the notion that we can actually hide from God. The truth is that we stand naked before him *every* day. He sees who we are even more than we do. The question is whether *we* are willing to see who we really are? Are we willing to let the probing truth beacon of the Spirit search into the depths of our hearts and expose attitudes of hatred, selfishness, pride, greed, lust, etc. and flush it out, or are we operating under the deluded belief that we can actually fool God by acting holy on the outside but harbor trash on the inside. If we live in a "naked and unashamed" manner every day, then on THAT day we will not be ashamed. If we live in THIS day trying to cover up our filth with the garments of self-righteousness and self-importance and self-protection, then on THAT day, when God tears off those clothes, the stench of our body will destroy us.

As we go into the world today, let's ask our betrothed to cleanse us and bring us out into the open. We want to live in THIS day as if it were already THAT day. This is our hope!

Lesson 4

- 2 Corinthians 5:11-6:13

Study Questions

Why is Paul explaining these things to the Corinthians?

What compels Paul to do what he does?

What effect does being "in Christ" have on a person?

How does Paul describe his ministry in 5:17-21?

What might it mean for the Corinthians to receive God's grace in vain?

How does Paul "commend" himself? Why?

How has Paul dealt with the Corinthians?

Food for Thought

A New Creation

I grew up solidly planted in the conservative Evangelical Protestant Tradition, and for that I am truly grateful. Having been raised in this tradition, 2 Corinthians 5:17 was a common verse that was memorized in Sunday School from a very young age. It is one of the fundamental truths of the gospel. When a person gives his life to Jesus, submitting to his authority as Lord of his life, then he becomes of "new creation; the old has gone, the new has come." For my entire life I have understood that verse to mean that I, in myself, have been rejuvenated and made into a new person – me, myself, and I. In the Evangelical understanding of salvation we emphasize the idea of accepting Jesus as our personal Lord and Savior. He is my Lord. It's all about me and getting my butt out of Hell and being made new.

I don't deny any of that. However, as I read this passage again, I believe it is time to expand the perspective beyond our ideas of American individualism and hear what Paul is really saying here. Look what he says in verse 16, "from now on we regard no one from a worldly point of view." Then look back in verse 15, "those who live should no longer live for themselves but for Him who died for them." Being true to the context of the passage, we see that the point of the transformation is not just for me. I haven't been transformed so that God can now love me. I have been transformed so that now I can love you!

As we continue the flow of the passage we see the truth of this interpretation through the bombardment of the word "reconciliation." In this word we find the heart and soul of the Gospel. The Greek word for reconciliation has at its root the idea of "change." When we say yes to Jesus we are not just making a legal transaction that expunges our record in the law courts of Heaven. We are entering into a restored relationship with the Creator of all things. We are a new creation. Not just us, but all things.

God created all things to be in fellowship – intimate relationship -- with Him. This was the first creation. Sin has spoiled the connection between God and His creation. God and man are estranged spouses. Humans cannot connect with each other. Humans and nature are at odds with each other. In an unconnected, uncreated state of existence, we cannot help but view each other as external threats to our sense of survival and well being. In my severed state, when I look at you, I see you as that naked mole rat that is "over there" who is threatening my stuff "over here." The Good News of Jesus is that God says, "Timeout! That's not why you were created! You were created to be in loving relationship with each other. Come back into that place for which you were made and allow yourself to participate in the "new creation" that God is doing in the world."

Paul is crying out to the Corinthians and begging them, "Please stop being divided among yourselves. Stop allowing these false teachers to tear you away from the simple message of Jesus by discrediting me and clouding my message. I am doing nothing but openly and honestly serving you so that you can see the glory of Jesus and be reconciled to God, to each other, and, hopefully to me as well."

My point is simply this. I'm not "saved" for me. I'm saved for you. We are being called into the community of God and all of his creation to live in peace with each other. Ask God today how you can more fully experience the "ministry of reconciliation" in your spheres of influence today.

Résumé of a Loser

Paul is beginning to build steam in his argument and come to a climactic finish in this passage. His opponents were concerned with résumés and credentials and letters of recommendation. Paul says, "You want my credentials, here you go." Then he lists off the worst possible scenario for a distinguished scholar and dispenser of wisdom.

In this passage Paul sums it up in verse 11 by saying, "Hey guys, I'm an open book. What you see is what you get. I've allowed you to see me for who I am, warts and all. I've held nothing back. My life has been hard, but I've done it all for Jesus and for you, nothing more, nothing less. Why can't we just make things right between us?"

Whenever you feel that you are nothing, come back to this passage. Whenever you see the person who is more educated, more successful, more "blessed;" remember that God used the "loser" Paul to do great things. It's not what's on the outside that matters, it's what's on the inside and is allowed to be seen from the outside that matters in the eternal scheme of things.

Lesson 5

- 2 Corinthians 6:14-7:16

Study Questions

What warning does Paul give the Corinthians concerning the false teachers?

What promise has God made to His people?

What attitude should God's promises elicit in our hearts?

What effect did Paul's reunion with Titus have on Paul's state of mind and his attitude toward the Corinthians? Why?

What effect did Paul's previous letter have on the Corinthians?

Food for Thought

Today we come to the bookend on the other side of Paul's train of thought that began in 2:12. In 2:12 Paul said, "I still had no peace of mind, because I did not find my brother Titus there." Paul was full of anxiety over the letter that he had sent with Titus to the Corinthians. He wondered how it would be received. Was this the end of their relationship? Was all his work in Corinth for nothing?

Between 2:12 and 7:2 Paul explains to the Corinthians the source of his anxiety. He knew that the church was being threatened by a deadly philosophy that, if embraced by the church, would jeopardize the relationship they had with God in the Grace of Jesus. Now that he had met Titus and heard that all was not lost you can almost hear the huge sigh of relief that comes from Paul as he writes chapter 7.

He praises this church. Like a soldier on the front lines who has heard nothing but bad news and bombs exploding and bullets whizzing by for months and months, when he gets one small shred of good news he goes crazy with effervescent rejoicing and praise over it. Finally, there is a ray of hope in his strained relationship with Corinth. In this chapter Paul allows himself to gush a bit over his not-yet-lost children.

There are two messages for us in this chapter:

1. **Don't mess around with dangerous philosophies.** Paul says, "don't be yoked together with unbelievers." The image here is of two animals joined together in a wooden yoke for the purpose of plowing a field or accomplishing some laborious task. Every good farmer knew that you can't put an ox and a donkey in the same yoke. They aren't compatible. They pull at different rates and have different styles. If you yoked those two together you would get nothing done.

Listen very carefully to what Paul is saying and what he is not saying. He is not saying "don't be friends with non-Christians or associate with people in the world." What he is saying is, "It is impossible to be in intimate community with someone who does not believe in the fundamental truth that Jesus is the crucified, risen, Lord of all things." Be careful who you let into the inner ring of your relationships. Be careful of those teachers that are winning your hearts. It is easy to buy into the tantalizing message of impressive speakers who seem impressive on the outside. Don't look on the outside. Look deep inside and you'll see that, at the core, they deny the simple message of Jesus.

Reading Paul's Mail

God has created us to be simple clay pots; an ordinary temple in which the glorious Spirit of God can freely move and flow for the purpose of reconciling the world to the Father. This stuff is real. It's not a philosophical proposition. It's not a self-help tool to make you feel better about yourself or give you a pipeline to material blessing. We are supposed to be a conduit of God's grace to the world, not a self-polished ornament. We serve Him, not ourselves. Because He has promised to love us and live through us, let's get rid of all that nonsense that clouds the issues. Let's grow up and seek to be mature (perfect) children who work solely for the glory of God – not for us or our favorite teacher.

2. **There is a time and a place for hard, in-your-face truth encounters.** Anyone who has ever had a drug addict in their family knows the painful truth of chapter 7. Sometimes the most loving thing we can do for someone is to confront them with their sin. That is what letter C was between Paul and Corinth. He had to be the loving father and spank his children severely. In this chapter of letter D (2 Corinthians) Paul reflects on the process and the results of this kind of intense truth encounter. As we read his words we can glean some principles that will help to guide us when we are forced to take this very difficult step.

- **You have to be in a place of authority to do it.** Either you have to be recognized as the spiritual parent in this relationship (as Paul was) or have been invited into the person's life to bring accountability. Too many times we, as "concerned Christians" take it upon ourselves to be the sin police for everyone in our communities. I don't believe that attitude coincides with the spirit of the gospel message.

- **You have to assume a position of humility to do it.** Paul bent over backwards to demonstrate to the Corinthians that he was not lording it over them, but was serving them in everything he did.

- **Your goal must be reconciliation, not punishment.** If you approach someone who is living in a self-destructive pattern with the idea that they deserve to be punished, then stop in your tracks and don't do it. The only way this kind of confrontation can work is if your goal is to come alongside the person and give them every opportunity to repent and be restored and reconciled.

- **Your motive must be love.** As with everything in the Kingdom of God we must flow out of love. God's discipline – His "wrath"— does not flow from hatred. It flows from the heart of a loving Father who loves His children enough to discipline them when they stray from the path. So should our motive be with a brother or sister who has been distracted and has gotten themselves into a dangerous situation.

Conclusion

We've covered a lot of ground in these seven chapters. Through Paul's painful defense of his ministry and his authentic love and concern for the troubled church in Corinth we have had the opportunity to look a little deeper into the heart of the true nature of the gospel and the Kingdom of God. At the core of all ministry must be three essential components: humility, compassion, and hope. In humility we submit ourselves to the Lord Jesus as supreme ruler of all things. In humility we acknowledge that we are nothing more than simple clay pots. In humility we submit ourselves to the possibility of being misunderstood by those around us. In humility we serve those around us. Through compassion we look to serve the needs of the other and be conduits of Gods' grace to them. Through compassion we become agents of the ministry of reconciliation for the world. Through it all we are able to withstand any amount of difficulty that may come our way because we place our hope in the fact that we have a glorious future with our groom. Someday the mortal will be swallowed up by the immortal and we will realize why we were created.

Spend some time today reflecting on what you have learned this week. In what ways can you take the message of the Gospel into your world and be the simple pot that is the conduit that overflows God's grace to your world?

(Footnotes)

[1]Kittel, G. (1995, c1985). *Theological dictionary of the New Testament*. Translation of: Theologisches Worterbuch zum Neuen Testament. (Page 65). Grand Rapids, Mich.: W.B. Eerdmans.

[2]Arndt, W. (1996, c1979). *A Greek-English lexicon of the New Testament and other early Christian literature : A translation and adaption of the fourth revised and augmented edition of Walter Bauer's Griechisch-deutsches Worterbuch zu den Schrift en des Neuen Testaments und der ubrigen urchristlichen Literatur* (Page 83). Chicago: University of Chicago Press.

Introduction

The second section of 2 Corinthians can be divided into two distinct parts.

Chapters 8-9 Paul reminds the Corinthians that he is heading their way to collect money for the suffering church in Jerusalem. He wants them to be prepared for the collection well in advance so that he does not catch them unaware and have to brow beat them to get them to give to this cause.

Chapters 10-13 Paul resumes his tone of self-defense as he harshly warns the Corinthians to sever ties with the false teachers that are stirring up so much doubt and controversy in the church. He warns them that if they do not change their current trajectory they will head into a nasty collision with him when he finally arrives. He would love to avoid that conflict and would prefer that the church repent and get back on the right track without any ugliness.

Lesson 1

- 2 Corinthians 8

Study Questions

What is Paul's purpose for mentioning the generosity of the Macedonians?

Why does Paul want the Corinthians to demonstrate generosity?

What is the purpose of giving? (verse 13)

What potential accusation could be made against a traveling band of teachers who are collecting a large sum of money? How does Paul try avoiding these accusations?

Why does Paul take pride in the Corinthians?

Food for Thought

What this passage IS NOT...

I'm going to start this lesson by breaking a long standing, unspoken rule of good pastors. I'm going to expose the myth of 2 Corinthians 8-9. Like it or not, this passage is not an instructional mandate to the church to give 10% of our income every week to our local church. AAAAGH! There, I did it. Every pastor knows that the survival of the local institution called the church is dependent upon hearty givers. Without the consistent giving of the membership the bills cannot be met. That's a fact. In light of this incredibly practical reality in the life of a church, it is easy for pastors to use this passage as biblical evidence for regular, weekly tithing to the local church. (I must confess that I have fallen into this trap before).

When we honestly step back and employ our proper lens of good Bible study methods and observe the text objectively, we must admit that Paul is not talking about the issue of giving to the local church at all. The truth is that he is talking about a one-time collection that he is taking up for the church in Jerusalem. The believers in Jerusalem had been hit with a double whammy: they were blasted with famine on one side and severe persecution on the other. Paul's collection campaign effort was akin to the way the country rallied around the victims of 9/11, or the way the world rallied to help the Tsunami victims in Sumatra or how "Katrina Relief Funds" popped up all across America after those fateful natural disasters. Paul, in an effort to affirm his desire for unity between the Greek and Jewish sectors of the church, and in a display of solidarity, was sweeping through Asia, Macedonia, and Achaia with a multicultural entourage in order to bring financial aid to this flagship church in need.

What this passage IS...

Now that we have let the proverbial cat out of the bag we can regroup and get some perspective on these two chapters. While it is true that the immediate context refers to the one-time collection for Jerusalem, there are some wonderful nuggets of transferable principles for us that will challenge us to the core of who we are...our pocketbooks. These chapters are all about one word: GENEROSITY. Paul goes so far as to say that generosity is the test – even the proof – of our sincere love.

Today and tomorrow we will look at some of these transferable principles. Ask God to open your heart to hear these challenging words.

Lessons on Giving

Generosity is overflow (8:1-5)

The Thessalonian church had suffered great persecution from the day it was founded. Much to Paul's delight, however, these difficult circumstances refined the church and produced inside of them joy which bubbled up into a manifestation of generosity.

I'm sure Paul's love and fatherly pride for the Thessalonians was 100% genuine, but it is somewhat humorous to see what he is doing in this passage. You can almost hear him speaking like the father who says, "Well, your brother got an 'A', I sure hope you're not going to let me down. Why can't you be more like your brother?" Perhaps sometimes a little bit of positive peer pressure is a good thing in the body of Christ. At least Paul thought so.

The question for us is what overflows from our lives when we get squeezed? When life's hazards press in on us do we overflow with joy and generosity, or do we cave in and become bitter and resentful? Perhaps we could be more like the Thessalonians, eh?

The Proof is in the Pudding (8:6-10)

Have you ever wondered what that phrase means, "The proof is in the pudding?" I looked it up on a website that cares about questions like that. Here's what it said,

> PROOF OF THE PUDDING IS IN THE EATING -- "The way to test whether something came out as it was intended is to try it. The pudding may look good when it is put on the table, but the only way to know for certain is to taste it. As you might expect, it is an old proverb. One version of it dates to the 14th century. A translation in 1682 of Boileu's 'Le Lutrin' offered this: 'The proof of th' pudding's seen i' th' eating.'" From "The Dictionary of Cliches" by James Rogers (Ballantine Books, New York, 1985).[1]

Paul's version of this phrase comes in verse 8. He is not commanding the Corinthians to give, but says,

> "I want to test the sincerity of your love."

Later, in verse 24, he says,

> "Show these men the proof of your love."

The Greek word being translated "sincerity" in verse 8 is the word, "gnesios" and literally means "to be legitimately born; not an illegitimate child." In other words, Paul wanted to make sure that the love of the Corinthians was not something that they just talked about, but was the real deal. The pudding looked good when everything was going well, but when the spoon of giving was plunged into it would their love be proved well cooked?

Simply put, our confession of faith and love means little when it is not demonstrated in the action of giving. This message is peppered throughout the Bible.

> Jesus said, "For where your treasure is, there your heart will be also. (Matthew 6:21)

> James said, "As the body without the spirit is dead, so faith without deeds is dead. (James 2:26)

> John said, "If anyone says, "I love God," yet hates his brother, he is a liar. For anyone who does not love his brother, whom he has seen, cannot love God, whom he has not seen. (1 John 4:20)

Are we willing to demonstrate our love by helping those out who are in need?

It's about heart, not amount (8:11)

Paul advised the Corinthians to give "according to their means." In verses 1-5 Paul was eager to compare the Thessalonians' generosity with that of the Corinthians. In this verse he gives an important corrective to insure that we do not fall into a trap of negative comparison. Paul never intended to compare the *amount* that people gave. That is irrelevant. What matters is the heart condition of the giver.

The spiritual discipline of giving has a back window of opportunity for the enemy to catch us in his trap. If we resist the temptation to be stingy by committing to help those in need we avoid one trap, but then, ironically, we can be tempted on the other side to be arrogant about our ability to give. This is like the time when Jesus pointed this principle out to His disciples in Mark 12:41-44

> Jesus sat down opposite the place where the offerings were put and watched the crowd putting their money into the temple treasury. Many rich people threw in large amounts. But a poor widow came and put in two very small copper coins, worth only a fraction of a penny. Calling His disciples to Him, Jesus said, "I tell you the truth, this poor widow has put more into the treasury than all the others. They all gave out of their wealth; but she, out of her poverty, put in everything—all she had to live on."

If a person gave a million dollars but did it grudgingly or out of shame and guilt, then it was not an authentic gift that blesses both the giver and the givee. Worse yet, if a person gave more than he could give, to the detriment of his family's wellbeing, just to impress others, then the gift was a destructive force in the body of Christ. On the other hand, one dollar, given out of an authentic overflow will produce waves of blessing to the heart of those involved. Before you give, check your heart and make sure your motives are pure.

It's about equal distribution, not poverty (8:12-15)

There is a myth that has been floating around the hallowed halls of Christendom from the time of its inception. Somewhere along the line people came to believe that poverty was a virtue. In an expression of this belief many monastic orders take a 'vow of poverty' in order to prove their devotion to Jesus and to not be distracted by the things of this world.

Let's think about that for a minute. What is poverty, really? Poverty is not having the things you need – food, clothing, water, shelter – for survival. A truly poor person is one of the most distracted people on the planet. They live in fear and anxiety every moment of their lives. They live from moment to moment, scraping to find a morsel to keep their bodies alive to the next day. A monk who takes a "vow of poverty" is not poor. He has shelter, food, and clothing provided for him by the monastery. His vow is not poverty, but simplicity. There is a big difference.

Look at what Agur said in Proverbs 30:8-9

give me neither poverty nor riches,

but give me only my daily bread.

Otherwise, I may have too much and disown you

and say, 'Who is the LORD?'

Or I may become poor and steal,

and so dishonor the name of my God.

Paul is driving this point home to the Corinthians. He does not want them to give to the point of becoming poor. He wants them to simply even things out. In the Kingdom of God there should not be filthy rich people or filthy poor people. God gives some people monetary wealth so that they can help those who cannot provide for themselves.

If Paul were writing this letter to the American churches today I'm sure he would double underscore verse 14: "Then there will be EQUALITY." As it was then, so it is now; the problem of poverty in the world today is not a production problem, it's a distribution problem. There is enough food and resources produced in the world every year to feed every single person on the planet with some left over. The problem is that the wealthy people have all the produce and the poor people don't have access to it. Paul screams out to us, "No! It shouldn't be that way. If you have extra, give it away. Then, when you are in need, others will give to you. That is how the Kingdom should work."

As rich American Christians (and, yes, 99.9% of us are rich according to global standards) the challenge is extended to us to help our suffering brothers in "Jerusalem" that are suffering and starving and have no way to help themselves. Let's pray that God could help us to find a way that we could eliminate poverty in the Kingdom of God.

Be careful when handling snakes!

What!?! The passage doesn't mention snakes! No, it does not. However, it does address the issue of handling an important, but potentially lethal item in your hands. In this case Paul is talking about carrying a large sum of money across the country.

Imagine how you would feel if a traveling band of "evangelists" came to your town and said they were taking up a collection to help the needy overseas and they wanted your gifts in hard, cold cash. Immediately you think, "Who are these guys? How can I trust them? How do I know they aren't con men preying on my tender heartedness?"

Paul was under the same kind of scrutiny. In this passage there are two important issues that we must address regarding financial integrity in the body of Christ. First, we must be aware that whenever we deal with money we will come under very close scrutiny from our critics. Money scandals are the favorite accusations of the enemies of the church. Secondly, we must remember that carrying large sums of money does bring with it great temptation. Whenever any organization receives donations of any kind it must always put into place the strictest safeguards possible to insure that no one succumbs to the temptation that money brings. If we lose our integrity in this area then our witness to the world will be severely damaged.

Paul knew this so he made sure to explain to the Corinthians that he was taking every precaution to ensure the safe delivery of the precious gift that he was carrying to Jerusalem.

Lesson 2

- 2 Corinthians 9

Study Questions

How did Paul represent the Corinthians to the Macedonians? What effect did this have on the Macedonians?

What was Paul afraid might happen when he arrived in Corinth?

What should be our attitude toward giving?

What promise does Paul make to the generous person?

What results does Paul say a generous gift from the Corinthians will produce?

Food for Thought

In the ancient world the common method of planting seeds was called "broadcasting." In this method the sower carried a bag of seed slung around the shoulder. As he walked along the field he would grab large handfuls of seed and, in a sweeping motion, would scatter them all across the ground. It is this image upon which Paul is drawing as he writes the key phrase of this passage,

> "Whoever sows sparingly will also reap sparingly, and whoever sows generously will also reap generously."

There are a lot of topics we could address from this chapter, but instead of going all over the map, let's simply focus in on the principle of the sower. Ultimately it lies at the foundation of the principle that Paul is presenting to the Corinthians, and to us.

The principle is really simple. If you want a lot of wheat to grow in your field, then you need to throw a lot of seeds out there. The more generously you broadcast the seeds the more likely you will be to produce a good crop. The problem is that seed is costly. As a farmer you may want to cover more acreage so you may be tempted to skimp on the seed and spread it out more widely. You may think that you could get more for your money if you hold back a bit. If you did that, however, you would be forgetting about one simple factor – the birds. The farmer knew that when the seed is broadcast it attracts birds to take away the seed. If you don't put enough out there then the birds may take it all away. If you want to have enough seed to withstand the birds, then you need to sow generously.

The analogy of the sower is used throughout the Bible. Let's expand the scope of our discussion from finances specifically and look at the parable of the sower in all aspects of life. Paul used the analogy of the sower in regard to spiritual formation. He said to the Galatians,

> A man reaps what he sows. The one who sows to please his sinful nature, from that nature will reap destruction; the one who sows to please the Spirit, from the Spirit will reap eternal life. (Galatians 6:7-8)

Jesus used the sower analogy in regard to human interaction in Matthew 7:2

> "With the measure you use, it will be measured to you."

In our vernacular we say, "What goes around, comes around."

It's really simple, yet so often we forget about it. If we all followed the simple rule that Jesus

107

taught us, "So in everything, do to others what you would have them do to you" then life would run so smoothly and there would be no inequality.

So, the question is, "why is it so hard for us to be generous?" The main reason we do not give is fear. We are afraid that we are being conned. We are afraid that if we give our time and money away that we will lose our financial security. We are afraid that the person who receives it will misuse it and the gift will be wasted. So, like the stingy farmer, we hold onto our seed and try to "maximize its potential."

Paul urges us to not slip into that line of thinking and succumb to those fears. "Give!" he says. Remember that God is the one who supplies for our needs. When you give you actually open your heart up to the very nature of God. God is the ultimate giver. He gave up everything for us. As we open ourselves to generosity then our spirit resonates with the Spirit of the Giving God and we become a conduit of blessing. When we become a conduit of blessing, and people see that our hearts are pure, then that kind of freedom sparks others to let go and give as well. Before you know it everyone is basking in the glory of God as we are touching each others needs and bringing about healing and reconciliation.

Ask God to show you ways in which you can open up your heart in generosity today and support a person who needs help.

Lesson 3

- 2 Corinthians 10:1-11:15

Study Questions

What accusations can you sense are being hurled at Paul? (found throughout the passage)

What kind of "weapons" does Paul use? What effect do they have?

How does Paul assess his opponents in verse 12 and in 11:13-15?

What should be the source for boasting? What does that mean?

What was Paul afraid might be happening to the Corinthians?

How did Paul treat the Corinthians when he was with them?

Why is Paul motivated to press on in his mission?

Food for Thought

What is Your Standard?

In this section Paul takes a hard emotional left turn. Up to this point he has been praising the Corinthians for not giving up and has been encouraging them to give generously for the purpose of unity in the global body of Christ. Now he resumes his intense warnings, corrections, and self-defense that he started at the beginning of the letter.

As we have discussed throughout the study of Paul's letters, it is important to always try to listen to the conversation that is happening on the other side of this letter. This principle is especially important in chapters 10-13. As Paul makes claims about himself and about the false teachers in Corinth it is obvious that he is making counter-point arguments to certain accusations that have been leveled at him. Let's try to reconstruct the basic attitude toward and presuppositions about Paul that his opponents carried, as well as the accusations that they brought against him.

Basic assumption: His opponents believed that Paul operated according to the same standard that all teachers do in the Empire. Paul says, "Some people ...think that we live by the *standards of this world*." The New American Standard Bible more literally translates it as "some people regard us as if we walked *according to the flesh*." The point is that the false teachers who were infecting Corinth operated under the commonly accepted idea that being an educated person made you better than everyone else. They used their high and lofty knowledge and their eloquence of speech to manipulate others, exalt themselves, and extort money from the ignorant. They assumed that Paul was doing the same thing, so therefore was lying to the Corinthians in his teaching. For the false teachers the debate with Paul was simply a game of who can be more convincing and win the hearts of the Corinthians.

Accusation #1: Paul is all bark and no bite. He speaks harshly in his letters, but in person he is small both in stature and in intellect. Pay no attention to the man full of hot air.

Accusation #2: Paul had no authority to teach in Corinth, or in any region of Greece for that matter. He should have never brought his crazy teaching here to confuse you in the first place. He has no papers of authority or letters of recommendation like we do. Don't listen to him, listen to us.

Accusation #3: Paul does not really love you. If he did he would have asserted himself in a place of authority over you and told you clearly how to live. When he came here he was nothing more than a common tentmaker full of crazy ideas. Listen to us, we'll show you the proper way to live.

In response to the assumption

Paul responds to the basic assumption in 10:3-7. This is a very famous passage that has been used by various theological camps to defend various theological positions. Allow me to attempt to read this passage in the context of the flow of Paul's logical presentation. Here is a literal translation of the passage (when I say literal, I mean it tries to be true to the grammatical structure of the Greek instead of read well in English)

> *For in the flesh we do walk around, not according to the flesh do we fight, for the weapons of military service of ours not fleshly but powers to God for the tearing down of fortresses, thoughts tearing down and all that is being lifted up on high against the knowledge of God, and taking captive every thought to the obedience of Christ, and in preparedness having to avenge all disobedience, when might be fulfilled of you the obedience.*

That's a little rough to read. Now, allow me to paraphrase for meaning.

> *Yes, we do live in the flesh, just like everyone, but living isn't what we're talking about. We're talking about war. We're talking about the battle between our teaching and the teaching of those false apostles. It's a battle for the truth and a battle for your hearts. When it comes to battle we do not fight according to the common sets of standards. We do not flaunt ourselves or exalt ourselves and believe that we are something special. Instead, we use the power of God that tears down all that pretense and pompous arrogance. Just like when the people in Genesis tried to lift up a high and lofty tower in Babel to make themselves equal with God, and God broke down their efforts, so do we use that same power to tear down the self-righteous who think they can achieve God's greatness through philosophical rhetoric. We are on the warpath to take all of those pointless and dangerous teachings as prisoners of war and are prepared to bring God's punishment on all of the people who are trying to persuade you to turn away*
> *from the truth of the Gospel. We want you to simply obey Jesus and move out of the line of fire so that judgment can be brought on those who are disobedient. So, don't presume that I am operating like they do.*

In response to accusation #1

Paul saves his response to this accusation until the end of the letter. We will explore his answer more in chapter 13. Simply put, he said, "On my return I will not spare those who sinned earlier or any of the others."

In response to accusation #2

(In the voice of Paul) You don't think I have authority? True, I'm not as well papered as those "super-apostles" that are so impressive. But I don't measure myself by those standards. I am what I am. I was chosen by Jesus, plain and simple. It appears you are impressed with teachers who flaunt their stuff and brag about all of their academic achievements and qualifications for being great dispensers of wisdom. You want boasting? OK... here goes. I boast in the Lord. Oh, that's not enough for you? Let me list all the things that make me great... (we'll pick up that train of thought tomorrow)

In response to accusation #3

This one has to hurt the most. Do you actually think I don't love you? I'm the one who has never been a burden to you. I didn't impose a financial burden on you. I didn't impose a heap of stupid religious rules and regulations on you. All I did was give you the message of freedom that comes through Christ. These teachers you are so enamored with are beating you up...and you like it? I don't get it.

I can't believe you don't think I love you. Let me show you how much I love you. I'm going to tell you the truth. Those teachers are nothing more than phonies. They are wolves in sheep's clothing. They are just like Satan who dresses himself up like a beautiful angel and then sucks out your soul. I love you so much that I am going to come to you and nip this problem in the bud. I'm going to cut down all the pretext and deception that these teachers have presented to you and expose them for what they really are. If I didn't love you I wouldn't care and would allow them to ravage you and steal you away from the Grace and Love of Jesus.

So What?

In this commentary, hopefully, we have been able to see Paul's words in the context of Paul's self-defense. Before we leave it, let's ask the practical question for us. What can we learn from Paul's words?

1. **Don't play by the world's standards.** As followers of Jesus we get into big trouble when we start evaluating our self-worth according to the conventional wisdom of our culture. Our culture says that you are only good if you are financially secure and vocationally successful. Failure is not an option. The pretty people are on top. The "successful" people rule the roost. The church can fall into a deep pit when it starts believing that it is only good if it has the biggest and the best facilities, the prettiest stage faces, and the best "growth rate" in weekly attendance. I have a hard time believing that is the measuring rod that God uses when He judges the hearts of His people.

2. **Understand God's standard.** God's standard is simple. If what you do is authentically submitted to the authority of Jesus and is flowing from an obedient heart, then it is right. If your actions are self-glorifying or self-protective or any other kind of destructive motivation, then it is not from God. Each person must stand before God and give account. Let's not fall into the trap of creating our own "spiritual measuring stick" and walk around measuring each other. If you are going to boast, boast only in what is for and from God.

3. **Watch out for wolves**. There are many teachers and philosophies in the world that tout themselves as messengers of God and bearers and protectors of the truth and have a more enlightened way. Whenever you encounter a teacher, be careful. Test what they say. Listen to more than their words. Listen to their heart. Are they angry? Are they shifty? Do they seem to have a hidden agenda or ulterior motives? Are they approaching the interpretation of scripture with integrity or are they ripping verses out of context and using them to bulldoze their own agenda? The only way to safeguard against wolves in sheep's clothing is to know your Bible well, be well connected to the Spirit of God, and be discerning in all things.

Lesson 4

- 2 Corinthians 11:16-12:13

Study Questions

What is Paul's attitude about himself as he writes this section? Why?

Summarize the kinds of things that Paul is "boasting" about.

Why did God give Paul a "thorn in his flesh?"

Why does Paul delight in weakness?

What question (or accusation) can you hear lying behind Paul's words in 12:13?

Food for Thought

This passage can be summed up in the words of 11:30, "I will boast of the things that show my weakness." In this section Paul elaborates and illustrates what Jesus said when He told the disciples in Mark 9:35

> *"If anyone wants to be first, he must be the very last, and the servant of all."*

Paul was a living testimony to the truth of Jesus' words. From our perspective we consider Paul one of the greatest Christians to have ever lived. Yet, if we were to see him as he actually appeared I think we might be incredibly underwhelmed. Paul had a miserable life. He was beaten, imprisoned, maligned, tortured, starved, and misunderstood. Then, in the end, he was beheaded. Not exactly a Hollywood hit.

Early in my ministry I heard a message from Pastor Rick Warren that deeply impacted me. It was about ministering from weakness. He used the story of Jacob's wrestling match with the angel of the Lord as his text (Genesis 32:22-32). When Jacob wrestled with God, the angel touched his hip and this caused Jacob to limp for the rest of his life. In other words, God allowed Jacob to have an infirmity in order to remember his place in the world and his encounter with God. Rick gave many examples of people who live with terrible suffering in their lives, and because of this suffering, are mightily used by God. Rick tells of his own suffering with a condition in which he is allergic to adrenaline. Anytime he gets a rush of adrenaline it sends him to bed with debilitating headaches. Anyone who has ever preached knows that preachers depend on adrenaline. Therefore, the more Rick preaches, the more he suffers. Yet, God has used his teaching ministry to impact literally millions of people all over the world.

Paul says the same thing. God sent a tormenting messenger from Satan to inflict Paul with a thorn in his flesh. Why? To keep him humble. Paul actually begged God to take the suffering away. Did God not answer Paul? Was Paul living in sin, thus making it impossible for him to be healed? Is God a vindictive God? Is Satan so strong that neither Paul's prayers nor God's desire could overpower this thorn? No to all of the above. God gave the suffering to Paul in order to keep him humble. God's answer to Paul's petition was, "My grace is sufficient for you."

Everyone who has served in church leadership knows the simple truth that with a position of authority comes the corollary temptation of pride. The more successful your ministry becomes and the more people start touting you as a "great leader" or teacher, or missionary, etc. the more you have the temptation to believe your own press. More often than not God assists leaders in the development of humility by allow difficult circumstances to be present in the lives.

There are many schools of thought within the Christian community that believe God's desire for each and every person is to live in perfect health, perfect finances, and perfect lives all around. They claim that people who do not experience this level of perfection are obviously living in sin and deception and therefore are cut off from the healing power of God and His perfect will for their lives. Be careful of this kind of thinking. Paul's life should be a good example for us. Very few people walked in step with the Spirit as closely as Paul did, and in the same vein, very few people suffered as intensely as Paul did.

Is it true that sinfulness and negative thinking will cause physical, emotional, and spiritual trauma in a person's life and dealing truthfully with these issues will promote healing? Absolutely. Is it true that healthy eating habits and proper rest and exercise will increase the potential for the body's natural healing processes to function and promote an overall increase in health? Of course. Is it true that being wise financially will bring about financial stability, and perhaps abundance? Yes. Is it also true that God loves us and desires to bless our socks off? Beyond doubt.

All of these things are truisms. However, we must be careful that we do not take these ideas and make them what they are not. As we discussed yesterday, these standards are not the measure by which God measures us. He measures the heart. He measures the integrity of our desire to serve him and be used by Him and to flow in the simple truth of the good news of Jesus and be a light to the world regardless of circumstances. The danger in the philosophies that teach perfect health, wealth, and prosperity are that they can become a breeding ground for attitudes like shame, blame, inauthenticity, hidden secrets, judging, gossiping, etc. When we buy into the idea that a good Christian can't be sick or be sad or have doubts or ever wear a frown, then we create an environment that is similar to that of Russia under the KGB. We live in fear that someone might find out that I had a fear, or a sniffle, or a doubt and "out" us in front of the congregation. We don't want to be judged, so we hide our pain and put on the happy Christian mask and go to church spewing sentimentalities like, "I'm just blessed today," or "God is good all the time, isn't He?" or, worst of all, "I'm fine." When all the while we are struggling inside and need someone to simply extend the loving and accepting arms of God out to us and take us in -- warts and all.

Paul put on no pretenses. He let it all hang out. He hid nothing from anyone. He knew who he was and that the only thing that mattered was what God thought of him. If false teachers wanted to discredit him for not "fitting the mold" then so be it. If he was misunderstood, then "oh well." All that mattered was that he served God by fulfilling his calling to serve the Corinthians and all the Gentile regions with the Good News of Jesus.

Lesson 5

- 2 Corinthians 12:14-13:14

Study Questions

What does Paul want from the Corinthians?

What are Paul's fears concerning his upcoming third visit to Corinth?

What is Paul's warning to the Corinthians?

What is Paul's prayer for the Corinthians?

How would you summarize the tone of chapters 10-13? Why?

Food for Thought

Paul ends his letter with a warning and a challenge. He warns the Corinthians that, even though Titus brought good news about them, they still had many problems that were troubling to him. He was coming to visit them for the third time and he really hoped the third time would be a charm. If they didn't clean up their act then he would have to get tough with them.

You can just hear the mixed emotions oozing from him as he writes these words. In one respect he is totally frustrated with the church. It's like the Mom who walks into her son's room and finds it a total mess for the thousandth time. Ugh! "How many times do I have to tell you to clean up this mess!!!" Then, in another respect you hear the agony of a father who is watching his teenage son struggle with drug addiction. The only thing that will help is to institute "tough love" and intervention. Nothing could be more painful than to watch your little boy go through physical pain of withdrawal. You also hear the genuine compassion of a parent/mentor who has invested untold hours of time and energy teaching, training, and walking alongside someone. Paul wants nothing more than to see the Corinthians walk with Christ, and he will do whatever necessary and within his power to discipline them and protect them.

Then Paul challenges the Corinthians. In verse 9 he says, "Our prayer is for your perfection." Then in verse 11 he says, "Aim for perfection." In our culture we need to be careful when we come across the word "perfection" in the New Testament. For us, as Modern, Westernized, American Christians, when we hear the word "perfection" we immediately think of getting a 100% on the final exam. We think of scoring the perfect 10 in the competition, or having the perfect body, the perfect smile, the perfect life. Then we slump down in discouragement as we realize that "perfection" is the unattainable goal. We buy into the apathetic life slogan, "nobody's perfect" and accept mediocrity as the standard of our lives.

The word translated "perfection" is the Greek word *katargizo*. It means to be equipped, to be restored, to be put together internally. Look at other verses where it is used.

*And the God of all grace, who called you to his eternal glory in Christ, after you have suffered a little while, **will himself restore you** and make you strong, firm and steadfast. (1 Peter 5:10)*

*Night and day we pray most earnestly that we may see you again and **supply*** *what is lacking in your faith.*

(1 Thessalonians 3:10)

*Brothers, if someone is caught in a sin, you who are spiritual **should restore him** gently. But watch yourself, or you also may be tempted. (Galatians 6:1)*

Paul is not telling the Corinthians to be perfect, as we understand it; rather he is telling them to pull it together. Be restored to one another, to God, and to me. That is why he continues on in verse 11 and says, "be of one mind, live in peace."

So, here we are at the end of 5 weeks of study in Paul's letters to this very messed up church in Corinth. They were divided over teaching factions and doctrinal differences and social status. They were being duped by false teachers who wanted them to enter into a legalistic, esoteric philosophy that denied the simple message of Jesus who lived in a physical form, literally died, was buried, and physically rose from the dead, and now is exalted to the place of supreme ruler of all things (higher than Caesar, even). The good news is that this risen Lord has set us free from all the divisions that keep us hating each other and calls us to enter into His Kingdom, under His authority, where we can, with Him, bring glory to the Father.

After all this study the message is simple. Love God with an undivided heart and love your neighbor without divisions. In this we will shine the light of God's Kingdom and bring emancipation to everyone who suffers under the oppression of the pettiness of human strife. May we walk in that Kingdom in our families, our churches, our jobs, and our neighborhoods today and always. Let's get it together!

(Endnotes)
[1] http://plateaupress.com.au/wfw/proofoft.htm

Reading Paul's Mail

Romans part 1

As we begin our study of Paul's letter to the Romans it is important to keep the correspondence between him and the Corinthians fresh in our minds. Over the past few sesions we have been looking at Paul's sordid relationship with the Corinthian church and have watched as he slowly moved toward that city on his "Jerusalem Relief Fund" tour. Finally, Paul arrived in Corinth. In Acts 20:2-3,

> *"He traveled through that area, speaking many words of encouragement to the people, and finally arrived in Greece [probably Corinth], where he stayed three months. Because the Jews made a plot against him just as he was about to sail for Syria, he decided to go back through Macedonia."*

It is most likely that it was during this tumultuous three month period that Paul wrote the letter to the church in Rome. Who were the Romans? What connection did Paul have to the church there? Why did he write the letter? These are important questions that must be answered if we are to understand the meaning of the letter.

First of all, the church in Rome was not started by Paul. That is an incredibly important thing to keep in mind. All of his other letters were written to people that had been either personally discipled by Paul or had been a direct product of his ministry. The Romans, however, were a church that was probably older than Paul's own Christian life. Although there is no hard evidence to validate this speculation, it is very safe to assume that the church in Rome was planted as a direct result of the day of Pentecost. On that day, as recorded in Acts 2, Jews from all around the Roman Empire were present to witness and partake in the outpouring of the Holy Spirit. It is most likely that some Jews who had traveled to Rome for Pentecost were exposed to the message of Jesus through Peter's teaching, received the Holy Spirit, and took that embryonic seed of the Gospel back to Rome with them.

Shortly after the church's establishment in Rome the Emporer became antagonistic toward this new movement and made life difficult for the followers of Jesus. Many of them fled the city and relocated in other places in the Empire. Two of those emigrants were the husband and wife team,

Aquila and Priscilla. In Acts 18 we learn that Paul made fast friends with this couple and worked with them in their tent-making shop in Corinth. There is no doubt that over the long hours of tent-stitching there were many conversations about what the church in Rome was like. It is also likely that Paul met many other Roman refugees scattered throughout the provinces of Asia, Macedonia, and Achaia during his travels.

Apparently the political climate had changed for the Roman church between the time of Acts 18 and Acts 20 and the refugees were allowed to return home. We know these things because at the end of the letter to the Romans Paul addresses many people that he knows (including Aquila and Priscilla). Given these personal connections with refugees and the hours of discussion with Aquila and Priscilla concerning the church, Paul probably felt that he already knew this church well even though he had never physically been there.

There are two likely reasons why Paul wrote this letter. First, he wanted to set the stage for his arrival. We might think of this as a kind of calling card or statement of faith that Paul presented to the church to let them know where he stood on the basic issues that the church was facing at that time. Paul's plan was to take the money that he had collected for Jerusalem, deliver it to that city, then sail to Spain to expand the gospel in that region. On the way to that mission field he desired to stop off in Rome and spend some time encouraging the church there and being encouraged by them. He made a special effort to point out that he did not presume to plant a church in Rome since the church was well established. After what he had just been through in Corinth the last thing he wanted was to be accused of moving in on someone else's "territory." He simply wanted to meet them and make a good connection with new brothers and sisters in Christ. In an effort to prepare the way for himself and insure the best possible time in Rome, he probably had a desire to circumvent any gossip that may have already spread to the Romans concerning all the false accusations that Paul had endured in Corinth. As you read the letter, with the Corinthian letters in mind, you can hear Paul still defending himself against some of these accusations.

Secondly, Paul may have been addressing some issues that had come to his attention through his association with the refugees he had befriended. Perhaps Aquila, during their many tent-making conversations, said to Paul,

> "You know, the church in Rome is still really confused about the whole issue regarding the role of the law and the Gospel. I mean, most

of us were born and raised Jews. Now we have Gentiles in our fellowship who have no regard for the Law of Moses and it still makes us uncomfortable. Paul, I've learned so much from you, it would be great if you could write a letter to my church and guide them through the scriptures to show them the truth about Jesus' Gospel. You know, the way you do it every time you go into a new synagogue. So, if you ever get a chance, could you do that for me?"

No one knows if a conversation like that took place, but it is definitely clear that Paul is addressing a predominately Jewish audience and explaining to them how the grace of Jesus for the whole world intersects with the nation of Israel and its many traditions.

Of all the letters that Paul wrote, the one to the Romans is the least "occasional" and the most "systematic" in its approach. In other words, when Paul wrote the letters to the Corinthians, he was responding to a list of very specific questions and addressing very specific issues in that particular church. He did not paint a broad-stroked theological treatise, but pinpointed specific issues with the understanding that the recipients already had the background teaching in place to make sense out of his specific directions. That is what is means to be "occasional." To the Romans, on the other hand, Paul did take the time to construct a fairly thorough and well crafted argument that created his basic theological grid through which he viewed the world. Building a logic argument is taking a "systematic" approach to communication.

In much of Paul's ministry his common practice was to enter into a town, go to the synagogue, and reason with them from the scriptures to demonstrate that Jesus was indeed the long-awaited Messiah. It is very likely that the text of Romans 1-11 is a rough outline of what that kind of presentation may have sounded like.

If you look at the illustration you will see a fairly detailed chart of the entire letter. Here is the basic flow of the text.

Chapters 1-3: Everyone is a sinner and everyone is welcomed into the Kingdom of God through faith. There is no favoritism or distinction between Gentile and Jew in God's eyes. This was an important foundational principle to establish because it flew in the face of conventional Jewish wisdom. In the Jewish theology, God loved the Jew and proved Himself "righteous" by upholding His covenant with Abraham and excluding all Gentile sinners. To put it abruptly, God loved Jews but hated Gentiles. Paul demolishes that belief and brings everyone onto an equal playing field. God loves everyone.

Chapters 1-8: Throughout the letter Paul uses a common teaching technique where the teacher will anticipate a question from the listening audience, voice it, then systematically answer and nullify the question. Basically you can read Romans like a conversation between the Jewish audience in Rome and Paul. It goes like this:

P: Being a Jew and following the Law doesn't make you better or worse than anyone else in the world. All have equally sinned and all are equally welcome through God's mercy.

J: What's the point of being a Jew, then?

P: God loves the Jews and entrusted you with scripture. However, being a Jew doesn't make you any better than being a Gentile. We are ALL sinners, and we are ALL are justified by the grace of Jesus.

J: What about the Law, then? How does it fit into the scene?

P: Abraham didn't have the Law, and he was considered righteous. His faith is what "saved" him. So it is for everyone. Anyone (Jew or Gentile) that has faith in Jesus is at peace with God and lives in the hope of glory. It all started long before the Law when Adam brought sin for ALL men. Now Jesus, apart from the Law, has brought grace for ALL men (not just Jews).

J: If you think we should abandon the Law then should we sin so grace can increase?

P: By no means! You weren't saved to feed your sinful nature. You died to that. You are now a slave to righteousness. You died to that old spouse and are now married to a new spouse so you can "bear the fruit" of God.

J: Are you saying that the Law is sin? Is something good now something evil?

P: Absolutely not! God gave the Law to expose the fact that we are sinful and desperately need His grace. Because of God's grace there is no longer any condemnation from God. We do not have to serve our sinful nature. We are set free. We are sons of God. We are heirs to all of God's glory. We walk in His Spirit and call him, "Daddy." Nothing can separate us from God's love!!

Chapters 1-9: We will continue the dialogue and cover these chapters in the next session.

Lesson 1

- Romans 1

Study Questions

What is Paul's attitude toward the church in Rome?

What does he hope to do with them?

Where does righteousness come from?

Why is the wrath of God coming on the people described in this chapter?

What was the result of the people suppressing the truth and turning to idols?

Food for Thought

What is righteousness?

A key concept that unlocks much of Paul's theology is to understand the definition of the word "righteousness" as Paul uses it. This term is so important that volumes have been written about it and much debate has swirled around it. The following commentary is a simple presentation. If you are interested in digging deeper into Paul's mind and thought then this would be a good place to begin.

The Greek word is *dikaiosune*. In ancient Greece the Goddess Diké was the goddess of Justice. She held the scales of Justice in her hand and meted out "just rewards" based upon people's behavior. Throughout the course of Greek culture the term *diké* and *dikaiosune* was used to discuss areas of justice, fairness, and more importantly, faithfulness to a contract. In the Hebrew Bible (which is what would have more dramatically impacted Paul's thinking) the idea of justice had much to do with God's faithfulness to His eternally binding promises that He made to His people. Simply put, the "righteousness of God" is God's faithfulness to His covenant.

During the period of time between the Old Testament and the New Testament an attitude concerning God's righteousness and the Law developed among the Jewish Rabbis. The Jews believed that God's righteousness and His blessing were for the Jewish nation only. God loved the Jews but hated the Gentiles. The heart of Paul's message was that Jesus came to dismantle that ethnocentric attitude and to declare to the world that God's righteousness (His faithfulness to His promise) was to the whole world. He made the promise to Abraham that through him God would bless all nations. The righteousness of God is that He is keeping His promise to everyone, not only to the Jews.

So, what does it mean for us to be righteous? We are to be righteous as God is righteous. God is faithful to His promise and has provided grace and mercy to us. For us to be righteous is to live a life of faithfulness to God. In the same way that a husband and wife pledge fidelity to one another, so we, too, are called upon to be faithful; to be righteous before God.

We will see Paul unfold this argument throughout the letter.

They are full of it

In chapter one Paul submits exhibit "A" of his two part opening argument. In this chapter he basically says, "All the people who have turned away from the true God and have given themselves over to idolatry are cut off from God's fellowship and deserve His wrath." Before you get up at arms and call Paul a "hellfire and brimstone" preacher, just wait and let the argument unfold over the next two lessons.

He paints a pretty grim picture of the Gentile world in this chapter, of that there is no doubt. As he lists all the things that the Gentiles are "full of" it is difficult to imagine any Gentile that could even be a nice person. Once again, Paul is building a case. Be patient.

Here are some observations from today to think about.

1. **God is accessible to all people.** Many skeptics ask the question, "What about all the people who have never heard the name of Jesus? Do they have no chance to be saved?" That is a really valid question. It seems that Paul addresses that issue in this passage. Paul's point in this passage is that Gentiles are culpable for sin in the universal scheme of God's justice. Yet, if they do not have the name of Jesus, what is the basis of that judgment? Paul said that God is present in all of creation. His "invisible qualities" are ever present and every person on the planet is confronted with His realities every day. While they may have never heard the name of Jesus, they have been exposed to the infinite presence of God. The sin in their case – the thing for which they will be judged – is that they denied a Creator and worshiped the creation. On the one hand this has positive implications for our present theology: It is possible to know God in an environment in which Jesus has never been presented. On the other hand, it is negative in the sense that all cultures also have the same temptations to give in to selfishness, greed, pride, lust, etc. These behaviors cut us off from God's presence – thus bringing "wrath" (separation from God's presence).

2. **Denying a creator will lead to self-destruction.** From the very beginning of time the core temptation for man is to think he is more than he truly is. We are tempted to think that there is no ultimate authority in the universe and that we can actually do whatever we want to do. When we sever ourselves from a Creator and an authority in our lives then all we have left is ourselves. Left to ourselves we tend to start seeking to fulfill our own desires. We create gods that look and behave like us, or like creatures, and we worship them. Other humans become objects for our own consumption. Eventually we destroy everything around us and implode on the shell of our hollow self.

3. **Be careful who you condemn.** Many Christians have used this chapter to hurl accusations and condemnations toward "sinners" in our culture. This is especially true in the issue of homosexuality. I think it is important that we be fair in this regard. Yes, the passage says that homosexuality does not line up with God's plan for humanity and is ultimately a destructive practice. However, look a little closer. Paul also lists a whole bunch of other attitudes that equally cut an individual off from the life-giving presence of God. How many of the self-righteous accusers have ever fallen into the trap of envy, gossip, slander, have been prideful, or...here's the clincher...have ever disobeyed their parents? The point is that ALL sin is sin, no matter what it is. ALL people fall into the category of "sinner" and it is foolish to cast stones in a self-righteous manner against anyone. Let's stay tuned as Paul continues his presentation and shed's more light on this matter.

Lesson 2

- Romans 2

Study Questions

Who is Paul specifically addressing in this chapter?

What does God's kindness lead toward?

What will happen to the human that passes judgment on another human?

What is God's standard for judging all people?

Restate verse 11 in your own words.

What is the relationship between the Law and God's judgment on people?

Summarize Paul's discussion regarding circumcision. What is it really all about?

Food for Thought

Here's a thought to chew on: God's judgment is based on kindness and leads to repentance. Man's judgment is based on arrogance and leads to condemnation.

Allow me to summarize this chapter in a paraphrase:

OK, Jews. You think you are special and "righteous" simply because you were born into the nation of Israel, your foreskins have been removed, and you have head knowledge of the Law of Moses. You think that those things give you some kind of special privilege to be able to judge and condemn the rest of the world. Well, you're wrong. God doesn't give a rip about your genetics, the status of your foreskin, or whether you can pass a Bible Trivia test. He cares about the condition of your heart. The truth is that only God has the right to judge a person's heart, and He judges by a standard that has nothing to do with the Law of Moses. He knows the intentions of a person. A person may look good on the outside and live according to the Law in every external way, but on the inside there could be all kinds of filth gurgling around. Yet, a Gentile, who has no access to the Law, could authentically be seeking God and the well-being of others. God knows this and will judge accordingly. When you "judge" others your motivation is to condemn them, cast them aside, and establish yourself and your nation as supreme in the world. That's not God's agenda. When God judges people His motivation is to bring them to a place of repentance. God is kind and merciful. He created everything for the purpose of knowing Him. Why would He desire to condemn everyone? It breaks His heart when people turn their hearts away from Him and He will do whatever it takes to get them to turn around and experience His love. Sometimes you religious people make that process very difficult. In so doing you are actually turning your heart away from God and bringing the 'wrath' you so desperately want to mete out to others onto your own head.

Now, what would this passage sound like today? I think Paul would be writing this to the church of today. In so many ways we have become the self-righteous, "law-abiding" Jews of Paul's day.

We think that just because we have the Bible, and just because we got wet one day in baptism, that God loves us more than anyone else and that we have the right to point the finger at all the "sinners" out there. Be careful! God doesn't give a rip about how wet we got on our baptism, or how well we can quote scripture, or how perfect our church attendance is. He looks deep into our heart and judges our intentions. Just as it was for the Jews, so it is for the Christian today; we were blessed to be a blessing. There is only one person who has the right to judge another; that is God Himself. The key verse in this chapter is verse 11, "God does not show favoritism." He loves everyone equally, regardless of their race, color, or creed. That is a tough pill to swallow for a group of people who believe they are the only ones that are "in" the God club. Let's keep an open mind as we explore this letter and see how Paul reconfigures the Jewish (and, I propose, the "Christian" mindset).

A note for deeper study

For those of you who would like to dig a little deeper, please keep track of all the times that Paul says "it is written" or directly quotes an Old Testament author. Remember, this letter is Paul's message in which he "reasons from the scriptures" with the Jews, pointing out that their own Holy Scripture teaches the message of Jesus that he is proclaiming. In this chapter he quotes Isaiah 52:5, "God's name is blasphemed among the Gentiles because of you". This is very significant because that verse is at the beginning of a long passage that describes the suffering servant that would come and take all of the sins of Israel on Himself and then open up the "tents of Zion" for the entire world. If you have time and desire, you may want to familiarize yourself with Isaiah 52-54 to get better context for Romans.

Lesson 3

- Romans 3

Study Questions

What question is Paul addressing in this chapter?

What accusation had been brought against Paul? Why?

What purpose does the Law play?

What is the source of righteousness?

Who has access to righteousness? Why?

Food for Thought

Today Paul ends his opening argument by saying that everyone is a sinner – Jew and Gentile alike – and everyone has access to God's grace through faith in Jesus – Jew and Gentile alike. As the Jews listen to his arguments, they are no doubt scratching their head and thinking, "OK, Paul. Now that you've totally insulted us and unraveled everything we believe about ourselves and our place in the universe, we have one question. If you are right and everyone is equal, then why in the world did God call Abraham and create the Jewish nation in the first place. Was it just a waste of time, or some kind of sick joke that entertained God for the past 1400 years?"

We need to sympathize with the Jews for a moment. They have a really valid point. Everything thing they had been taught told them that their hope rested in the fact that God would restore Israel and bring them a future of great abundance. That notion is actually reflected in the question itself. In our English translations verse 1 reads, "What *advantage* is there in being a Jew." The word "advantage" in our culture can have some connotations of pride and arrogance or "getting ahead of the Joneses" mentality. The Greek word *rrisos)* however, means "overflow, abundance." The question is really saying, "Hey, I thought we have endured all this suffering and oppression throughout the centuries so that God will one day give us great abundance. If we aren't really His special people and our adherence to the Law of Moses doesn't really set us apart from the world as His chosen people, then where is our hope in a better future?"

I love the way Eugene Peterson paraphrases this section. It is so right on that I'm going to have you read it for yourself,

> So what difference does it make who's a Jew and who isn't, who has been trained in God's ways and who hasn't? As it turns out, it makes a lot of difference—but not the difference so many have assumed.
>
> First, there's the matter of being put in charge of writing down and caring for God's revelation, these Holy Scriptures. So, what if, in the course of doing that, some of those Jews abandoned their post? God didn't abandon them. Do you think their faithlessness cancels out His faithfulness? Not on your life! Depend on it: God keeps His word even when the whole world is lying through its teeth. Scripture says the same:
>
> "Your words stand fast and true;
>
> Rejection doesn't faze you."

> But if our wrongdoing only underlines and confirms God's rightdoing, shouldn't we be commended for helping out? Since our bad words don't even make a dent in His good words, isn't it wrong of God to back us to the wall and hold us to our word? These questions come up. The answer to such questions is no, a most emphatic No! How else would things ever get straightened out if God didn't do the straightening?
>
> It's simply perverse to say, "If my lies serve to show off God's truth all the more gloriously, why blame me? I'm doing God a favor." Some people are actually trying to put such words in our mouths, claiming that we go around saying, "The more evil we do, the more good God does, so let's just do it!" That's pure slander, as I'm sure you'll agree.

Equal at the foot of the cross

We need to remember that Paul is "reasoning from the scriptures" with the Jews. In the second half of this chapter Paul is basically saying, "If you don't believe what I'm saying, then read the Bible that you hold to so dearly. It says it in plain black and white; *everyone is a sinner.* All the scriptures I'm quoting to you are referring to the people of Israel, not the Gentiles. So, don't tell me that I'm just pulling this stuff out of thin air."

If you have time, look up these verses and see for yourself what the Old Testament says regarding these things.

Psalm 14:1-3;

Psalm 53:1-3;

Eccles. 7:20

Psalm 5:9

Psalm 140:3

Psalm 10:7

Isaiah 59:7-8

Psalm 36:1

These are the passages that Paul uses to barrage his listeners with "Biblical evidence" for his case.

In the final section Paul states that all people have fallen short or are deprived of God's glory because all have sinned. In order to interpret this passage correctly we have to read it in the shadow of verse 27. "Where then is boasting?" Paul's point in this passage is not to condemn the whole world to Hell. His point is to wake the

Jews up into realizing that their perspective on God's eternal plan has been painfully distorted. His primary objective here is to break down the ethnic division, arrogance, and prejudice that lay between the Jews and the Gentiles. At the foot of the cross EVERYONE has severed their relationship with God by being selfish, arrogant, prideful, etc. In God's eyes we are all equal and always have been. God set apart Israel to be the bearers of His objective revelation and to be a blessing to the world, not to be the only people in Heaven.

Here's something to ponder. If ALL people are equally condemned by their sin, then no one can enter into God's presence. However, God loves EVERYONE equally and desires to be in fellowship with His creation. A holy God cannot tolerate sin. Yet a loving God does not want to lose anyone. What is He to do? Enter Jesus. God demonstrated His justice (the same word we translate righteousness) by sending Jesus to die and pay the price for sin. God conquered sin through love. Now EVERYONE is welcome.

As Christians we need to remember that God's eternal plan and His love for ALL humanity is deeper and wider than anything we can imagine. We need to be careful that we don't fall into the trap that the "chosen" people of Israel did and start throwing everybody into the lake of fire because they don't agree with us or our interpretation of the Bible. God's grace through Jesus is big enough to take care of the whole world, even if we don't understand how or why.

In closing, I think Jesus' parable about the lost son in Luke 15 is very appropriate for this chapter. That parable is not really about the lost son. It is actually about the older brother. The older brother was the "good kid." He didn't go out and squander his inheritance. He stayed home and worked hard and did everything right. When he saw the prodigal son come home and get a big party he thought, "That's not fair. I've done everything right and I never got a party." The Jews (and we as good evangelical Christians) are like the big brother. We look at the world and all the terrible things they are doing and secretly think, "I hope they get what they deserve." Then when we see that God welcomes them in with their tattoos and wild music and strange lifestyles we think, "Hey, that's not fair!" God looks at us and says, "You don't really want me to be fair do you? Why don't you just rejoice in my Grace and be happy that these lost ones have come home."

Lesson 4

- Romans 4

Study Questions

Upon what basis was Abraham considered righteous?

Where was the Law when Abraham was considered righteous?

Did the Law have anything to do with it?

What place does circumcision have in Abraham's righteousness?

Summarize this chapter in your own words.

Food for Thought

Paul gives one last "Biblical Proof" of his message by going right to the source. The Jews boasted in the fact that they were the children of Abraham. God had chosen Abraham and called him out from among the Sumerians and told him to go to the land of Canaan. God promised that He would bless him and make him a great nation and that through him all nations would be blessed. (If you aren't familiar with the story, go back and read Genesis 12-21) When God made this promise, Abraham and his wife, Sarah, were old and childless and beyond the age of conceiving a child. For God's promise to come true it would take a true miracle. So, Abraham said, "OK." He simply believed. That's it. In fact, he even messed up a lot and wavered in his ability to maintain his faith (he conceived a child with his slave woman, he lied to the Pharaoh, etc.) Yet, God still worked with him.

The miracle child – Isaac -- was finally born and the family line was started. From Isaac came Jacob, who had 12 sons. These 12 sons became the 12 tribes. Those tribes were enslaved in Egypt for 400 years, and then Moses led them into freedom. So, 600 years after Abraham said, "OK," God gave a Law Code to Moses to instruct the newly freed slaves how to live and not get themselves into trouble when they headed into the treacherous land of Canaan.

In Paul's day, the Jews looked back on that story and lumped it all together into one big pie. The Jews took all of those components -- Abraham, circumcision, the 12 tribes, Moses, and Law – and made them into inseparable parts of God's plan for the universe. Paul points out to them the narrowness of that perspective. Abraham was the father of more than one nation. He was the father of Ishmael who then became the father of all the Arab nations. Then Isaac was the father of Jacob and Esau. Were Esau's offspring any less children of Abraham than Jacob's, even though they aren't in the 12 tribes? There were a lot of people out there who could legitimately claim to be children of Abraham, so Israel couldn't claim exclusive rights to that. "Ah," they would retort, "what about circumcision and the Law? That is what makes us special." Paul reminds them that neither of those things was in place when Abraham said, "OK." It was his simple faith; his belief that God was real and that God was his advocate. That faith was what "credited" him as righteous.

Paul pleads with the Jews to open up their eyes and widen their perspectives. GOD LOVES THE WHOLE WORLD. God looks at every person's heart, just like He looked at Abraham's, and asks,

do you believe in me? To prove God's love for us and to cancel out all the destructive garbage that we have built up against ourselves over the millennium, God sent Jesus to be crucified for our sins and raised to life again to bring us righteousness. Righteousness is faithfulness to the promise. God does not back down or give up on us. Jesus reaches out to us and demonstrates that God loves us more than we can ever imagine. He is faithful, even when we are not.

Lesson 5

- Romans 5

Study Questions

What do we have because of faith?

What is the purpose of suffering?

What have we received through Jesus? What does that mean?

What came through Adam? What was the scope of this event?

What came through Jesus? What was the scope of this event?

Food for Thought

In chapter 5 Paul moves away from his opening argument in which he stated that all men are equal, regardless of ethnicity, and moves onto the second part of his argument. He now starts to explain the current situation in the wake of Jesus' death and resurrection. What are the benefits of God's grace and His universal Kingdom?

In verses 1-11 he states it very clearly. Because of Jesus' death and resurrection we are at peace with God. Did you hear that? *Peace with God.* That means God is not against us. Isn't it amazing how many religious systems (including many Christian ones) paint a picture of an angry God? It's like the Far side cartoon where God is looking at a computer screen which shows a picture of a man standing on the sidewalk with a big piano hanging over his head. God is hunched over with his finger ready to strike the "SMITE" button. So many people think that God is just waiting for us to mess up so that He can throw us out into the trash heap. NO! God is our Father. He created us. He loves us. Through Jesus He settled the score and paid the debt that we accrued for us and in spite of us. He is not at war with us; He has made peace and calls us into reconciliation. Through this reconciliation He urges us to be reconciled to one another. He wants us to stop living in the hellish prison of self that we have created and walk in the glorious life of His Kingdom and walk in reconciliation with Him and all people.

In verses 12-21 he draws from another pre-Law Bible story to demonstrate the scope of what he is talking about. The discussion of Adam accomplishes two things. First, it demonstrates that the sin issue is not about the Law but is something that separated humanity from full fellowship with God from the very beginning. Once again, it has nothing to do with obeying or disobeying the Law of Moses. Secondly, it demonstrates the scope of God's plan. God is not concerned only with the children of Abraham and the 12 tribes of Israel. God is concerned with the entire world. Adam was the father of ALL people. If Paul didn't make the point of God's love for all people clear enough in his Abraham analogy then he was definitely going to drive it home by discussing Adam. The sin issue is for everyone because Adam is the father of everyone.

Now, this is the really important part. Just as sin came to everyone through Adam, so does grace come to everyone through Jesus. Let's think about this. Paul is making a one to one comparison between Adam's impact on humanity and Jesus' impact on humanity. They both work the same way. If Adam's sin affected everyone, then shouldn't Jesus' gift affect everyone? Did we get a choice of whether we would receive Adam's curse, or did it affect the whole world? Do we get a choice about whether we will accept Jesus' gift? Do you see the problem? The traditional, evangelical teaching says that all are condemned, but, because of God's grace through Jesus, only those who say the sinner's prayer and accept Jesus into their hearts will be saved. Everyone else is condemned to Hell, and only a few will receive the free gift of grace. That sounds great if you are one of the lucky ones who grew up in a culture where Jesus was preached, but what about the millions of people who didn't? To be true to the passage we need to at least question that line of thinking and ask how Jesus' gift impacted the entire world in the same way that Adam's sin did. It seems to be an all or nothing scenario. Jesus opened up the door to reconciliation for all people, everywhere, in all time. That is huge and the implications of it are something that we need to seriously dwell upon.

Before we leave today, let's reconnect to the point of this passage: through Jesus Christ and the simple, Abraham-like faith, we are at peace with God. As you go out into the world today and you hear those negative voices in your head that say, "God doesn't love you." "You don't deserve to go to Heaven." "Why don't you just indulge in that favorite addiction and numb yourself out again." Stop right there and say out loud, "NO! Those are lies. God does love me. I have been reconciled with God. I am at peace with God and we are on the same side. I don't have to hide from Him or be afraid of Him. I don't have to hurt myself or mask my pain. I'm free and I'm going to live with the grace of Jesus overflowing out of my life today and be a blessing to everyone I meet."

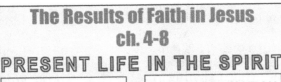

The Simple Message ch. 1-3

EVERYONE IS CONDEMNED

-but now-

EVERYONE IS WELCOME TO FAITH IN JESUS CHRIST

Shall we sin to increase Grace?

Shall we sin because we are free?

No wAy!
You were saved for transformation!

The Results of Faith in Jesus ch. 4-8

PRESENT LIFE IN THE SPIRIT

PEACE WITH GOD   NO CONDEMNATION

What about the Law?

ADAM vs. JESUS not LAW vs. JESUS

Law intensified sin to show our need for GRACE.

Jesus defeats sin

slave to sin

realize inheritance of glory

acknowledge adoption as child of God

become slave to righteousness

must cross a line of faith

FUTURE HOPE OF GLORY

NOTHING CAN SEPARATE US FROM THE LOVE OF GOD

Romans part 2

This session there are two sections to our text. The first is chapters 6-8. The second is chapters 9-11.

In chapters 6-8 Paul continues his dialogue with the Jews over the issue of the Law and sin. It is important to keep a constant view of the forest before you zoom in and examine the trees in this text. We must always keep in mind that Paul is discussing, first and foremost, the nature of the Law in God's overall plan of redemption for the world with people who have always identified themselves as the only nation loved by God. For the Jews the Law was their identifying mark of God's righteousness. By obeying the law they were demonstrating faithfulness to God and thanking Him for saving them from the wrath that He was going to mete out on the Gentile barbarians. For Paul to say the things he was saying was incredibly difficult for them to imagine, let alone accept. Let's highlight the "forest" of the dialogue before we explore the "trees." In order to get the flow we must back up to chapter 4 and then proceed into this week's text.

Chapter 4

Abraham was saved through his faith, not the Law or circumcision. It is our faith in Jesus that saves us, not following the Law or being circumcised.

Chapter 5

Since we are saved through faith, we are at peace with God (the Jews believed that all Gentiles were God's enemies). Sin came through Adam to all men (before the Jews were even invented); now grace comes to all men, regardless of race.

(Now, here's the key to understanding our text for this week.)

Verses 20-21: the Law (carried by the nation of Israel) was added to the human story to increase the intensity of the sin that was introduced through Adam. Since the Law showed us how sinful we really are, now we can appreciate the depth of God's grace, walk in righteousness, and know eternal life through Jesus.

Chapter 6-7

In these two chapters Paul proposes a list of questions that the Jew would naturally ask. Here are the questions:

Shall we go on sinning that grace may increase?

Shall we sin because we are not under Law but under grace?

Is the Lsin?

Did that which is good, then, become death to me?

131

As you listen to these questions you can hear in their tone the painful tearing sound that happens when a person's inherited worldview with its deeply set root system gets torn out. This painful process happens to all of us when we encounter the level of worldview-shattering teaching that Paul was presenting to the Jews. We oscillate between many emotions. On the one hand we are appalled at the foreign teaching and want to attack the teacher. On the other hand, if we sense there is truth in the teaching, we become mortified and don't know how to function in the new world of these ideas. In these four questions you can hear the Jews both attacking Paul while at the same time honestly questioning him. As we study his answers to these questions we will gain some great insight into the life of spiritual transformation that God has called all people to experience.

Here are the summaries of his answer to the questions:

Shall we go on sinning that grace may increase?

No way! You died to sin. You are no longer a slave to sin. Sin is not your master, you are under grace.

Shall we sin because we are not under law but under grace?

No way! You are now slaves to righteousness; your whole body is under its authority. God's gift to you is eternal life. Dying to the Law and to sin has now freed you to live with Jesus and bear His fruit.

Is the Law sin?

No way! The law helped us know what sin really looked like. Since the Law exposed the sin, the sin brought death.

Did that which is good, then, become death to me?

No way! The Law didn't bring death. The Law exposed sin and sin brought death. The Law showed me that there is a powerful force of sin in me that wrestles against my desire to love God. Apart from God I am dead. Who will save me? Jesus saves me from myself and the sin that keeps me down! The Law was part of God's plan to expose our need for grace.

Chapter 8

Now that we are justified (brought into true relationship with God) we are not condemned by God, but are His children. We do not have to follow the Law, but are led by His Spirit living within us. We are adopted as His children and have an inheritance of His glory forever. Nothing can separate us from His love!

In chapters 9-11 Paul answers the really big question. The Jews throw up their hands and say, "Alright Paul, let's say you're right and the Gentiles are just as acceptable to God as the Jews and it is all about faith in Jesus, not about being a Jew. If that's true, then what was the point of creating the nation of Israel in the first place? Should we throw out our heritage and the scripture? Was God just messing with us? Is the nation of Israel lost forever?"

Paul addresses these questions and gives us a good perspective on how we, as finite humans, are to approach the subject of trying to understand the eternal plan of God.

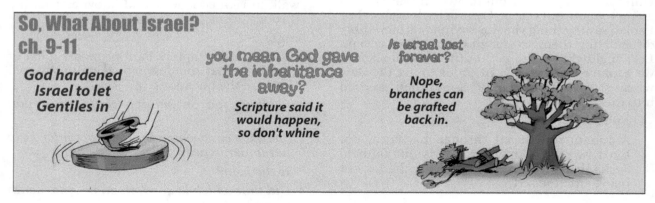

So, What About Israel?
ch. 9-11

God hardened Israel to let Gentiles in

you mean God gave the inheritance away?

Scripture said it would happen, so don't whine

Is israel lost forever?

Nope, branches can be grafted back in.

Lesson 1

- Romans 6:1-7:6

Study Questions

What question does Paul set up and knock down in verses 1-2?

What is this question a reaction against from the previous chapter?

What metaphor does Paul use to answer this question? Do you think it is a helpful metaphor? Why or why not?

What question does Paul set up to knock down in verse 15?

What metaphor does he use to answer this question?

Do you think it is a helpful metaphor? Why or why not?

Food for Thought

Dead to Sin

Paul ends chapter 5 by saying, "The law was added so that the trespass might increase, but where sin increased, grace increased all the more." At that statement all the Jewish eyebrows shot up and the heads tilted. "Huh? Are you saying that sin is actually a good thing? Here's what we hear you saying, Paul. You are saying that by having knowledge of the Law we have a heightened understanding of God's standard. Thus, we have a heightened clarity for how to sin more effectively. The more we sin the more we need grace. Therefore, I'm actually doing God a favor by sinning because I allow Him to rescue me and make Him look good. Bring on the sin!"

Paul responds to this idea with a resounding, "by no means!" In the Greek this expression translates the phrase *may genitor* literally translated, "may it never be given birth or come into being." Never, ever, ever, should a person who is walking in the grace of God entertain the idea that sin is OK or is part of God's plan.

In Paul's response to this question he gives us a very important aspect of the Christian identity and life. In Christ we are dead to sin. Although this may be a morbid image, think of a corpse in a coffin. Let's call him Fred. What would happen if we came up to Fred with a Playboy centerfold and said, "Hey, Fred, check this out?" Nothing. Fred is dead. He doesn't flinch. He is not affected by it.

Perhaps you have heard about this idea of being dead to sin before and you think that it is too idealistic. You think that it is a good idea to think of oneself as dead to sin, but the reality is that you are very much alive. When the centerfold is displayed (or whatever your temptation of choice may be) you see it and it has an impact on your body and your mind. How can you be dead to it? Here's the key to dying to sin. You can't kill yourself. It's not your death. You attach yourself to the death of Jesus. You take your sinful desires and nail them to the cross with Jesus. You bury them in the ground with him. Then you leave them there. When you rise from the dead you are no longer under the oppression of those desires but are filled with the power of the Spirit of God.

Let's talk a little about the "sinful desires." We need to not get into the pettiness of the Pharisees and their legalistic tendencies to categorize every external act as sinful or righteous. The Law is over. The grace of God is not a legalism issue, it is a heart issue. The only way that we can truly be dead to sin is when we are dead to our own pride and need to be right or special or powerful. After all, what is at the heart of sinful desires such as sexual addiction, gluttony, power struggles, etc? Selfishness. We desire to be in control of our own lives. We desire to play God. When we see a beautiful woman or man, we think, "I can have her and she can do for me the things that I want." When we look at that woman we only see ourselves and our own desire. That is not love.

Let's look at the example of the Playboy centerfold again. (While this example leans heavily toward male issues, women can easily replace it with an equally intense temptation to lust) When that centerfold is presented to our sinful nature, what do we see? A woman? Not really. We see an object that we can have for our own gratification. That happens because we think that our sexual urges were given to us to meet our every whim and fancy and we can do whatever we please with them.

What would Jesus see if He was shown the same centerfold image? Would He start drooling, and play out His sexual fantasies in His mind? I don't think so. Why? Is it because He is God and is asexual, thus eliminating the desire? No. Jesus was fully human. That means He experienced normal sexuality.

Jesus wouldn't lust over that women or covet her because He had the correct perspective on His life and His purpose. He also had the correct perspective on sexuality. Some people would say that the very presence of the sex drive in humans allows us the freedom to use it whenever and however we want. Jesus knew this was not true. The sex drive was not created for the needs of the self. It was actually created to meet the needs of the other person. It was created to bring a man and a woman together for the purpose of intimacy and procreation, not self-indulgent recreation.

When Jesus looks at that centerfold I believe He would not see an object of desire, but a scared little girl. He would see a child who was probably abused by a parent or an elder in some way. He would see a girl who didn't love herself enough to say no to men who pushed her too far. Jesus would see through the façade and see the truth. He could do this because He was dead to selfish indulgence and was walking so intimately with the Father that all He could see was truth and the legitimate needs of others.

Slaves to Righteousness

What does it mean to be dead to sin? It doesn't mean to walk around and flail your body with whips and deny yourself access to anything that may be a distraction or a temptation. That is physically impossible because you can never escape your

own thoughts. To be dead to sin means to be more focused on the mind of God than you are on your own agenda. It means to take everything in your life and nail it to the cross. Everything. That is why Paul goes on in the chapter to say that we are slaves to righteousness. The key to dying to sin is to realize that you are not your own. You are not an autonomous self wandering aimlessly through the cosmos. You are a created child of God who is part of a family. You are a member of the family of God called humanity. You are part of the body of Christ. What do we call it when a part of our physical body turns against the other parts of the body and starts living on its own? Cancer. When the human being believes that he is an autonomous self and has the freedom to do whatever he chooses and starts living for himself, then he becomes cancerous to the body. We are dead to sin. We are slaves to God. He owns us and our lives work best when we realize that everything we do must be done for the glory of God.

Everyday when we get out of bed we must die. We must say, "This is not my life. Lord, I bow before you and I worship you. My worship to you is my day. Every step I take, every breath I breathe, every thought I have, I submit to your authority. You are my king. I serve you today. Take my life and do with it what you will." When we orient ourselves in that way, then God transforms our minds and we can begin to see the world through the truth lenses of Jesus. Then, when we see the pretty woman we see just another hurting soul that needs to know God, not a hunk of meat for my appetite. When we see the fancy car we see a big car payment and a burden, not something that will make me feel good about myself.

Death sets us Free

In 7:1-6 Paul continues his metaphor of dying to the law by using an example from the law. When a husband dies, the woman is legally set free from her commitment to that man. In our culture where divorce is at epidemic proportions and the covenant of marriage is viewed as having little more worth than the paper the certificate is printed, on this analogy loses its punch. In Paul's day a Jewish woman had no rights to divorce her husband. She was bound to him until death, even if he was a wretch. Imagine how painful and debilitating it would be if your arranged marriage eternally joined you to a drunken wife-beater and there was nothing you could do about it. When that man died the woman was set free and was legally able to pursue a new husband. With that culture in mind you can see the power of Paul's analogy. As human beings we have been set up in a pre-arranged marriage to sin by our father

Adam. We are legally bound to this terrible force of self-destruction called sin. We can't escape it. But now, Jesus has killed that terrible, wife-beating husband and, in so doing, has freed us from the law that bound us to him. Now we are free to pursue another lover. Jesus is our groom who welcomes us into His household where we can bask in the benefits of His love, grace, and glory. We are now free to live in the Spirit and life, not under the law of sin and death.

Today, may we take a step closer to knowing what it means to die to sin and live for God.

Lesson 2

- Romans 7:7-25

Study Questions

What question and answer does Paul set up in verse 7?

What question and answer does Paul set up in verse 13?

What is the relationship between the Law and sin?

Restate verses 15-25 in your own words.

Food for Thought

Sin Gets Outed

For centuries people have debated over the nature of sin. In the fourth century Augustine argued with Pelagius over whether humans were born sinful or if we were born innocent and became sinful based upon the incredible pervasiveness of sinful behavior in the world. In the 16th century Calvin argued against similar ideas and further propagated Augustine's doctrine of "original sin" that stated that all human beings are born sinful and are doomed to the flames of Hell because of Adam's sin. Others have countered with the argument, "How could a loving God knowingly create a race of humans that were doomed to Hell?" The debate has raged on and has not been easily resolved. The scope of this little study does not have room to treat these questions with the respect and depth they deserve.

The one thing that everyone agrees on at some level is that something seems wrong with the world. This is classically called "The Problem of Evil." Truth be told, most people that began in a "Christian/Western" culture are atheists or agnostics or have turned to Eastern/Pantheist philosophies because of this issue. Yet, even atheists and pantheists agree that something is not quite right. No matter how much a naturalistic atheist may believe that we are nothing more than highly evolved mammals crawling around on a speck of dust in a meaningless universe, they still would object to someone raping their daughter. Why? Because it is *wrong*? Upon what standard is that act considered wrong? No matter how you slice it, no matter what theological jargon you want to dress it up in, the fact remains that man is sinful and, for some reason or another, has a natural propensity to hurt himself and others.

In this passage Paul is helping the Jews understand just how the Law fits into the universal scope of God's plan for redeeming this sin-sick race. As he stated in chapter 1, the Gentiles were conscious of sin apart from the Law because of God's natural revelation and their own conscience. Yet, under those circumstances things are very fuzzy. The one true God, the Creator of all things, the eternal, life-giving Spirit is present in all things and is accessible to all people that wish to be open to Him. Yet, in this infinite, abstract form of energy He is very fuzzy. It's like He is out of focus. In that state, God is a vague idea and, therefore sin is a vague idea.

An Analogy

In order to understand Paul's concept, let's create an analogy. Imagine a dark room where only faint moonlight shines through the window. It is nearly impossible to distinguish the details of objects in the room. Now, let's say that humanity lives in this dark room.

God is in the room as well, but His presence is like a quiet song. It is a faint whisper that can only be heard when the room is silent. God wants humanity to sing along with the song.

There is another presence in the room. Sin. It wants nothing more than to drown out the sound of the song and distract humanity from hearing.

Before the Law of Moses existed, Sin hid in the darkness of the room. It was vague and its features were hard to distinguish. Humanity knew it was there, like an ominous threat, but couldn't tell what it looked like and couldn't call it by name. In this darkness, Sin hounded humanity and tried to drown out the song.

When the Law came it was like a flashlight that allowed humanity to shine light on sin and see what it looked like. Humanity was now able to describe it by name, saying, "Oh, that feeling I have to take that man's woman for myself is called covetousness. Now it is clear. Now there is no mistaking what it looks like."

The flashlight didn't destroy the sin; it simply brought it into focus and made clear what it was. In fact, now that there was light in the room covetousness actually had a little more power to jump on the human and distract him from the song.

Paul says that the Law, like the flashlight, is good, but it does not have power to defeat sin. It simply exposes the fact that sin is in the room and needs to be run out.

The Jews responded to this idea by saying, "does that mean that the Law is death?" "No!" Paul responds. The Law is not death; it simply was a tool of God to expose the true nature of death itself.

Let's continue our analogy of the dark room and flashlight to explain. The light of the Law exposed the fact that the room was full of nasty little sin-creatures. They continually pounced on humanity and drown out the song. Humanity knew the song existed and wanted to hear it, but the vermin did not allow it.

The more humanity entertained the Sin, the more Sin grew and the more sin-creatures entered the room. Humanity was trapped and enslaved by a room full of sin and could not hear the song. Since the Law was shining the flashlight on the scene humanity knew exactly what the sin looked like and could call it by name, but was powerless to defeat it.

For the humans who don't have the Law, the Gentiles, they live in the dark room without a flashlight. With or without a flashlight, the sin is the same. Without the Law humanity simply struggles against a faceless enemy. Under the Law he struggles, but at least knows the face of his opponent and knows his name. It is sin.

The Good News of Jesus is that He brings more than the little flashlight of the Law. Jesus turns on all the lights in the room. In fact He is the light in the room. He is like a flaming sword that sweeps into the room and starts hacking the sin creatures one by one and sends their mutilated carcasses flying out the windows. The human stands in awe at the sheer power of Jesus' ability to destroy these things against which he has been struggling his entire life.

At first the human lies huddled up in the fetal position, curled up in a ball in the corner. All the lights are on, the sin is gone, and Jesus stands in the room. The human is scared. He doesn't know what to do. Then he notices something strange. He can hear the song. Only this time it is not as faint as before. As he looks around he notices that the song is actually coming from Jesus. Yet, the strange thing is that Jesus' mouth isn't moving. Somehow Jesus is the song itself; just like Jesus is the light itself. No longer is the song a vague whisper from outside the room. Now the song has popped into clear focus and is the person named Jesus. Jesus stands before the human and reaches out His hand and motions for him to get up. At that point the human is faced with a choice. Is this a dream, or is it real? Do I believe that all the sin has been defeated by Jesus and that the song is actually standing right in front of me, asking me to get up and run into His arms? Or, do I turn my back on Him and hide in the corner, doubting that it is real.

I realize that this analogy is a bit melodramatic and could be as harmful as it may be helpful. Yet, I think it demonstrates what Paul is trying to get across to the Jews. The Law served its purpose to expose sin for what it really is, but it had no power to defeat sin. Jesus has defeated sin once and for all and is now offering freedom in His Spirit to all people from every nation. They simply need to believe that it has been done for them and realize the gift God has given them.

What is Sin?

Before we move on there is one issue that needs to be touched on briefly. As we stated at the beginning of today's study, people have been arguing over the nature of sin for centuries. What is it? Where did it come from? How did we get infected by it? Did God create it? Is God powerless to defeat it? How can we be saved from its power? Are we held responsible for it even if we didn't start it?

Every culture and every theological camp has its own answer to those questions. Even those who deny that man is inherently sinful admit the presence of evil in society and are calling for a savior of some sort. As Christians we have some competing ideas about the nature of sin. On the one side some say that sin is nothing more than an attitude of our own heart. Therefore, we are culpable for it. When the Bible speaks of sin in a personified manner it is just a metaphorical device that helps us to discuss the internal battle we have with ourselves. Ultimately we are responsible before God for our own sin. When covetousness creeps up behind me and takes over my heart it is just the exposure of the fact that I have surrendered my heart to God and am a covetous person. It's my fault. On the other side of the spectrum there are those who claim that sin is actually in the form of spiritual beings called demons. The chief among them is Satan. These spiritual beings have names, like covetousness, bitterness, anger, lust, self-destruction, etc. Looking at my earlier analogy of the dark room, this camp would say, "Yes, they do have faces and names. The only way to defeat them is to call them by name and cast them out of the room."

The question for us is which view is right? There are strengths and weaknesses to both sides. In the former view, the strength is that it places all responsibility on the human for sin and emphasizes personal repentance and reliance upon Jesus' grace to be transformed out of the sinful nature and into a clean heart that can sing His song. The criticism of this view is that it tends to lend itself to a denial of the spiritual world and the Biblical witness to the presence of angels and demons in the universe, thus opening the Bible reader up to the potential of slipping into a revisionist or demythologizing of scripture. The strength of the latter view is that it does take into account the Biblical language of the reality of the spiritual world and openly acknowledges the presence of demons and angels in the universe. The criticism of this view is that it tends to give room for the idea that the individual is not responsible for his own sin. One can slip into a "the-devil-made-me-do-it" mentality that can be dangerous. Also, this view tends to be enemy-focused and keeps the believer's eyes focused on the demons and the struggle, rather than on Jesus and the victory.

The truth is that both views are wrong and both are right. Both take into account Biblical data and both fall short in some way. As is the case in every issue in theology, there is a continuum of ideas and the truth lies somewhere in the middle, or in the tension of two extremes.

To further muddy the waters, neither view addresses the issue of God's role in the presence of sin in the first place. If God is sovereign and all-knowing, then He knew sin would happen and is, therefore responsible for sin. How can He hold us responsible for sin, then? We'll deal with that issue more in chapters 9-11.

Here's a word of encouragement for the Christian whose head is spinning right now; for the Christian who is feeling defeated because they are overwhelmed by so many theological perspectives that are competing for the status of being "right" while condemning everyone else for being "wrong." As followers of Jesus it is our job to know what the Bible says and to recognize that these debated issues are bigger than the scope of the Biblical data and the scope of the human intellect to understand. In every case the Bible gives evidence to support both perspectives. That means they are both right and that there is something bigger above it that is beyond our ability to comprehend. So we accept them both and live with the tension of the mystery. We live in the unity of Spirit in the body of Christ and work together for the glory of God.

Here's the bottom line of what Paul is saying regarding sin: We've all got it, and we are all under its control. But now, Jesus has defeated it and, if we believe that, we can walk in the freedom of His Spirit. We don't have to understand it to walk in it. We need the faith of Abraham to look into the eyes of Jesus and say, "OK" as He lifts us up from the corner and breathes new life into our heart through the breath of His spirit. Now we are His bride and we can walk in victory and allow Him to transform us into what He created us to be.

Lesson 3

- Romans 8

Study Questions

What is our standing before God because of Jesus?

How did Jesus bring about this condition for us?

Contrast the mind controlled by sin vs. the mind controlled by the Spirit.

What metaphor does Paul use to describe those who are led by the Spirit of God? (verse 14)

What is the hope for the person who lives in the Spirit?

What can separate us from the love of God?

How does that promise affect you today?

Food for Thought

Today we reach the climax of Paul's argument. He is done answering the questions of the Jews and presenting the logic behind his message of the gospel and is now ready to cut loose and gloriously proclaim the good news itself. Sin has been defeated by Jesus. The Holy Spirit is accessible to all people through faith in Jesus. We are sons of God and cling to the hope of future glory. God loves us and nothing can change that!

This chapter is so rich that we could spend weeks unpacking it. Obviously we are not going to do that. In a spirit of celebration let's spend today simply highlighting the promises that God makes to us through Paul in this chapter.

- **There is no condemnation.** Jesus has defeated sin. God is not condemning us. We simply need to acknowledge that fact and step into the Spirit that He has freely offered. Even though He is holy and the great cosmic judge, God does not stand with pointed finger and call us sinner. He looks at the sacrifice of Jesus and says, "Not guilty." There is great freedom to know that God is not against us but is actually for us. He is not waiting for us to mess up, He is empowering us to grow and mature.

- **We have the Holy Spirit to empower us.** The key to the Christian life right now is the Holy Spirit. The Father is the omnipotent "other" that stands in the distance, holding all things together and setting the standard of holiness and justice in the universe. The Son is the creative song that brings life to all things, that defeated sin through His sacrifice, and makes the way possible for us to access the holiness of the Father. But it is the Spirit that indwells us. It is the Spirit that is the breath of God; the vibrant energy of the universe that is pulsating and singing the song at the core of every molecule. The Spirit is the spring of living water that flows to and from the heart of God. When we step into it, and let it flow in us, then we can resonate with the song of God, we can swim in the ebb and flow of God's purpose and plan for the universe. We can walk in power and authority to be exactly what we were designed to be. Not in our own strength, as if we were autonomous selves that area clever enough to manipulate the Spirit, but in a sense of abandon as we let the current of the Spirit guide us and move us through life to be used by God for His glory and purpose. In the Spirit we become an integral part of His body. It is not slavery, it is fulfillment.

- **We are children of God.** Paul brings the enigmatic language of life in the Spirit into a concrete metaphor by calling us children of God. There are two aspects to being a child. First, as a child of the King, we have access to the King and are able to call Him "Daddy". We do not cower in fear like a slave, we respectfully, yet confidently approach in the full knowledge that we are welcomed and desired as kin. Secondly, as a child we are inheritors of the estate. All that is God's glory is ours as well. What does that mean exactly? No one knows. All we know is that it is good and it is, somehow, the reason we were ultimately created. The very core of our being yearns for it. Every molecule in the universe longs for it.

- **We have hope.** This inheritance we have is a future transformation that will catapult us into a state of existence that will be the fulfillment of our creation. We don't know what it is, but we know it has been promised. When you have trouble getting out of bed in the morning because you think that today will be another ho-hum day, when you wonder if you will be able to bear the suffering that you experience in life, remember your hope. This is not the sum of all things; this is the beginning of things. If we truly believed that, then we would hop out of bed in the morning and be ready to take on whatever God had for us today.

- **We have strength for the journey.** Paul says that the Spirit gives us strength in our weakness and that Jesus intercedes for us because we do not know how to pray. It is a good reminder for us that there is a difference between our current state of existence and our promised future. Traditionally, theologians have called this the difference between Justification, Sanctification, and Glorification. Because of Jesus we have been justified. That means that we have been set free from sin and have been adopted into God's family as a child. Positionally, we are 100% a child of God. Yet, just like an infant has no idea who they are or what it means to be a child, so we, too, are weak and don't know how to be a child of God. The Holy Spirit comes along side us and teaches us and empowers us to grow up. This gradual maturing and refining process is called sanctification. It is the process of being made holy. Finally, the hope that lies before us is our future state of existence that we discussed above. That is called glorification; that state in which we will be ultimately transformed into God's glory and be with Him forever

in truly intimate fellowship. For now we stumble along on the journey and rely on the grace of God and the power of the Spirit to guide us.

- **We are safe.** Nothing can separate us from the love of God. Did you hear that? Nothing. Look at the list of things that Paul presents. It seems as if Paul is going through all the arguments that he has heard in his years of teaching and rolling them into a big pile. People have said that these things have power to take God's children away from him. No way. Nothing can do that. God loves His people, all people, from all nations, and nothing can stop Him from loving them. It's just like a child with a good Father. The Father looks at his child and thinks, "I love that kid so much. Even when he's sassing me and disobeying me, I love him. Yes, I have to punish him in order to correct his behavior, but nothing he could ever do would ever stop me from loving him." That is how God feels about us.

Today, as you go into the world, let these promises soak into your heart. Let them rumble around in your mind. Meditate on them and see if they don't lighten your step and transform your lenses a bit. Let us walk in the Spirit and in the knowledge that we are children of the King!

Lesson 4

- Romans 9-10

Study Questions

Chapter 9

What is Paul's attitude toward the nation of Israel? Why?

Who are considered God's children?

What question and answer does Paul set up in 9:14?

What question and answer does Paul set up in 9:19?

What question and answer does Paul set up in 9:30?

According to this chapter, how is God dealing with the nation of Israel?

Chapter 10

What is Paul's desire for Israel?

To whom is salvation available?

What does it take to be saved?

Food for Thought

In chapters 9-11 Paul is dealing with one basic question: What about Israel? If God loves all nations equally, apart from the Law, then why in the world did God create the nation of Israel in the first place? It seems as if God has changed the rules on us and then blames us for breaking the new rules when we didn't even realize it had changed. Where's the justice in that?

Here's the basic flow of chapters 9-10. Once again, this is in a dialogue format.

Paul: God did set aside the people of Israel through Abraham. However, it has never been about his genetic descendents, it has been about his spiritual descendents. Anyone who follows in the faith of Abraham, according to the promise, is a child of Abraham. Anyone who doesn't live in the faith of Abraham, even if they have his DNA and follow the Law, is not really Israel. God has set this up from the beginning.

Israel: Is God unjust?

Paul: Not at all. God is sovereign and He can do whatever He wants.

Israel: Then why does God blame us? Who can resist His sovereign will?

Paul: Who are you to talk back to God? He's potter, you're the pot. You don't get to call the shots.

Israel: Are you saying that the Gentiles, who didn't pursue God through the Law, have found God, but Israel, who has spent its whole existence following the Law, has not found God?

Paul: Yup. It's all about faith, not the Law. Always has been, always will be. Let me put it clearly. There is no difference between Jew and Gentile in God's eyes. Jesus put that issue to rest. The opportunity to have faith in God's promise is open to all people, everywhere. Anyone who calls on the name of the Lord will be saved. That's the bottom line. So don't think your circumcision or Law-abiding will get you a front place in line, because it doesn't.

There is an issue that must be addressed in the study of Romans and this passage is the most appropriate place to do so. The issue is predestination and election. For centuries Christians have argued over this issue. They've even gone to war over it and the blood of thousands of brothers in Christ has been shed in civil war. Once again, the nature of this study does not allow us to delve deeply into the subject; however it is important to touch on it.

There are two camps on this issue. On the one side there are those who say that God is absolutely sovereign and that man has no ability to make any choices in life. While he may seem to be making choices, God actually predetermined what choices he would make. God predetermined that Adam and Eve would disobey and that sin would infect humanity and severe humanity from the holy presence of God. Then God chose the people He would save. Therefore, the only people who will be saved on the Day of Judgment are those who are elected by God for salvation and the rest have been elected for eternal condemnation. If we are the elect then we can't help being saved, no matter what we do, and if we are not elect, it doesn't matter how much we try, we can't be saved.

In the camp on the other side of this continuum are those who say that God created humanity with free will. God set up the universe with free will and then sent it spinning. God created us for love, but in order for love to be real it must be chosen. So, God created Adam and Eve and hoped they wouldn't make a stupid choice. They did. Bummer. God loved humanity so He continually provided a way for man to make the choice to come back to him – the sacrificial system of the Old Testament that was ultimately fulfilled in the sacrifice of Jesus. Now God just sits back and waits to see what choices man will make. If you say "Yes" then He welcomes you in. If you say "No" then you have made your own bed and you have to lie in it.

So, who's right? Before we can answer that question we have to keep something in perspective. We have to ask ourselves where these camps are getting their ideas. Are they just making this stuff up? No. The tricky part of this issue is that both sides of the equation are drawing from the Bible. Here's the really tricky part...both sides are drawing from the letter to the Romans! Look at it. Chapter 9 basically says, "Hey, quit your whining, Israel. God is the sovereign Lord of the universe and He will do whatever He wants to do whether you like it or not. Your job is to fall in line and deal with it." But then, in chapter 10 he says, "Hey, salvation is for anybody and everybody. Anyone who calls on the name of the

Lord will be saved. All it takes is faith." Chapter 9 presents the sovereign will of God and chapter 10 presents the free will of man. Now, of course, both sides have clever ways of explaining away the chapter that presents the opposing view. But, no matter how clever they are, the fact remains that both here and throughout the Bible, both views are presented.

So, who's right? Both are right, and both are wrong. Before we throw up our hands in frustration, let's look and see why both sides fight so diligently for their perspective. Each side is both promoting a key Biblical principle and defending against a terrible and dangerous heresy. Let's start with the Sovereignty side. They are promoting the Biblical principle that God is in control of the universe. God is not a God of chaos. God is not at the whim of the fates or of the puny human will. The Bible clearly states that God is Lord and Sovereign of the universe. And so He is. And so should they defend that foundational Biblical principle. They are also defending against a terrible heresy. From their perspective, if the Free Will side is correct, and if you carry their position to its logical conclusion then you have a weak and powerless God that is being pushed around by the sovereign will of man, or by a higher power of fate. If that is true then man has no hope that God will be ultimately victorious in the end and we all live in the potentiality that evil and chaos may triumph. Without hope in God's power all is lost and we can't let that happen.

Now let's switch to the other side. Those who promote the free will of man are keying off of the very clear passages throughout scripture where God extends a choice to people between good and evil. From Moses' declaration of choice in Deuteronomy 30:19 to Joshua's invitation in Joshua 24:15 on down through the messages of the prophets to John the Baptist's and Jesus' invitation to repent and believe, we have a clear Biblical precedent that God has given man a choice. This camp is defending against a terrible heresy. If the sovereignty camp's position is carried out to its logical conclusion then life is nothing more than a deterministic animated feature film that God is watching on a screen. He wrote it, He drew the characters (us), moved them around according to His whims, and it's nothing more than that. Ultimately what the free will camp is opposed to is the idea that, if God has determined everything, then He is the cause of evil, thus ultimately evil Himself. So what's the point?

The irony is that on both sides there is a deep love and respect for the authority of scripture, a deep love and respect for the sovereignty and love of God, and a deep desire to not misinterpret the nature of God and distort the truth. So, who's right? As difficult as it is for our minds to grasp, they are both right. Somehow, far above our ability to see it, there is a higher truth in which both aspects of the Biblical data are correct.

In the context of Romans, I don't think Paul was even talking about this issue, and that's part of the reason we have been fighting about it ever since. We want to make Romans about this issue, as if Paul sat down to write a definitive thesis on predestination vs. free will. He didn't. His agenda was dealing with the Jew vs. Gentile issue. In order to demonstrate to the Jews that God has the right to love the Gentiles he draws upon the intuitive knowledge that God can do whatever he wants, so they need to just back down and accept the fact that their circumcision doesn't get them a 'get out of jail free card' without having the proper heart condition of faith. Then, in chapter 10, to further demonstrate the truth of the gospel, Paul draws upon the intuitive truth that God always has and always will invite everyone to simply trust in Him and be saved regardless of their race.

As we move into the 21st century, we, as the Western Church and the inheritors of this very tired debate need to lay it to rest and move on. It is time for us to embrace the tension of the two extremes and get on with the business of walking in the Spirit of God and being the conduit of blessing to the world that God commissioned Abraham to be from the beginning. It is time for us to stop splitting theological hairs and using the splinters to stab each other in the back and work toward peace and mutual edification so that we can be salt and light in the world.

Lesson 5

- Romans 11

Study Questions

What question and answer does Paul set up in verse 1?

What Old Testament story does he use to demonstrate his answer?

What question and answer does Paul set up in verse 11?

What metaphor does Paul use to explain the relationship of the Gentiles to the plan of God?

What is the plan and the hope for the nation of Israel?

Summarize Paul's message to the Gentiles in this passage.

Food for Thought

There are two final questions in Paul's dialogue with the Jews. Here's the summary:

Jews: Did God reject Israel?

Paul: No. God didn't reject them. He had to harden them so that the Gentiles could also be accepted. Yet he has not abandoned the people themselves.

Jews: Is Israel beyond recovery?

Paul: Of course not. God's grace is open to everyone, even the hardened Israel. Hey, if God could graft a bunch of wild Gentile branches into His tree, wouldn't it be even easier to graft back into the tree the branches that were native to the tree. It is an easy step for the Jews to have faith in the Messiah and they are welcome to come, just like everyone else.

There is one simple message for today. It is sprinkled throughout the chapter. DO NOT BOAST! Paul looks the Gentiles straight in the eye and says, "Now look. Just because God has opened the door to you and closed the book on the Law and the Jewish distinctive, that doesn't give you room to gloat. Just because you aren't under the Law doesn't mean you can flaunt your 'freedom' in your Jewish brother's face. The fact is that if you do walk around in arrogance then that is a pretty good indication that you really haven't gotten the message and the Spirit of God isn't really living in you. Remember, if God was willing to cut off Jewish branches, don't you think He'd be willing to cut off Gentile branches too? Remember, God doesn't care about race or culture; He cares about the heart and faith. Don't get cocky, stay humble."

There is an important message for us in this chapter. Modern Western Christianity has been marked by the division of denominations. Every denomination has broken away from its parent group in a spirit of "we don't agree with you. We have a better grip on God's truth than you do. You are wrong and we are right. God loves us better. We don't even know if you're saved." Bottom line -- that is the very arrogance that Paul warned against. The gospel is simple, yet so complex and mysterious that it can't be explained. It can only be lived. God is Lord, He loves us, and faith in Jesus saves us. We follow Jesus. Everything else is up for discussion and the discussion can lead to growth. When the discussion turns to ridicule or slander then the enemy has taken root and we lose out. Let's pray that we can come together and be the body of Christ so that the world can see that God does love everyone and that a life of transformation through the power of His Spirit is possible.

Notice how Paul ends this section. In verse 32 he states the reality of living in the tension, "God has bound all men over to disobedience so that He may have mercy on them all." Then he submits to the mystery of it all by quoting from Isaiah and Job,

"Oh, the depth of the riches of the wisdom and knowledge of God!

How unsearchable His judgments,

and His paths beyond tracing out!"

"Who has known the mind of the Lord?

Or who has been His counselor?"

"Who has ever given to God,

that God should repay him?"

For from Him and through Him and to Him are all things.

To Him be the glory forever! Amen.

Reading Paul's Mail

So, How Do We Live in the Kingdom of Jesus?
ch. 12-15

LIVING SACRIFICES

HUMBLE BODY PARTS

that's me

SINCERE LOVE

GLORY

ACCEPTING UNITY

JOY

PEACE

HOPE

Romans part 3

As we move into our final session of Romans we can take a deep breath. We've been swimming in the deep waters of theology as Paul "reasoned from the scriptures" with the Jewish Romans and demonstrated that the grace of God is for all nations and not just for the Jews. To our 21st century, western, Christianized minds Paul's arguments may have been difficult to follow and confusing at times. This lesson we pop our head up for air as Paul gets very practical and answers the really important question, "So what?"

Here is the entire letter to the Romans in a simple paragraph:

Nobody's "good" enough to match up to God's holiness, so God's grace has been poured out to all nations, regardless of race and ethnicity. Jesus conquered sin and gave us the free gift of reconciliation with God and life in the Spirit of God through faith. Now, live in the freedom of the Spirit. Freedom is not freedom to sin, but freedom to love others in everything you do, and, in so doing bring glory to God.

Here is a little more detailed outline of chapters 12-16

- Since God has been merciful, live your life as a sacrifice to Him. After all, its your heart He has always wanted, not your cows. (ch. 12:1-2)

- God has given you all spiritual gifts, as members of one body. The one gift He has given to everyone is love. (12:3-13)

So...

* Love each other deeply. (ch. 12:14-21)

* Love each other by obeying the civil authorities and paying your taxes. Don't be annoying trouble makers. (13:1-10)

* Love each other by avoiding pagan revelry which ultimately tears down your own body and debases the lives of others. (13:11-14)

* Love each other by accepting one another and not getting worked up over disputable matters. (14:1-15:13)

- Paul expresses his plans for delivering the Jerusalem Relief Fund and his hope to visit Rome on his way to Spain. (15:14-33)

- Paul gives personal greetings to many people in Rome from many people that are with him in Corinth, and then gives a final blessing. (16)

Lesson 1

- Romans 12

Study Questions

Why should we be living sacrifices?

How are we transformed?

What should be our self-perception according to verses 3-8.

Summarize Paul's description of love.

Food for Thought

In chapters 12-15 Paul is answering the question, "So what?" Paul, now that you've established that being a Jew does not make us better than anyone else and that Gentiles and Jews alike are welcome to the grace of God, how are we supposed to live? What does it mean to live like a child of God and walk in the Spirit? Without specific laws to govern us, how will we know how to function? Are we free to follow any cultural whim that blows our way? Are we free to live like the pagans, then? Give us some practical guidelines, please!

Paul's response is simple. In verses 1-2 he redefines the idea of worship to God. Then in verses 3-15 he redefines the law of God. There is only one law in the life of the Spirit, child of God: walk in humble and sincere love. In verses 3-8 he deals with humility and in verses 9-21 he deals with love. Then in chapters 13-15 he gives practical scenarios for what love looks like in action.

Real Worship (1-2)

The word "therefore" is the great hinge upon which the direction of Romans swings. In chapters 1-11 Paul was establishing the fact that God's grace is open to everyone, not just to the Jews. Therefore...since God is so incredibly merciful...offer yourselves as a living sacrifice, which is your reasonable act of worship.

We must hear the word "sacrifice" through the ears of a 1st century Jew. At that time the temple was still functioning in Jerusalem. Three times a year there was a great festival in the holy city to which the most devout Jews would travel in order to bring a sacrifice of livestock to God. This sacrificial offering was defined as "worship" for the Jew. In this verse Paul is, once again, breathing new life into these ancient traditions by redefining their terms and connecting them to the heart of God. He reminds the Jews that God's plan has never changed from the beginning. God is not interested in your livestock; He's interested in your heart. Like David said in Psalm 51:16-17,

> You do not delight in sacrifice, or I
> would bring it;
>
> you do not take pleasure in burnt
> offerings.
>
> The sacrifices of God are a broken
> spirit;
>
> a broken and contrite heart,
>
> O God, you will not despise.

In our churches we need to take pause and ask what "reasonable worship" is. When God calls us to worship Him, is He asking us to break out the guitars and have a sing along? The Greek word that is translated "worship" is the word *latreia*. It means "to serve." Paul is reminding the Romans, and us, that real worship isn't about the religious rituals in which we partake, it is about how we live our lives from day to day. It is about offering up our whole selves to God in submission to His will and service for His Kingdom, not ours.

Humble Body Parts (3-8)

The key to humility is to realize two important things. 1. There is a head honcho in the universe around which everything revolves. 2. You're not it. Paul uses the analogy of the human body to describe our place in the universe. Jesus is the head of the body and each of us is a part in the body. Body parts are not identical to each other, but are equally valid and important to the health and functionality of the body as a whole. Some people are one thing, others are another. If we can all remember that we each play a role and that it is counterproductive to slip into the comparison game, then it will be easier for us to love each other in mutual support.

If you have some time, take a moment and review 1 Corinthians 12-14 in our previous study of that passage. It is interesting to note the contrast between the way Paul deals with the issue of the body and spiritual gifts in 1 Corinthians with his approach here in Romans. Notice that in the Corinthian letter the gift of tongues was the dominant issue, but in Romans it isn't even mentioned. This observation gives further evidence to the great need to always keep the context of the letter in mind when reading. In Paul's less urgent and more methodical approach to the issue of spiritual gifts in Romans, he gives a nicely balanced presentation of what they are: prophesying, serving, teaching, encouraging, contributing to needs, leadership, showing mercy. While this list is by no means exhaustive, it does represent the vast spectrum of human personality and the need for all types of people to be active in the body of Christ.

Do you know your place in the body? Are you functioning within that place right now, or are you trying to be something that someone has convinced you that you should be?

Love Poem (9-15)

The second part of the law of life in the Spirit is to walk in love. But, what is love? How do we know if we are really being loving or are just being manipulative? In verses 9-21 Paul gives us a wonderful exposition on the nature of love.

If you read these verses in English (any version) it chops it up into small sentences that begin with an imperative (a command). Below I have emphasized the imperatives.

Love must be sincere.

Hate what is evil;

Cling to what is good.

Be devoted to one another in brotherly love.

Honor one another above yourselves.

Never be lacking in zeal, but

Keep your spiritual fervor, serving the Lord.

Be joyful in hope,

[Be] patient in affliction,

[Be] faithful in prayer.

Share with God's people who are in need.

Practice hospitality.

As you read this you can imagine Paul wagging his finger at you saying, "You had better do these things if you want to be a good person." I would like to propose that it is possible that Paul was not taking this tone at all. Let's look at the structure of the passage in the Greek. First of all, between vv. 9-13 there is not one imperative found in the Greek language.

(You may be wondering, "why, then, do all English translations make it into the imperative?" Good question. The construction of this passage is so foreign to the English language that it is nearly impossible to directly translate it. Since the verses directly following these verses do have the imperative where Paul does say "Bless those who persecute you..." "Rejoice with those who rejoice..." etc. The translators chose to keep that tone and assume that Paul had that tone in this passage. Let me be very clear. I am not saying that the standard translation is wrong. Nor am I saying that my translation is better. I'm simply sharing with you a structure that I found in the original text that, in my opinion is inherently beautiful as it portrays the love of God.)

This passage is all about describing love. There is only one propositional statement in the mix. Paul says, "Love is not hypocritical" That's it. The rest of the passage simply defines what "not hypocritical" looks like. This definition has two layers. First it begins with a negative, and then gushes forth a list of positives. Love abhors anything that is useless, unfruitful, or contrary to God's way of living. That's what being "not hypocritical" doesn't do. What it does do is cling to that which is excellent and beneficial and congruent with God's way of living. The key word here is *kollomenoi* which is translated "cleave" in the KJV and means to join together intimately, in the way a husband cleaves to his wife.

When you cling, you have to cling to something. You need a direct object to which you cling. The structure of the rest of this passage is a list of nouns that are in the dative form (meaning they receive the action). In other words, Paul is saying, "love clings to all kinds of good stuff. What kind of good stuff, you may ask? Well, let me list them out for you..."

Here is the actual structure of the Greek text,

love is non-hypocritical

abhorring that which is useless for God

joining intimately...

> with that which is excellent
>
> with the affectionate love exchanged between brothers
>
> with honor outdoing each other (considering others as better than self)
>
> with diligence that is not apathetic or hesitant
>
> with the spirit being pumped up and excited to work (literally boiling)
>
> with the Lord, serving
>
> with hope, rejoicing
>
> with suffering, enduring to the end
>
> with prayer, remaining continually
>
> with needs among the church, sharing everything together
>
> with the love of those outside the church, vigorously pursuing.

You see, this is not a list of "Do's." Paul isn't saying, "You must behave in this way." In the verses immediately preceding this passage Paul said that God had given many gifts to people within the body. If you a have particular gift, use it well. Then he flows immediately into this wonderfully poetic description of love.

Here's what I think Paul is saying. Love is a gift. Love is the gift that all of us have been given by God. This passage is a description of the kind of love that God has for us and, through Jesus, has set as our example. Immediately following this passage he says, "Do this" In other words, he is

saying, "in light of this amazingly wonderful gift of God's love...

- Bless those who persecute you; bless and do not curse.

- Rejoice with those who rejoice;

- Mourn with those who mourn.

- Live in harmony with one another.

- Do not be proud, but

- Be willing to associate with people of low position.

- Do not be conceited.

- Do not repay anyone evil for evil.

- Be careful to do what is right in the eyes of everybody.

- If it is possible, as far as it depends on you, live at peace with everyone.

- Do not take revenge,

- Do not be overcome by evil, but overcome evil with good.

At the beginning of the chapter Paul said, "don't get squeezed into the mold of how this age operates, instead, be transformed by remapping your brain and thinking along new lines." The age in which Paul lived – under the shadow of the Roman Empire, the Greek gods, magical arts, and secular Greek philosophy – was dominated by selfishness, greed, and fear. The truth is that every age is dominated by these basic human impulses. This is the mold that wants to squeeze you into its shape and pop you out as a mindless clone that follows numbly along with the current of contemporary culture. Paul says, "No!" It doesn't have to be that way. Jesus came to break the molds and give you freedom in His Spirit to be what God created you to be. Freedom in the Spirit is energized by selfless love for others. We walk in life because we realize that saving our own skin is not the primary motivation in life. We don't have to hold grudges or draw party lines or hate our enemies. We have been set free from all of that and we are called to love one another as God has loved us!

Lesson 2

- Romans 13

Study Questions

If you were living in Rome at the time of Paul's writing this letter, who would be your "governing authorities?"

Who established these authorities? What is their purpose?

How is a Christian supposed to interact with the local government? Why?

According to this passage, why is love the fulfillment of the law?

What is the motivation to put aside the "deeds of darkness?"

What are the "deeds of darkness?"

With what are they contrasted?

Food for Thought

Love in the Public Square

As Paul reasoned with the Jews about the grace of Jesus, he continually presented the message, "no law, no law." If you wanted to, you could hop onto that idea, distort it, and take it to all kinds of places that Paul never intended for it to go. You can, and many did. One of the greatest accusations against Paul, and one of the greatest distortions of Paul's teaching, was that Paul was advocating Libertarianism and/or anarchy. "There is no law! No one can tell me what to do! I have my rights, you know!" Thus many people, in the name of Jesus, were wreaking havoc in the public square and being common pests as they refused to pay taxes, were disrespectful to the "pagan" government officials, and running wild.

It seems that Paul felt the need to set the record straight for the Romans on this manner. Freedom in the Spirit of Christ was NOT license to be bad citizens. After all, God is the supreme ruler of all things, God is a God of order, not chaos, and it is extremely necessary to have civil law in order to bring about justice for the victimized. Law is good. Even if the law has been established by a "pagan" ruler, it is still better to have some semblance of social order and structure than it is to have people running wild in the streets, killing each other, looting, and doing whatever they please.

But, how could Paul possibly say these things? Is he actually asking us to bow the knee to Caesar? That is blasphemous. If we pay our taxes then we are acknowledging that Caesar is a god, like he claims himself to be. We can't have any part of that...we are Jews! We are Christians! We are supposed to come out from among them and be separate!

Paul patiently shakes his head and responds. Listen to yourselves. Is Caesar really a god? Do you believe that? Of course you don't. Does paying your taxes mean you worship Caesar? No. However, paying your taxes does contribute to the roads and aqueduct systems that make life in the Empire better for everyone. Is that a bad thing? Your taxes provide for the courts that bring criminals to justice. Is that a bad thing? Of course not. We must always remember one very important thing. The issues of the Kingdom of God are above these issues. The Kingdom of God is eternal. The Roman Empire is temporal. It will fade away some day, but God's Kingdom will remain. Even though the Roman Empire is pagan at its core, and is opposed to Christians, it is still a government that has been allowed by God and is being used to do good things in the world. It is what it is, and we need not get worked up over it. If you owe a tax, just pay it. What's the big deal? If a dignitary walks by, show him respect. Why not? Don't make unnecessary waves in the political arena just because you are "free from the law."

The law you are under is the law of love. Love isn't rude and disrespectful. It doesn't run around like a crazy man ranting against the system. It loves the system in spite of the system. It looks out for the good of others. The fact is that if everyone walked according to the law of Jesus' love, then there would be no more need for civil law. Now, what do you think is going to be more effective to throw down the need for civil law: a. running around breaking the law and being generally rude and disrespectful in the name of Jesus, or b. actually loving those in the government and demonstrating a higher law at work in your life, thus setting an example that Christians are not a threat to civil peace, but are actually the backbone upon which civil peace must be built?

Here's a simple word for us today. Be careful how you navigate political waters. As American citizens we have the right to speak our mind. Granted. We also have the right to promote the kind of lifestyle that we would prefer to live. True. However, there is a subtle trap that lies before us if we, in trying to promote our "Christian lifestyle" in our democratic system, behave in very non-Christian ways to achieve that goal. Better to live the life in authenticity, than to speak the life in hypocrisy. Republicans and Democrats come and go. The Kingdom of God is eternal. Let's live for the King and keep our focus clear.

Lesson 3

- Romans 14:1-15:13

Study Questions

What is the issue that is causing problems in the church?

How are we to treat the person who disagrees with us? Why?

What makes something clean or unclean for the individual?

What should be our goal and motivation in the body of Christ? (14:19)

What is Paul's definition of sin in this passage?

Restate 15:1-13 in your own words.

Food for Thought

The Key to God's Love: Acceptance

Today Paul continues giving the Romans practical examples of demonstrating God's love in the real world. No issue could be more practical for the church in Paul's day than the issue of meat that had been sacrificed to idols. We covered that topic in the Corinthian letters. Please refer to that study for more on the context of the subject itself.

For our purposes today, rather than rehash the subject of meat specifically, we are going to look at the spirit behind Paul's message and find the timeless principle that will help us in our practical "meat" issues that are causing division in the church today.

Let's begin by looking closely at verse 1. If you compare English translations you will find a wide variety of readings. Anytime you find large discrepancies between the English translations it is a good indicator that there is something messy going on the in the Greek language. The syntax of Greek is so different than English that sometimes the translators come to a phrase in the Greek text and simply scratch their head. There really is no direct way to translate this into English. It could mean a few different things. At this point the translator has to draw from the context of the letter as a whole and try to interpret the intended meaning. Let's unpack this a little...

Here is a very wooden, literal translation of the text:

"But the one being weak in faith take to yourselves, not into dividing doubtings."

Let's look at three words:

"take to yourselves" = *proslambano*. This has behind it the picture of opening up your arms, letting someone get near you, and then giving them a big hug.

"dividing" = *diakrisis*. This word is tricky. It's root word is "krino" which means to judge. But the form of diakrisis has a flavor that is hard to pin down. The TDNT (Theological Dictionary of the New Testament) says, "This word has such varied meanings as "separation," "distinction," "strife," "appraisal," and "exposition." In the NT it usually means "discernment" or "differentiation" (between spirits in 1 Cor. 12:10, between good and evil in Heb. 5:14). In Rom. 14:1 the point is obscure. The meaning might be "not for disputes," but another possibility is "not for evaluation."

Reading Paul's Mail

"doubtings" = *dialogismos*. The root word here is "logos" which means word or reasoning or thinking or intelligent reflection. The word "dialogismos" has various shades of meaning in the New Testament. The TDNT says, "1. "Evil thoughts" is the predominant sense in the NT (Lk. 2:35; Mk. 7:21; Lk. 9:47; Rom. 1:21). In view of the more flexible LXX [Greek translation of the Old Testament] use, we see here how deep is the NT conviction that our sinful nature extends to our thinking and our very heart. 2. Sometimes the term denotes "anxious reflection" or "doubt" (Lk. 24:38: torturing doubts; Rom. 14:1: worrying about trifles; Phil. 2:14: murmuring; 1 Tim. 2:8: probably questioning rather than contention). 3. "Discussion" or "argument" is probably the sense in Lk. 9:46. 4. "Bad decisions" rather than deliberations or thoughts fits best in Jms. 2:4."

Now let's see how some English versions translated this verse:

Him that is weak in the faith receive ye, but not to doubtful disputations. (King James Version)

Now accept the one who is weak in faith, but not for the purpose of passing judgment on his opinions. (New American Standard Bible)

Accept into your group someone who is weak in faith, and do not argue about opinions. (The New Century Version)

Welcome all the Lord's followers, even those whose faith is weak. Don't criticize them for having beliefs that are different from yours. (The Contemporary English Version)

Welcome with open arms fellow believers who don't see things the way you do. And don't jump all over them every time they do or say something you don't agree with—even when it seems that they are strong on opinions but weak in the faith department. Remember, they have their own history to deal with. Treat them gently. (The Message)

So, what's the point? Where did all that ink get us? Simply put, Paul's message in this passage (14:1-15:13) could be summarized like this:

"Listen guys, life is full of more gray areas than black and white ones. We could occupy 100% our time debating

over the 'issues.' Is that really what we are called to do and be in the body of Christ? We are called to 'accept' one another because God has accepted us. God looks at us, with all of our crazily distorted perspectives about Him and opens up His arms to us anyway. He is not sitting back waiting for us to get all of our theological ducks in a row before He will accept us. He simply accepts us first, and then works from there. Here is the key to all of this. We need to remember that each one of us is answerable to one person only, and that is God. We are all servants out in the field. We are doing what God has asked us to do. It is not our place to play master in each other's lives, or to question the orders that the Master has given to another servant. All we are asked to do is:

1. *Have an authentic relationship with the Master so that we can know clearly what He wants us to do.*

2. *Trust that all the other servants in the field have a relationship with the Master and are doing what He asked them to do.*

3. *Accept the other servants so that we can have an encouraging community that helps us carry out our individual orders.*

4. *Believe that if any of the servants are cheating the Master that the Master will work all that out at the end of the day and I don't have to worry about it.*

Our jobs are to build each other up, not tear each other down. The last thing we need to do is exercise our 'freedom' and our 'rights' in such a way that we hurt people or distract them from their relationship with the Master. Just be humble, do your job, and look out for the best interest of the other, even if that means holding certain things inside that aren't really that big of a deal. Remember, ultimately, at the end of the Day, God is the Master and He made all people, Jews and Gentiles, to be His servants. Our first and primary purpose is to bring Him glory. The best way that we can do that is to behave like Jesus, walk in love, accept one another, and trust that God has it all under control. This is our hope."

Before we end today, ask yourself a very important question. Are there issues that you have allowed to become divisive in your heart and in your community? What are they? Think carefully. Why are they divisive? What is at stake in your thinking that causes you to pull away from someone? Are you willing to accept that person and strive for "peace and mutual edification" even though you disagree on many things? Ask God to sort these things out in your mind for you and set you free from any negative thoughts or feelings that may be clinging to your spirit over these issues.

Lesson 4

- Romans 15:14-33

Study Questions

What is Paul's general attitude toward the church in Rome?

What has been Paul's mission so far in his life?

What was Paul planning to do next in his life?

What was Paul's "prayer request" to the Romans?

Food for Thought

Paul's Prayer

Technically, we could say that the substance of Romans ends in 15:13 as Paul comes to the crescendo of his instructions on love with the words, "may the God of Hope fill you with all joy and peace as you trust in him, so that you may overflow with hope by the power of the Holy Spirit." – let's pray...message is over...where's the food?

In verse 14 he changes the tone, comes back down to earth, and begins his final words to the Romans by informing them about his travel plans. It could be very easy to start skimming at this point. God sent me to the Gentiles...yadda, yadda...I've preached the circuit here already... yadda, yadda...I'm taking the gift to Jerusalem... OK...when I'm done there I hope to stop by and see you on my why to Spain...great. Oh, yeah. Pray that I don't get hurt or in trouble when I go to Jerusalem...thanks.

While we could glance over the passage like that and not miss anything of substance that has to do with the main thrust of the letter itself, there is a very interesting, and perhaps profound little nugget in verses 29-32 that is worth examining. Paul says,

> I know that when I come to you, I will come in the full measure of the blessing of Christ. I urge you, brothers, by our Lord Jesus Christ and by the love of the Spirit, to join me in my struggle by praying to God for me. Pray that I may be rescued from the unbelievers in Judea and that my service in Jerusalem may be acceptable to the saints there, so that by God's will I may come to you with joy and together with you be refreshed.

From the point in Paul's life where he extended that prayer request, we must jump over to the book of Acts and see what happens next in the story. In Acts 20:3 Paul leaves Corinth and travels back through Macedonia, over to Troas, down past Ephesus, then on to Judea. When he gets to Judea what happens? In Caesarea he is warned not to go to Jerusalem because the Jews there are very hostile toward him and want to kill him. He goes anyway. When he gets there he is attacked and beaten by an angry mob, only to be rescued by Roman guards. In order to save his life the Romans escort him to Caesarea where he is imprisoned for two years. After being batted around between three government officials, Paul finally appeals to Caesar and is shipped off to

Rome as a prisoner aboard a prison ship. On the way he is shipwrecked on a small island. When he finally arrives in Rome he is placed under house arrest for two more years. When he finally gets to meet the recipients of the letter we just read, he has manacles shackled to his hands and feet.

Now here's the question. Did God answer Paul's prayer in Romans 15:29-32? Did he arrive in the "full measure of the blessing of Christ?" Was he "rescued from the unbelievers in Judea?" Did he come to them "with joy and together with you be refreshed?" The answer is "Yes" and "No." It all depends on how you want to look at it. Yes, Paul was rescued from the angry Judeans, and, yes, he did arrive in Rome. Is it the way that he pictured it? Most likely it is not. In fact, I'd venture to guess that this story line would not have been Paul's "best case scenario" for his trip to Rome – beatings, imprisonment, embarrassment, shipwreck, hunger, etc. Yet, that is what God had for him.

Allow me to get very personal for a moment. Right now my sister-in-law is very ill and is on the brink of death. She is lying unconscious in an ICU with a respirator keeping her breathing. She has had Cystic Fibrosis since childhood and has overcome it for most of her life, beating the odds and living actively into her forties. Two years ago she got a cold from which she never recovered. She has been on oxygen for two years. Five months ago she received a double lung transplant. Of those five months she has been in the hospital for over three months fighting infection. This week it took a turn for the worse and she "coded" two nights ago, putting her in her current state. At this point the physicians are baffled. They've never seen this scenario before. From this point on they are working with educated guesses for her treatment. It will take nothing short of a miracle to save her life.

Since the day of her transplant our family has prayed every single day for her recovery. We ask that God would heal her body from the infection. That God would encourage her and strengthen her and my brother and their family. And yet she slowly has been deteriorating. We are on an email list that one of her friends puts out to keep everyone apprised of her situation. Through that list literally hundreds of people have joined together to petition God for her healing.

The game is not over. God can still work a miracle, of that there is no doubt. But, what if He doesn't. Even if He does heal her, has the last five months of suffering really been what we have prayed for? Does God not hear our prayers? Is there sin in all of our lives to the point that our prayers become ineffectual? Does God not care? Is it God's "will" that she should suffer and that my brother should suffer?

If you are honest with yourself, you have asked these questions as well. What is the purpose of prayer? I wonder what Paul was thinking on day number 567 as he sat in the prison in Caesarea, staring out the small window at the tiny patch of blue sky. "Is this really why God stopped me on the road to Damascus? Is this really what my 'Gentile Mission' was all about? I'm rotting here in this place and not getting anything done. Did God not hear me when I asked Him to let me go to Spain? What is happening here?"

Throughout scripture we see this scenario. How did Jeremiah feel as he watched his beloved city burn to the ground? What was going through his mind as he was taken off into to Egypt, never to return? How did Jesus feel when He buried the headless body of His cousin John? How did the apostle John feel when he buried his brother James after he had been executed by Herod? As we discussed in the Corinthian letters, Paul prayed that God would remove his thorn in the flesh, but it didn't go away. Where was God in all of this?

What I am saying could affect you in one of two ways. It may completely depress you. You may say, "Yeah, where is God in all of this? If that is God's MO, then I'm out of here." While those emotions are valid, I hope you take the time to look at the second option.

Before we look at the second response, let's look at the real question. Why do we pray? Do we pray to get the results we want? That's part of it. God invites us to bring our requests to Him. Yet, just like a Father with a small child, God wants to hear our requests, but He also has a bigger perspective than we do. We don't pray to get out of God what we want, we pray to get our eyes on God and off of ourselves. After all, what do we typically want? We want what's best for us. We want perfect health, riches, comfort, peace, freedom from pain and suffering. Right? Who wouldn't want those things? Yet, when you really analyze that motivation, what is at the heart of it? Selfishness. We ask for what we want and expect God to give it to us because we have "faith." But, how did Jesus teach us to pray? He said, "Our Father...your kingdom come, your will be done." Not my will, God's will. Isn't that what we studied throughout this lesson in Romans? Living in God's love is placing the needs of others and, ultimately, the will of God above our own. Prayer is not the process of getting God to do what we want. Prayer is the process of getting our eyes focused on God and figuring out what He is doing, even if it doesn't make any sense to us, and joining Him there.

Your second response may be one of hope. That would be my desire for you. We pray because we have hope. Our hope is not that God will give us everything we desire. Our hope is in the confidence that God is in control and that no matter what happens it is all flowing from His love and grace.

I don't know what will happen with my sister-in-law. I know what I want to happen and I will not stop asking God for it. But, I also know that I want it because I don't want to suffer the pain of loss for my brother and my family. I also know that, when you pull back from the picture to the broader perspective, she has already defied the wisdom of modern medicine and lived 30 years beyond her predicted lifespan. That IS a miracle. We often miss the miracle before our eyes because we are asking for something else.

Please be encouraged today. Paul made it to Rome, it just wasn't how he envisioned it. God is working to bring the greatest blessing in your life because He loves you. Sometimes that is a more painful process than we would have originally signed up for. Yet, in the eternal perspective, it is all flowing from the love of a Heavenly Father. Let's rest in that hope today.

Lesson 5

- Romans 16

Study Questions

As you read through this list of names, write down as many observations as you can regarding the descriptions of these people.

What are Paul's final instructions/ warnings to the church?

Do these final thoughts shed any light on the purpose of the letter? Why or why not?

Spend a moment to reflect on the study of Romans for the past three weeks. What has God taught you through it?

Food for Thought

In this last chapter of Romans Paul says his final greetings. This passage really is a potpourri of names and ideas. It's kind of like the things you would shout back to someone in the doorway as you are walking down their front sidewalk after having spent a wonderful weekend at their home. "Bye! We had a great time! We'll miss you! Don't forget to write! Say hello to aunt Mildred! Remember to brush! We love you!"

Since this passage is a potpourri, let's make a potpourri of observations before we sign off on this study.

Observations:

Paul knew a lot of people in Rome, even though he hadn't been there yet. The fact that there are so many names on this list gives evidence to the fact that Paul's heart was really with the people in Rome. Many of them are probably refugees that he had met in his ministry around the Aegean Sea that had recently been allowed to return to their home town of Rome. It is important to keep this personal element of the letter in mind. Paul was not writing an abstract theological textbook, he was writing to a very specific group of people. He had their faces in front of him as he dictated this letter to his scribe. Theology is a real-life, person to person endeavor. We should never lose sight of that very important fact. If we don't, then our words and our ministry will always stay close to the earth and be helpful and practical for living out the Good News of Jesus in our own culture.

There were men and women. As you study the ministries of Jesus and of Paul, it is hard not to notice the fact that women played an important part. It seems evident that the women listed in this chapter played significant roles of leadership in the church and were vital to Paul's ministry. When we look at that contextually and realize the role women played in the mainstream of society (not much of one) then this list of names is revolutionary in the issue of gender roles in the church.

There were Greeks and Jews. This list is evidence that Paul practiced what he preached. Some of these names are obviously Jewish and some are obviously Gentile. If we looked closely and knew our geography and ancient sociology better we could discern that there were actually different ethnic regions of the Empire represented in this group as well. The church in Rome was an excellent example of the cultural melting pot that the ideal church should strive to become.

The churches met in homes. Of course being a church was illegal in those days so the churches were forced to meet in homes during this period. Given that fact it is naive to be dogmatic about the idea that all churches must meet in homes to be authentic "New Testament" churches. However, it is a valid observation that the original church did meet in homes all across the Empire. That means that when Paul is addressing local churches, he's probably only referring to small groups of 20-40 people. When you put it in that light it changes the scope and tenor of the writing. The fact is that the church is a community of people, not a massive horde of numbers. The church is a meeting of members for mutual edification and participation, not a mob of onlookers who absorb and go home.

Aquila and Priscilla were back in Rome. Something must have happened between Acts 18:25, when Aquilla and Priscilla instructed Apollos in Ephesus, and Acts 20:1-3 when Paul stopped off in Corinth and wrote the letter to the Romans. During that period Paul spent two years working in Ephesus. Perhaps during that two year period the political climate in Rome changed and the refugees were allowed to return. This would be all the more reason for Paul to be motivated to visit that city since many of his good friends now lived there.

Paul gives two final "quickee" instructions.

Watch out for divisiveness. Herein lies the heart of the message of Romans (and many of the other letters). In these words we hear the echo of the Corinthian letters. As Paul sits in Corinth he is painfully aware of the false teachers, the "super-apostles" who were hell-bent on tearing the church apart by convincing the Christians to become Jews and to shun the Gentiles. Paul urges the Romans to be wise and innocent. He wants them to be wise concerning what is "good," and innocent about what is "bad." What does it mean to be innocent? When we think of the innocence of children we tend to mean that they are ignorant and unaware of the things that will taint their young minds. That is healthy for a child, but is that really what it means in this context? The Greek word

is "akeraios". "The original meanings of akeraios are a. "Unravaged," "unharmed," of a city, walls, country. b. "Intact," "innocent." c. "Pure," e.g., of wine, or gold. The sense is always figurative in the NT: Christians are to be innocent (Phil. 2:15); to maintain their integrity in face of evil (Rom. 16:19)." The "evil" of which Paul speaks is divisiveness. As the church we should give it our best effort to maintain peace and unity in love within the body. In this we will stay "pure" and free of intrusive, divisive elements.

The Gospel is for all nations. The final word further emphasizes the point of Paul's mission. Paul's purpose in life was to demonstrate, both in words and in deeds, that God was tearing down the wall of hostility between the Jews and the Gentiles and was, as He had always been doing, embracing the entire world with His Grace, His love, and His Kingdom. As we move into the 21st century, and as our culture becomes more and more culturally diverse and pluralistic, let's keep these words in mind. God loves all people, from all nations. There is no privileged status in the Kingdom of God. Jesus died for all, and faith is all that matters. Let us live in the love of God and demonstrate that love to our world.

Introduction to the Prison Letters

This session we shift into a new phase of Paul's Letters. In this phase of Paul's life he wrote what are traditionally called the Prison Epistles because he wrote them from Rome where he was under house arrest. As Paul sat in prison he received visitors back and forth from the churches that he had planted in Asia and Greece. Since he was not free to travel, the next best thing was to send letters to the churches to encouragement them and instruct them. Four of those letters have been preserved for us – Ephesians, Philippians, Colossians, Philemon. There is no particular chronological order for these books since we can't know which was written first. For this study we will approach them in the order listed above.

In order to gain better context for these letters it is important to pick up the Paul's story from where we left him in Acts 20. Between the writing of Romans in Acts 20 and the writing of the Prison Epistles, the entire saga of Acts 20-28 takes place. After Paul sealed up the letter to the Romans and handed it to Phoebe for delivery, he set his face toward Jerusalem. His time in Corinth had not gone very well and the Jews there were so upset with him that they plotted to kill him. In order to escape this plot Paul retraced his steps and traveled north through Macedonia, and then over to Troas. After stopping on the beach to say a tearful goodbye to the elders in Ephesus, Paul set sail for Caesarea.

In that coastal city Paul was warned that great danger waited for him in Jerusalem. He was ready for whatever came his way and was even prepared to die for the cause of Jesus if need be. Nothing was going to stop him from delivering the "Relief Fund" that he had collected for the suffering church in Jerusalem. So on he went.

In Jerusalem he was met by a hostile mob that assumed he was unclean after being with the Gentiles. They thought he was intentionally desecrating the Temple. This was not true, but when did truth ever dissuade an angry mob from violence? Paul was beaten severely. Had the Roman guards not intervened Paul would have surely been killed. Instead, he was brought before the Jewish Council (Sanhedrin) for trial. The council was divided on what should be done with him, so, for his own protection, the Roman government had him shipped off to Caesarea to stand trial before the governor, Felix.

For the next two years Paul was cooped up in prison and jostled back and forth between three rulers. First it was Felix. He simply wanted Paul to bribe him and then let him go. Paul would not pay the bribe, so he was detained. Felix was replaced, so Paul was passed on to the next governor named Festus. He did not know what to do with Paul, so he invited the Jewish King, Herod Agrippa, to evaluate the case.

The truth was there was no case. The Jews had no legitimate case against Paul other than the fact that they didn't like him and the things he taught. The Jews begged Festus to send Paul back to Jerusalem so that they could ambush him on the way and kill him once and for all. Paul was informed of this murderous plot and, playing the only card he had left, invoked his right as a Roman citizen to appeal directly to Caesar in Rome. His appeal was granted and he was shipped off to the capital city along with several other prisoners.

On the sea voyage they came across a terrible storm that destroyed their ship. Miraculously no one died, but they were all marooned on a small island off the coast of Sicily called Malta. Paul, the prisoners, and the guards all stayed on the island for a few months while they waited for a rescue ship to retrieve them. Finally Paul arrived in Rome, chained to a Roman guard. For the next two years Paul was under house arrest while he waited for his trial. While he was there he met with the Jews, the Gentiles, and the Church, teaching them about Jesus' Kingdom. It is during these two years that Paul writes the Prison Letters.

Reading Paul's Mail

Ephesians

Introduction to Ephesians

If you pay close attention to Paul's letter to the Ephesians you'll notice something very strange about it. Compared to all of his other letters it is the least personal. He doesn't greet anyone by name at the end of the letter. His comments about the recipients at the beginning make it sound like he only knows them by reputation, not personally. Yet, here's the strange part, Paul ministered in Ephesus for two years. He wept bitterly with the Ephesian elders when he left for Jerusalem. He obviously knew these people as intimate friends, so why didn't he write with more personal passion?

There are many theories to answer this question. Some have proposed that Paul did not actually write this letter, but that it was written in the next generation under Paul's name. That wouldn't make it a fake. This kind of thing was common practice in the ancient world. If you were writing an important document and you really wanted to get your point across, it was accepted practice to write it under the name of a highly respected figure that represents the essence of

the perspective that you were trying to present to your audience. Those who purport this position claim that there is further evidence to support it in the actual structure and theology within the letter. While it sounds like Paul's words, there appears to be a more developed understanding of church structure than was evident in the church during Paul's lifetime.

While that position has merit, there is another answer to the question that addresses the "distant tone" of the letter while still allowing it to be authentically from the mind and pen of Paul himself. In the earliest manuscript copies of this letter that we have today, there is a strange phenomenon. In many of the manuscripts, in verse 1, the phrase "in Ephesus" is actually left blank. In other words, verse one reads.

Paul, an apostle of Christ Jesus by the will of God.

To the saints _____, the faithful in Christ Jesus.

Many scholars believe that the Ephesian letter was intended to be delivered to all the different churches throughout the region of Asia. This theory makes a lot of sense. When you examine Acts 19 you see that Paul used the city of Asia as the hub of a church planting ministry in the surrounding region. He did this through setting up a daily teaching ministry in a Greek lecture hall where he would present the Gospel of Jesus to the people who were traveling in and out of Ephesus from the outlying region. Apparently several churches were formed through this ministry. Now Paul, a few years later, sitting in house arrest, and probably hearing about some conflict happening in the Asian churches, decided to write a letter to all the churches. As a general letter to many different contexts, Ephesians could not single out individuals and speak to specific personal problems that the specific houses churches may have been facing.

This is a wonderful fact for us as we read the Ephesian letter through the lens of the 21st century. Due to its more generic flavor Ephesians is the most universal and non-specific of all of Paul's letters. That means that the teaching of Ephesians has a higher level of direct transfer to our lives.

However, that does not mean it was written in a cultural vacuum and has no contextual issues. The Ephesian letter is dealing with the universal themes that the church of the 1st century was facing. Those themes were:

How can Jews and Gentiles live together in peace?

What does it really mean to be free and to live apart from the Law? (both Jewish Law and Roman Law)

How is the church supposed to function in the shadow of the Roman Empire?

In this letter Paul deals with these issues and paints for the churches a beautiful picture of the ideal state of the church in the world. Here is the basic flow of the letter:

Chapters 1-3

The wall of hostility between Jews and Gentiles has been broken down. All people are equal and are under the supreme authority of Jesus. We need to strive to become one building – a holy temple – and one body, so that we can become mature and fully realize the reason for which we were created: Living in the Love of God.

Chapters 4-6

We must remember that our enemy is not "those guys." Our battle is not Jew vs. Gentile, husband vs. wife, older generation vs. younger generation, masters vs. slaves; our battle is against the darkness. Our battle is against sin. Let us stop walking in the self-centered, other-hating mindset that comes so naturally to us and start walking in the light of God by seeking how we can love one another. When we do this then we will be able to stand strong and the self-destructive patterns of sin will fade away in the light of God's truth and love.

Lesson 1

- Ephesians 1-2

Study Questions

In what person are 1:1-12 written? (First person = I, we, us; Second person = you; third person= he, she, it, them)

In 1:13-18, what person is emphasized, first (I, Paul) or second (you)?

Compare and contrast the emphasis in 1:1-12 with 1:13-18.

How is Jesus described in 1:19-23?

If you were the Roman emperor, or a member of his government, how would you feel if you read 1:19-23? What action might you take?

Describe the before and after contrast that Paul explains in 2:1-10?

What is the basis for the salvation that Paul describes in 2:8-10? What does this mean?

What has Jesus done to the barrier that existed between the Jews and the Gentiles? How?

What metaphor is used to describe the way Jesus wants the world to be in light of what He has done for it? What does this mean in practical living?

Food for Thought

Us + you = we

In chapter 1 we are confronted with that nagging old problem again. It is the problem of "us" and "them." It is the problem of "Jew" vs. "Gentile;" the ones God loves and has chosen vs. the ones God hates and has discarded. By now in our study of Paul's letters you can tell that this was on the top 5 list of pressing problems in the life of the church. Paul's message was so radical that it caused him trouble everywhere he went. How could he possibly think that God could love a Gentile? To the Jewish mind that was just unheard of. To think that God could love an uncircumcised barbarian was so far outside of the theological box that it was nothing less than heresy.

Yet that is the Good News that Paul proclaimed. He went to his death defending that message. Here in Rome his heart must have broken when he heard that this issue was raging hard and fast against his beloved church in Ephesus and the many churches that he helped start in the surrounding region. In this letter he, once again, takes on this issue head on as he describes to the churches the ideal picture of what Jesus had in mind for his people.

In chapter 1 there are three sections:

Us

The key word here is "us." God chose us. God gave His grace to us. There are two senses in which Paul is using the term. In the first sense he is playing to the ethnocentric pride of the Jews. "That's right," the Jewish mind would agree, "God chose our father Abraham and set us aside to be His holy people." Yet, Paul springboards from that foundational idea and further applies it to himself and his apostolic ministry. God chose him to be the messenger of the Gospel for the world. In the same way that God chose Abraham to be the bearer of His blessing, so God chose Paul to be the bearer of His Good News for the world. Paul did not choose to be the apostle to the Gentiles. Quite the opposite; he was on his way to destroy the Christians when he was supernaturally confronted with the presence of the risen Jesus. Paul's faith in Jesus was thrust upon him in a way that few of us could ever claim. It's not that God forced Paul to believe, but He definitely chose him specifically and revealed Himself so clearly to Paul that there is no way he would deny it. So, the language of predestined and chosen applies to Abraham and Paul. They are the fathers of the "us" crowd.

You

The people of Asia were predominantly Greco-Romans. They were fully entrenched in the pagan worldview as they worshipped the goddess Artemis, practiced divination, magic, and sorcery. In other words, through the lens of the "us" crowd of the Jews, the Asians were the scourge of the earth, the abomination that offended God, and the outcast from God's Kingdom. And yet, when the message of Jesus came to them they received it. What's more, they received it without circumcision or Hebrew school or following the Levitical laws. God had freely given to "them" the same Holy Spirit that He had given to "us."

We

In verse 19 we see the blending of "us" and "you" into a revised "us." No longer is it "us" who are the descendents of Abraham, rather it is the "us" who believe. Paul prays for this new human identity that it would understand the magnitude of this sociological shift. This was not just a simple little peace treaty between a couple of clans. This was a cosmic shift in the right direction. This was the kind of shift that started to crack open the fabric of Heaven and allow the truth of God's Kingdom to shine in on the darkness of human existence. This was the truth that Jesus Christ is the supreme ruler of all things. He was not just some carpenter/teacher dude from Judea who had some whacky ideas. He was the infinite Creator who, because of His infinite love for His creation, penetrated the darkness, destroyed the sin and gunk that keeps people destroying themselves, and brings all things together in unity!

It's a Gift

In chapter 2 Paul echoes the same message found in Romans 1-3. Salvation is a free gift from God. It is important that we connect to the mind of Paul's audience, once again. To the Jewish mind the idea of God's grace was that He graciously chose the nation of Israel to be His people. In response His people were to obey the Law in order to maintain their position in God's grace. To the Jew, the Gentiles were out of luck because they did not obey the Law. Paul is destroying that mindset. He is redefining the terms of theology (or more accurately, recalibrating the terms to their proper meaning). In chapter 2 he is saying that both "you" and "us" are equally sinful. All of us cater to our selfishness and self-destructive tendencies. As a result we are dead inside. But God loves us to much to let us stay that way; ALL of us. Both the Gentiles who were supposedly "far away" and the Jews who were supposedly "near" were equally in need of God's free gift of salvation.

So, here it is. Come one, come all. God's desire for humanity is that we live in unity under the authority and love of Jesus. He desires to build us up into one new man. He does not want us to be a divided and warring people. A body that is divided and fighting itself is a body with cancer. God wants to heal us from that garbage and set us free. Paul then mixes metaphors and declares that God wants to reconstruct us into a strong building that can be used as a temple for Him. All of this is by God's grace, because He loves us... ALL of us.

God's Will

Before we move forward, we must take a brief moment to speak about God's will. The fact that the concept of God's will is so strong in these two chapters and the fact this has been a hotly debated topic for centuries necessitates that we address it. Allow me to throw my two cents into the conversation. When you look at the Greek word translated "will" it means desire. As humans we have lots of desires. We want the best for our children. We want to be successful in our endeavors. Yet, just because we desire them doesn't mean they will happen. Over the centuries the idea of God's will has been blended with the pagan concept of fate. In the height of the Middle Ages and into the period of the Reformation, God was perceived as the distant, unchangeable dictator who governed all things in the universe with rigid, unswerving certainty. This idea is not far removed from the Greek idea of fate. Those who believed in fate believed that they were destined to do certain things and were powerless to "change their stars." On the one hand this can be a comforting concept if you are under "good stars" but can be quite disconcerting if your stars have you bound for pain and destruction.

I believe that Paul's discussion of God's will does not fall under that paradigm of thought. God is the Creator and Father of all things. He created humanity for the purpose of loving Him. Yet, true love cannot be reciprocated unless it is freely chosen. It was God's will that humanity would always love Him, yet, in His sovereignty (meaning, He's the boss, no matter what happens) He made provision for the worst case scenario. Just like a good Father, no matter how rebellious His children may become He will never give up on them. From the moment sin entered the world God has been chasing us, reaching out to us, and making every means possible for us to reach out to Him and say "Yes" to His love. Peter tells us

that God "is patient with you, not wanting anyone to perish, but everyone to come to repentance." (2 Peter 3:9) Jesus said that "God did not send His son into the world to condemn the world, but to save the world through Him." (John 3:17)

When Paul speaks of God's predestination and His choosing, he is playing to the theology of the Jews. The Jews had distorted the idea of predestination to believe that Jews were destined for glory because of their race, and all Gentiles were destined for condemnation because of their race. That is not God's will. As Christians today, we need to be careful that we do not fall into the same trap that the Jews did in Paul's day. We have been the dominant "in" crowd (as far as we're concerned) for 1500 years. It is very easy for us to be smug in our "salvation" and feel very little compassion for "those guys" who are "outside the camp." Remember what Paul said. ALL sin and ALL are freely justified by His grace. God's will is for all to be saved. We don't get to determine God's will or tell Him who He can and cannot love. Our job is to simply accept His gift, be filled with His Spirit, and let the flow of His love direct our steps.

Reading Paul's Mail

Lesson 2

- Ephesians 3

Study Questions

How does Paul describe himself?

Where does Paul get his authority to make the bold claims about God, Jesus, and salvation?

What is Paul's motivation to persevere through suffering?

What is Paul's prayer for his audience?

Spend a moment to meditate on Paul's description of God's love. Write some responses to that meditation.

Food for Thought

Paul validates his message

You have to love the way Paul's mind works. He is the king of the ramblers. Look closely at verse 1. It stops in mid-sentence. Paul says, "I, Paul, for the sake of you Gentiles....What? You didn't know I was the apostle to the Gentiles? ... surely you have heard about the administration of God's grace..." Then he rambles on for 11 verses. He resumes his original thought in verse 14 when he says, "for this reason I kneel before the Father." What reason is that? He's referring to the fact that Jews and Gentiles are, together, being built up into a dwelling in which God lives by His Spirit.

Let's press pause on that stream of thought for a moment and look at Paul's side bar in verses 2-13. Paul is defending himself again. It is very likely that the "super-apostles" that we encountered in the Corinthian letters (or people like them) were spreading dissension and doubt among the Asian churches, trying to convince the people that Paul was not an authentic apostle. Perhaps their argument went like this. "How can you trust Paul? Who is he anyway? By what authority does he preach? Who died and put him in charge? Just look at his life. Right now he's rotting away in prison. Obviously God is not on his side. Be careful of his dangerous and heretical teaching."

In this passage Paul reminds the churches of several important points:

- My message is a mystery. This is an important message for us today. In the Protestant world we have prided ourselves in understanding God; in having our theology nicely tied up with a bow. This is a dangerous place to live. How could we possibly have God figured out? The message and method and nature of God are nothing less than a mystery to us. That doesn't mean we can't know God. Of course we can, that is why God continually reveals Himself to us throughout history, and ultimately in Jesus Christ. Yet, we can't understand it fully. Part of the process of spiritual growth is to embrace the mystery and plunge into the cloud of unknowing, allowing it to humble you before God and be used as a vehicle of His love for the world.

- I am a servant, not a lord. Paul's strength was in his utter weakness. When Jesus confronted him on the road to Damascus Paul was stripped of all the earthly things that would have made him "somebody." From that moment on he was simply serving the Master and doing his job. As Christians,

168

and especially as leaders, we should take note of Paul's attitude and make sure that we are walking with a servant's heart.

- The purpose of the church is to display the truth of God's loving unity to the world. The church's job is to demonstrate what the Kingdom of God was intended to be and what God calls all men to. This demonstration is to send a message to the 'rulers and authorities in the heavenly realms." Many have debated the true meaning of "rulers and authorities in heavenly realms." We will discuss that in chapter 6. For now suffice it to say that it represents the present, darkened, sin-sick way in which the world is functioning apart from God's love. The church is to shine the light of God's love to the world, not by talking about it, but by BEING it.

- My suffering has a purpose. Don't think that my imprisonment is a sign of defeat or God's curse upon me. Anytime you shake the tree you are bound to have stuff drop on you. My suffering is evidence that the Kingdom of God is shaking things up. I'm willing to do it if it means that Gentiles and Jews will be able to come together in peace, unity, and the love of God.

You can't help but say thanks

Now let's return to his main train of thought. In light of God's plan of building a new, unified building out of previously warring people, I pray for you. What does Paul pray? He is basically saying, "I pray that you would get it. Do you understand the magnitude of what I'm talking about? I'm talking about the fact that God's love is bigger than we could have ever imagined. God is our Father. His love dominates every fiber of the universe. It is the energy that spins the atoms. You can't get away from its presence. If we simply accept it and flow with it, then we will be transformed by it and made into what we were designed to be. God loves us and has freely given us access to His love. That is so powerful and so rich that you can't help but fall on your face and say 'thank you' to the Father."

As I read this I am reminded of the story when Jesus healed ten lepers. Do you remember what happened? Jesus freely healed 10 men from a heinous disease. They didn't do anything for it; He simply did it out of pure love. Then what happened? Only one of them actually came back and said 'thank you.' Jesus said of the "foreigner" that it was his faith that made him well. I believe this demonstrates the truth of God's Kingdom. God has given salvation to all people. All have been freely justified by His grace. The question is, have we come back to say "thanks?" Do we actually realize what God's love is all about, or do we keep it hidden deep under the shackles of our religion and our self-righteousness? Paul wants the Asian churches to "get it." He doesn't want them to be persuaded by the false teachers to slip back into an "us" and "them" religious system that hardens their hearts and separates them from the love of God. Paul wants them to dive into the mysterious and glorious love of God which is lavished upon us and is free for the taking. He wants us to be rooted in it so that we can be transformed by it and walk in the love and the Spirit of God always.

Lesson 3

• Ephesians 4:1-16

Study Questions

In what attitude should we live?

How is unity described?

What are the types of people Paul describes in this passage?

What is their purpose?

What is the goal of the body?

Food for Thought

In chapter 4 Paul switches gears in his flow of thought. In chapters 1-3 Paul builds the case that God's eternal purpose has been to have a united humanity and, through Jesus, has broken down the wall of hostility in order to build up a new, united humanity. Then everyone says, "Nice ideal, Paul, but how in the world does that happen? What does it look like in everyday life?" Chapters 4-6 answer that question.

In today's passage Paul paints a picture of what the new "man" (church) should look like, how it should function, and what its purpose should be. In 4:17-6:9 he contrasts the way of light with the way of darkness by giving specific attitudes and behaviors that should be both avoided and embraced. Finally, in 6:10-24, Paul summarizes it all with the metaphor of armor that will help us to stand strong in the spiritual battle.

The Body

Here are some observations from this short, but potent passage:

• **There is only one body.** If you survey the spiritual landscape you would find this statement hard to believe. Many have said that the most segregated hour of the week is Sunday mornings. The "Christian" church is divided between Roman Catholics, Greek Orthodox, Presbyterians, Anglicans, Episcopalians, Methodists, Baptists, Pentecostals, Charismatics, etc. God must just shake His head as His children run around shooting at each other in the front yard while the supper of His love feast grows cold in the dining room. Yet, in spite of our divisions, the truth remains that there is only one body. There is one Lord, one Spirit, one baptism. There is not a smorgasbord of gods and philosophies from which we can order ala carte to fit our self-indulgent nature. There is one body, of which we are a part. The question is; are we are a healthy part or a cancerous part?

• **There are many parts.** We've discussed spiritual gifts in the study of past letters. It is interesting to compare this list with the lists found in 1 Corinthians and Romans. In this passage I believe Paul is specifically zeroing in on the kinds of gifts that God gives to the leaders of the body. That does not mean that there aren't other gifts. As with the human body there are many, many parts and each part plays its role to the greater good of the body. So do we, as members of God's body, play our part for the benefit of the greater good of all. Or so we should.

- **Leadership is plural.** If our premise is true that the five gifts mentioned here are leadership gifts, then it is safe to say that good leadership in the church must be diverse and pluralistic. Notice what some have called the five-fold ministry of leadership:

- *Apostle*: Apostle means "one who has been sent out to represent; an ambassador". If the church is going to be healthy there must be people in leadership who are constantly pushing the envelope and venturing out into uncharted territory with an entrepreneurial spirit to expand the Kingdom of God and take the light of Jesus into new places and in new ways. These people are not necessarily nurturers, they are go-getters.

- *Prophets*: The prophet has always played a special role in the Kingdom of God. The prophet is the finger pointer and the mouthpiece of God. He points the finger in two ways. First he points to sin and calls it out. He says, "There is no place for that in the body, get it out before it destroys us." Secondly, it points out the people and places that God calls. The prophet says, 'there is where God is calling us," "you are the person God is calling." Prophets are rarely popular or a well-integrated part of the cozy community. They often find themselves out in the desert preaching to the rocks.

- *Evangelists*: The word "evangel" means "good news." The evangelist is bristling with the joy and energy that comes from the Good News of God's love for us. The evangelist is the person who stands in the gap between people who are not yet connecting to a loving, nurturing community and those who are. The evangelist creates the bridge of hospitality between the stranger and the community and makes both feel at ease.

- *Pastors*: The word pastor means shepherd. The pastor is the nurturer of the flock. He is the one who spends time living with the sheep day in and day out, leading the sheep to water, protecting them from wolves, and guiding them to good food and shelter. The pastor is the relational glue that holds the community together.

- *Teachers*: Teachers are the ones who inspect and prepare the food and shelter for the flock. They make sure the food, water, and shelter that the flock is using is safe and beneficial for health. They sit up on the hill, slightly apart from the flock, so they can survey the landscape and find the best grazing spots. Once the food is found, they make sure it is presented in a way that the sheep can digest it well.

When you look at all five of these gifts and leadership types you will notice that they form a continuum. On the left is the outer focus of the world and action. On the right is the inner world of the Word and contemplation. In the middle is community. The apostle pushes the envelope into the world and is constantly on the move, always turning over new stones. He starts a community, and then leaves it to start the next. The prophet is not fully integrated in the community, but stands to the left of it. He speaks both to the world and to the church. Right in the middle is the people's person. The Evangelist loves everyone and is equally comfortable with people inside his community and outside his community. The Pastor is at the center of the community of faith. He is not reaching out to the world, but is concerned with protecting the sheep from the destructive elements of the world and leading the sheep to food. The teacher stands to the right of community. He is in it, but not necessarily fully engaged. His mind is in the word as he provides teaching and direction in order to equip the shepherd. The brilliance of this passage and the truth about the foundation of the church is that ALL TYPES are needed for healthy and balanced leadership. If the leadership team is myopic in its vision (being too heavily one of those things to the exclusion of another) then the church will become deformed and will be built upon an unstable foundation, unable to sustain growth.

- **The purpose of leadership is to equip the saints for service.** In Jesus' Kingdom the first will be last. Notice how the foundation blocks of the illustration are half buried in the mud. Church leadership is not about power, control, and glory. It is about service and equipping others. There is only one head, which is Christ. A good leader allows people to step on his shoulders in order to grow and become the fully mature follower of Jesus that he was meant to be.

- **The pinnacle of maturity is the balance of truth and love.** To be a healthy community is to be able to authentically speak the truth in love in all circumstances. This requires the ability to both speak the truth in love and receive the truth in love. Most people err on one side or the other. Some people are truth champions and they love pointing out error in others and pounding others over the head with "correct doctrine" for the sake of "truth." They figure, "hey, the truth hurts, don't it?" On the other side there are those who err on love. They are so worried about hurting peoples' feelings that they do not speak up when they should. They allow people they love to continue doing things that are self-destructive and end up enabling them in hazardous ways, all in the name of "love." Maturity strikes the balance – or lives in the healthy tension of the two extremes.

In the body of Christ we are being formed into the likeness of Jesus in that He exemplified for us the perfect blend of truth and love. He was the truth. There was no pretense or hypocrisy in him. Yet, he was also love itself. When He spoke the truth people were not condemned from a self-righteous finger-pointer, they were transformed by the Lover of their soul. In the community of God, our goal is to provide an environment where people can be equipped to come to a place in their life where they can allow God to transform them into a mature person who walks with truth and love in perfect balance in every aspect of their life.

Lesson 4

- Ephesians 4:17-6:9

Study Questions

How does Paul describe the way of the Gentiles?

According to verses 20-24, what does it mean to follow Jesus?

In 4:25-5:20 Paul contrasts the ways of darkness and the ways of light. Summarize this list.

What area of "darkness" is the biggest struggle for you right now?

What area of "light" is calling you the strongest right now?

How will you deal with each?

Describe the nature of the relationships that Paul discusses in 5:21- 6:9?

What is his point in this passage?

Reading Paul's Mail

Food for Thought

What gets you drunk?

When I first read 4:17 it seemed to stick sideways in my mind. Paul had just spent 3 chapters breaking down the Jew/Gentile hatred barrier and then he turns around in this verse and bashes the Gentiles. He says, "You must no longer live as the Gentiles do..." What's going on here? Whenever I have these kinds of questions I first turn to the original language for some clues. I noticed that the word translated "Gentiles" is "ethnos" from which we get our word "ethnic." It means "people" or "nations." It is used in various ways throughout the Bible. In Jesus' great commissioning of the disciples He tells them to go and make disciples of all ethnos. I believe that in 4:17 it is not necessary to translate it "Gentiles," in light of the previous chapters, but would be better to translate it, "you must no longer live as all the nations live."

I love the way the Message puts it,

> And so I insist—and God backs me up on this—that there be no going along with the crowd, the empty-headed, mindless crowd. They've refused for so long to deal with God that they've lost touch not only with God but with reality itself. They can't think straight anymore. Feeling no pain, they let themselves go in sexual obsession, addicted to every sort of perversion

In 4:20-24 Paul makes an important distinction about what it means to follow Jesus. This is very helpful for us today. Many people think that since the Gospel is not a message of religion and legalism (which it truly is not), and since the message is that God loves all of us (which He truly does), then I'm good just the way I am and God is satisfied with that. That is not what the Gospel is saying. The Good News of Jesus is that, since He has defeated sin and death, and since He has torn down the wall of hostility between people, we are now free to become the fully formed creatures that we were intended to be. Jesus set us free for transformation. We are to put off all that old junk – the selfishness, addiction, greed, and impurity – that clogged our spiritual arteries and numbed out our minds, so that we can see clearly the truth of God's plan for the universe; His plan of love and unity. The message of freedom is not a message of self-indulgence; it is a message of God focused and other focused growth into maturity. In other words, God says, "Grow up!"

From 4:25-5:19 Paul lists many virtues and vices and uses the metaphor of light vs. darkness. There is so much we could say about each of these items individually, but there is not enough space

to do so. To summarize this passage let's focus on two metaphors. First there is the contrast of light and dark. Light is something and darkness is nothing. Light and dark are not in a cosmic power struggle against each other. When light is present the darkness has to flee. God's light is always shining, we just have to choose to step into it and face it. Basically Paul is saying, "Get out of the shadows. Crawl out from underneath the basement steps and let God's light purge you of all the junk you've allowed to accumulate. God's truth will expose your sin. Yes, it may be painful at first, but your eyes will adjust and you'll be so much freer and happier when you do.

The second metaphor is found in 5:18. I think this metaphor sums up the whole passage nicely. What gets you drunk? Paul says, "Don't get drunk on wine." Why? When you are intoxicated you are no longer in control of your higher faculties. You are "under the influence" and you can do some pretty stupid things that would dreadfully embarrass your sober self and may even cause serious damage or death to others. Sin and the darkness is like wine in that it will dull out our minds and keep us in a stupor, bumbling around aimlessly, doing things we know we shouldn't do.

Interesting note: The Greek word for "drunk" is "methuo." Do you recognize the word "meth" Methamphetamines is one of the worst killer drugs that our society currently experiences. Back in Paul's day they didn't have the high powered drugs that we do. If Paul were writing this passage today he might say, "Don't blow your mind on stupid drugs or get all cranked up on meth and think that you can run at hyper speed. If you do that you're destined to crash and burn."

Instead, Paul urges, we should be filled with the Spirit. The Greek word here is "playrao" and it means to be filled up to the full. In some senses it is like the way sails are filled by the wind in order to propel the ship through the water. There is a wonderful contrast between "methuo" and "playrao." Methuo promises to fill you, but leaves you hollow. It talks a great talk and gives you an initial rush or euphoria that is way better than real life. Yet, the rush is artificial and it leaves you feeling empty and hollow after it wears off. Playrao has no fanfare in its invitation. It only speaks the truth. It tells you that its way is not easy, but it is real. If you follow playrao then you will actually be filled and fulfilled. To walk in the light instead of the darkness is to be filled with the Spirit of God, so that you can actually know what God desires from you and fulfill your intended purpose. Then you will know true and lasting fulfillment. That is why Jesus set us free and that is the journey to which He invites us.

174

Leveling the Playing Field

Ephesians 5:22-6:9 has been the source of much contention for many in the modern world. Wives submit to husbands!? Slaves obey masters!? Does the Bible promote male domination and slavery? I thought God was a loving God. I can't follow a God that would promote such heinous attitudes and behaviors!

One of the reasons why this passage has caused such outrage is that many people have forgotten to read it in the context of the overall flow of Ephesians. What has Paul been presenting in this letter? First he said that Jesus had destroyed the dividing wall of hostility between the Jew and Gentile. In the Kingdom of God – the body of Christ -- there is equality among the nations. Then he demonstrated that leadership in the body of Christ is the opposite of human standards and lowers itself to serve people rather than exalts itself to be in power. Next he lists several attitudes and behaviors that should be flushed out of the system so that the people of God can walk in the light of God's love and truth. In 5:18 he says, "Be filled with the Spirit." The next logical question is, "What does it look like to be filled with the Spirit?" To answer that he makes a list of things:

- • Speak to one another with
  - Psalms
  - Hymns
  - Spiritual songs
- Sing and make music in your heart
- Always give thanks to God for everything

And then, the grand crescendo of the list...

- SUBMIT TO ONE ANOTHER OUT OF REVERENCE FOR CHRIST

This is the ultimate picture of equality in the body of Christ. When we are filled with the Spirit we are connected to the Head – Jesus – and realize that we are simply parts of the body, all playing our specific roles. No one is dominant over another in the body. We all submit to each other and use our gifts for the betterment of the other.

To further demonstrate the radical nature of this claim Paul lists three relationships that were commonly understood in his day to be relationships of dominance and subservience and turns them on their head. In all three cases – husbands and wives, fathers and children, masters and slaves – the one was considered to be the absolute ruler and the other was expected to bow in abject humiliation. Paul says,

"No! That is not how things work in the body of Christ. Wives submit to your husband and actually respect them. Don't resent them. Husbands, actually love your wife. She is not your property. She is a child of God and your whole purpose is to serve her."

That was radical thinking in Paul's day.

Then he goes on. "Father's, you don't have the right to beat your children. Your job is to train them justly so that they can grow in maturity. They are not your property, they are on loan to you from God and He has entrusted you to care for them."

That was not the "way of the nations" let me tell you.

Then, finally, Paul addresses the masters. "Look, guys, do not for one minute think that you can actually own another human. Yes, slavery is pervasive in our culture, but as a child of God, you know that God does not acknowledge it. If you own slaves then treat them fairly and treat them well, because, in truth, they are your equal."

Now that was definitely radical and counter-cultural teaching!

Lesson 5

- Ephesians 6:10-24

Study Questions

Why should we put on the full armor of God?

Against what is our struggle? What does this mean?

What are we to "put on?"

What are we to "take up?"

Make a chart that describes the armor of God.

Food for Thought

Standing Firm

Ephesians 6:10-18 is one of the most well known metaphors in the Bible. In this passage Paul speaks of a battle -- a "wrestling" to be more precise – and encourages the Christian to put on the armor of God. Over the centuries many groups and theological camps have taken this passage and run wild with it in many different directions. Each camp has given their own interpretation for the meaning of "rulers, authorities, powers of this dark world, and spiritual forces of evil in the heavenly realms." They have used it to vilify certain groups or ideas and then led the charge for Christians to ATTACK!

I would like to make some observations of my own and, perhaps, challenge the idea that Paul is calling Christians to be on the offensive in the battle.

- **The idea is to STAND.** Throughout the passage Paul instructs the church to stand firm, not to attack. Yes there is a struggle going on against darkness, but it is the darkness that is trying to penetrate us, we are not trying to claim ground from the darkness. Here is one very important thing to remember when it comes to spiritual warfare. Jesus has already won the victory. He has already claimed the ground for us. The Kingdom of God is firmly established for us. Our job is to stand on it and be strong, because he has done all the work.

- **The enemy is sinfulness, not people.** Paul says that our struggle is not against flesh and blood, but against something else. We need to look at this in two ways:

  - **What it isn't.** The main thrust of this letter was to tear down the wall of hostility between the Jews and the Gentiles. The Jews believed that the Gentiles were the enemy because they were sinful Gentiles. Paul is saying, "NO! The Gentiles are not the enemy. Sin is the enemy. The destructive patterns of thinking and behaving that I listed in chapters 4 and 5 are the enemy. God loves people. He created flesh and blood and it is good. Stop seeing people as "bad" or the "enemy" and start realizing that it is the darkened thinking within them that is the enemy. It is our job to shine the light of truth for them to see that Jesus has won the victory and they need simply to accept His love and step into the safety zone of His light.

- *What it is.* Paul mentions four things to define the enemy. All of these terms would have been very familiar to the Greco-Roman mind. The first three refer to the power structures of the Roman Empire. Rulers, authorities, and powers of this dark world mean the forces of a governmental system that is greater than the sum of its parts. There is no one person that is the enemy, not even Caesar. It is the system itself that takes on a life of its own that is governed by greed, power, lust, and corruption. The Kingdom of God is the antithesis of this kind of world system and will be engaged in a continual wrestling match until the day Jesus returns. The fourth item is the "spiritual forces of evil in the heavenly realms." The Greco-Roman world was very conscious of the presence of gods, demi-gods, angels, and demons that lived in the space between God and Man. Throughout history different cultures have had various explanations for the mystery of the spiritual world. Some have leaned toward a heavily anthropomorphized typology that pictured demons as gruesome gargoyles and angels as handsome warriors of light. Others have swung to the other side of the spectrum and said that the spiritual world is simply a projection and extension of our own inner moral struggle as we wrestle with the negative attitudes of chapters 4 & 5. No matter where you fall on this spectrum, I believe the result is the same. Sin is an attitude or behavior that is contrary to the love of God and results in self-destruction. Our battle is against these attitudes, not against people.

- **What we HAVE.** When we investigate Paul's catalog of armor pieces it is important to notice that there are two major sections. The first section follows the phrase "Stand Firm" in verse 14. Paul says to stand firm with...then lists four things. In the Greek it literally says, "Stand firm, already having ..."

  - The belt of truth
  - The breastplate of righteousness
  - Feet fitted with the Good News of peace
  - The shield of faith, which covers all of it.

So, here is what Paul is saying, "You can stand firm because you know that God has already provided you with truth, righteousness, peace, and faith. The truth is that God loves you. You have a relationship with the Truth itself, Jesus Christ. Because of Jesus you have been made right with God and your heart is protected. No one can steal that from you. The good news is that you can stand firm on feet that are at peace with God. Do you hear that, you are at peace with God, not war! You don't have to worry about the struggle, because the battle has been fought and you are at peace. To top it all off, and to cover everything, you believe these things to be true – you have faith. With your belief you can snuff the stupid lies of the enemy before they even get to you."

- **What we TAKE UP.** In verse 17 Paul changes the tense and adds two more pieces of armor. He gives the imperative for us to "take up" the helmet of salvation and the sword of the Spirit which is the word of God. The Greek word here for "take up" is *dechomai* which literally means "welcome; extend hospitality; receive joyfully; be in fellowship with." There are other words in the Greek language which mean more specifically to pick something up with your hand. So, why does Paul use such a strong relational word to tell the church to take up the helmet of salvation and the Word of the Spirit? He does so because that is exactly what these things are – relationships. We are in a relationship with God. Yes, we have truth, righteousness, peace, and faith, but those things can tend to be static. They are statements of fact and position. In adding these two elements Paul is reminding us that the strength of our victory over the darkness is the fact that we are not static, but are engaged in a dynamic relationship with a loving Father. God is not an abstract idea way out there. He is not a Cosmic King on a throne way above the celestial dome who hopes we can fight hard enough to get to Him some day. Just the opposite. God is with us through the salvation provided in Jesus and the dynamic presence of God's word in His Spirit.

The word translated "word" here is not the typical word for "word" in the New Testament. It is *rhema* which specifically means the spoken word. Once again this emphasizes the relational aspect of the Holy Spirit in our lives. We can talk to God through His Spirit. He is present with us. How do we talk to God? We pray. That is why Paul ends the analogy with the instruction to pray.

Now, let's put this into plain English.

We have a struggle in life, but it is not against people. It is a spiritual struggle against sin. However, the key to winning the struggle is not to "rage against the machine" or "take it to the enemy." The key is to stand strong in the truth that the battle has already been won. You are standing in the light and the light repels the darkness. You have been set free, you are righteous before God, you are at peace with God, simply believe it. If you will keep your eyes focused on the source of light and engage in the dynamic daily relationship with your loving Father through prayer, and not focus on the darkness, then you will stand strong and be transformed by the light.

Paul ends the letter to the Asian churches with the key to the Christian life: Love the Lord Jesus Christ with an undying love. May we live that way today.

Introduction

When you boil it down to its bare bones, Paul's letter to the Philippians is essentially a thank you note for a gift. Paul had been under house-arrest in Rome for some time, waiting for his day in court. One day, as he sat, possibly wondering what God was really up to with this extended incarceration, in walks an old friend.

"Epaphroditus! What a pleasant surprise. You've traveled all the way from Philippi just to see me; that touches me deeply. Oh, and what's this...a gift, for me?"

Paul has a catch in his throat as the emotions overwhelm him. Just when he was on the verge of giving in to discouragement, God sends a gracious gift and a physical token of true love from the family of believers he had left behind in the Roman colony of Philippi.

I'm sure his mind must have flashed back to the story we find in Acts 16. Paul had been planning to set up his mission outpost in Ephesus, but God diverted his course and had led him to the northern town of Troas instead. From there Paul received the vision of a man from Macedonia, beckoning him to cross the Aegean Sea and bring the good news of Jesus to the Macedonians. Macedonia. He hadn't thought that far in his vision, but he was willing to go.

It was in Philippi that the first Macedonian (and European) church was formed. This city had a rich, pagan history. It was named after King Philip, the father of Alexander the Great, and was a strategic port city for the Macedonian and Greek Empire. In 168BC it fell into the hands of the Romans and became a true colony of Rome. It was transformed into a mini-Rome and was a favorite retirement spot for officers of the Roman army.

Unique in Paul's missionary endeavors, Philippi was one of the few cities that did not have a strong Jewish population. Therefore, the group of believers that formed there was emerging from a predominately Roman worldview.

During his time in Philippi Paul drove a demon out from a little girl. This exorcism threatened the financial well-being of the slave-girls owners and caused a commotion among the citizens which ended up in Paul and Silas being thrown into prison. During the night the prison was shaken by an earthquake that opened all the cell doors. Paul and Silas did not flee, however, but instead led the prison warden to Jesus. Being a Roman citizen himself, Paul was spared a brutal beating and was simply led out of the city and asked to move on. During the next part of his journey, as he traveled through Thessalonica, Berea, Athens, and Corinth, the believers in Philippi kept in contact with Paul and supported him financially.

Now, once again, the Philippians demonstrate their love for Paul and their tenacious desire to support him in his ministry by sending Epaphroditus with a gift of money. He did not only bring a gift, Epaphroditus also brought news of the state of the Philippian church. Apparently some of the Judaizers – Paul's nemesis that we have discussed in several other letters – had moved into Philippi and were trying to pull the Gentile church apart. The pressure must have been getting to the people, because even the strong members and leaders, like Euodia and Syntyche, were beginning to get at each others throats.

Paul must have been heartbroken at this news. He knew he must write back and tell the church "Thank You" and also warn them to not give in to the pressure of the Judaizers. But, before he had a chance to write the letter, Epaphroditus became ill and almost died. Paul felt the urgency to write the letter and so wanted to send it with Timothy. But he also knew that the Philippians would be worried sick about Epaphroditus. Paul decided to wait until Epaphroditus became well again, and then sent the letter with him.

As you read this letter keep two important factors in mind:

1. Paul is in prison as he writes. It is a very real possibility that Caesar may find him to be a threat to the Empire and order him to be executed. With this dark background the bright colors of the words "joy" and "rejoice" jump off the page for us, and give us the encouragement we need to press on through difficult times.

2. The church in Philippi was predominately from a Gentile background and was being faced with the pressures of a Jewish, legalistic system. Notice the antidotes that Paul prescribes to fight off these viruses and to keep back the "dogs" that seek to destroy the church.

Lesson 1

- Philippians 1:1-26

Study Questions

How does Paul feel about the church in Philippi?

What is Paul's prayer for the people?

What is Paul's attitude toward his present situation?

Food for Thought

A Prayer (1:9-11)

I'd like to hone in on three verses from this section; 1:9-11. These verses are special to me because they are my life verses. They became this because of a very special "aha" experience I had early in my teaching ministry. While I was teaching a course that we called GED (Growth through Education and Discipleship) we were studying the topic of Bible Study Methods. I was simply trying to teach the class how to use the proper methods to get to the accurate meaning of the text. Our 'lab' text was the letter to the Philippians. The students were assigned to analyze the letter, chart it out, and present it to the rest of the class.

It was during my prep for that class, and specifically while analyzing these three verses, that God hit me right between the eyes and changed my perspective forever. Prior to this time I was purely a "head" guy. To me, the most important thing that a person could acquire was proper knowledge of the scripture. I was motivated to teach people the Bible to free them from the bondage of ignorance. My prayer for the church was that they would "abound with knowledge, and then the knowledge would set them free." Then I read Paul's prayer for his people in Philippi. What does Paul want to abound in their lives? Not knowledge. His prayer was for love. BAM! Then it hit me. Love is the core of God's plan and purpose for creation, not knowledge. I stood before the class and confessed this to them and asked that God would transform my character from being a knowledge seeker to that of being a love gusher.

In light of this experience, and my fondness for this passage, plus the incredible message that it holds for all of us, let's spend a few moments walking through this prayer.

And this is my prayer: that your love may abound more and more

There's that word again: "abound". It is the word that is elsewhere translated "overflow." Paul doesn't just want the church to love some of the time. He doesn't even want it to be filled with love. Paul wants the church to gurgle and gush and overflow with love. He throws two extra "mores" on top of overflow to say that he wants the church to never stop growing in love so that, more and more, it wells up and pours over the top, touching everyone it meets. When love gushes out of us, we have little room for anger, bitterness, envy, greed, complaining, etc.

The question is, "how do we get to the place where we can love like that?" The answer is in the next phrase.

in knowledge and depth of insight,

Here we have two Greek words that merit definition: "knowledge" (*epignosis*) and "depth of insight" (*aesthesis*). If we are to know how love can abound it is important that we truly understand the meaning of *epignosis*. This is where I made my big mistake. Knowledge is not the acquisition of information. *ginosko* emphasizes understanding rather than sensory perception...and suggests the act of knowing rather than knowledge as such. This act embraces every organ and mode of knowledge, e.g., by seeing, hearing, investigation, or experience, and of people as well as things. Supremely, however, knowledge implies verification by the eye; hence the dominant concept is that of knowledge by objective observation. In other words, knowledge is actively participating in reality and accurately perceiving it. Then, Paul adds, for love to abound we must be *aesthetes*. The word *aesthesis* is where we get our word "aesthetics." It means to use the senses to perceive beauty.

Paul is saying, "Let love gush out of your life in an accurate perception of reality and the comprehension of beauty. Don't just theorize about things, really look at what is going on around you and see the good in it!"

Why? So you can do the following...

so that you may be able to discern what is best

This is a very difficult phrase to translate. It literally reads, "into the testing you the things that are different" Huh?

Many translations read this as "so that you can approve what is excellent" or "that you will see the difference between good and bad and choose the good."

I like to translate it, "so that you can figure out what makes a follower of Jesus different from the crowd; special, a cut above the rest, not following the selfishness of man, but flowing in the love of God."

Paul goes on to describe what being "different" looks like...

and may be pure and blameless until the day of Christ, filled with the fruit of righteousness that comes through Jesus Christ—to the glory and praise of God.

Here are three descriptions of the follower of Jesus:

Pure, blameless, and filled with the fruit of righteousness.

- Pure. The Greek word is *heilikrineis*. *Heilos* = sun. *Kriei* = to judge. To be pure is to be tested by the sun. It is the same as a previous discussion we have had regarding the word "sincere;" to be without wax. In the ancient world if a potter had a crack in a pot and wanted to trick his customer he would fill the crack with wax. A shrewd buyer would hold the pot up to the sun to see if the sunlight would shine through the wax. Thus, a "pure" pot was "sun-tested." A love-gushing follower of Jesus has no wax-filled cracks. That doesn't mean there aren't any cracks; it just means that there isn't any pretense. As followers of Jesus we are up front about our cracks, we don't hide them from anyone, and we allow God to fill them in with true clay that can make us whole and "pure."

- Blameless. The Greek word is *aposkopos*. "1. "not causing to fall," "not stumbling," "intact," and 2. "not giving offense," "inoffensive," "blameless," "not taking offense" (e.g., a clear conscience)." As followers of Jesus we do not get offended, nor do we intentionally cause offense to others. How can we do this? We do it through the knowledge and aesthetics that we discussed above. We look through the eyes of God and see people for what they really are; they are children of God that are in process. When people hurt us, we can realize that they are probably in a state of inner pain themselves, so we can let the hurt bounce off of us and we can respond with God's love to them.

- Filled with the fruit of righteousness. Here we could launch into a study of Galatians 5:22-25. The fruit of righteousness is synonymous with the fruit of the Spirit. The important thing here is twofold. 1) The fruit comes from Jesus. He is the vine, we are the branches. It is His fruit, not ours. Our job is to stay connected to Him and let Him produce His fruit. 2) The Father is the Gardener. The fruit exists, not to bring glory to us, but to bring a harvest for the Gardener. God's glory is our ultimate motivation in all that we think, say, and do.

Read Eugene Peterson's translation of this passage in The Message:

> *So this is my prayer: that your love will flourish and that you will not only love much but well. Learn to love appropriately. You need to use your head and test your feelings so that your love is sincere and intelligent, not sentimental gush. Live a lover's life, circumspect and exemplary, a life Jesus will be proud of: bountiful in fruits from the soul, making Jesus Christ attractive to all, getting everyone involved in the glory and praise of God. (Philippians 1:9-11 The Message)*

A Prayer Answered

Before we leave today we must address a very important topic in this passage. If you will remember at the end of Romans we discussed Paul's prayer and his plans to travel to Rome on his way to Spain. In that section we discussed how Paul's prayers were not answered in the way that he requested and we postulated on how that may have emotionally affected Paul and how those kinds of events affect our lives. In this passage we bring resolution to those questions. Here Paul reassures the worried Philippians that his difficult circumstances are actually working out for the good of God's Kingdom.

Originally Paul had wanted to simply stop off in Rome on his way to Spain so that he would not be accused of "building on someone else's foundation." Had he done that, he would probably have never experienced the depth of ministry that he was having during his time of house arrest. Just think about it. Can you imagine being the guard that was chained to Paul 24/7. Those poor guys couldn't help but be inundated by the gospel, not just in words, but in the consistency of a life-pattern lived out before their eyes. Paul was making a deep impact on the palace guard, which, in turn, would have a ripple effect in the very foundation of the Empire itself.

As hard as it may be for us to swallow at the time, God truly does work out every situation for the good of His Kingdom. How does this happen? It is a simple matter of perspective and attitude. As we will see throughout this letter, Paul encourages the church to realize that everything is a matter of attitude. There is good in everything if we will only allow ourselves to see through the eyes of God. Too many times we find it easier to whine about our pain and suffering. When we do that it takes us off the hook. We get to crawl into a hole and disengage from the world and say, "Oh, I don't have to be loving today, because my circumstances are bringing me down." Paul says,

"No way. Our circumstances come and go, but the fact of God's love is what holds it all together."

Where are you today? Are you hurting because of circumstances? Here are two words for you: First, don't deny your feelings. It's OK to cry. It's OK to emote authentically before God. In fact, given the proper environment, it is cathartic and necessary for you to process through your grief and pain. Secondly, don't let your pain blind you from the blessing. God does love you and there is something good in every circumstance that He can use to build you up and make you a better love-gusher in His Kingdom.

Lesson 2

- Philippians 1:27-2:18

Study Questions

What circumstances were the Philippians facing?

How did Paul encourage the Philippians to deal with these circumstances?

What example did Jesus set for the church?

How should followers of Jesus conduct themselves in the world? Why?

Food for Thought

What do you do when people throw stones at you? How do we typically react? As children, when the bully came by and pulled on our hair, or threw rocks at us, or called us all sorts of cutting names, what did we typically do? We either melted and ran away, feeling crushed and demoralized, or we got riled up and fought back. As adults we are still faced with similar situations. For some our "bullying" is little more than snide remarks or a misunderstood labeling and dismissal. For others, especially those in other countries, the "bullying" may be as severe as imprisonment and death. How should we respond? In this passage Paul gives us the answer.

The Philippians were being bullied. In 2:30 Paul says, "Since you are going through the same struggle you saw I had, and now hear that I still have." Apparently the Philippians were coming under attack for their belief and allegiance to Jesus as the Supreme Ruler of the universe. The "struggle" that Paul had when he was in Philippi was being thrown in prison. The "struggle" he was currently experiencing was that of being under house-arrest. Therefore, we can assume that the Philippians were being thrown in prison as well. That is a serious form of "bullying", to say the least.

So, how does Paul coach them in dealing with their oppressors? Paul encourages the Philippians to be united. If the church stands strong then the oppressors will see their own destruction and the church will be saved! At this word I can just see huge sections of the "Christian" population shouting "Hurrah!" They may be led to think, "That's what we need to do. Christians unite! Let's form coalitions and go on marches and tell this crooked world how sinful it is and how right we are. Let's stand up for what's right and fight off all those 'sinners' that are bringing our great nation down! Fight back, unite!"

Stop right there. That is not AT ALL what Paul is proposing. Think about it. What is really at the heart of that kind of attitude? It is pride and anger. Many of the Christians who are thumping their Bibles and pointing the fingers are doing so out of fear, pride, and anger. They are afraid that their comfortable standing in society is being torn out from under them. They are afraid that they may lose their control over the situation. In fear we tend to blame. We tend to point the finger and find the scapegoat towards whom we can channel all our anger. We look at other denominations that look at things differently than we do and blame them for bringing on the wrath of God. But, what does all of this accomplish? Nothing but division in the church, not unity.

Philippians

Paul pleads with the Philippians to be unified. But, how can we be unified? Obviously the church of today is anything but unified. What is the secret to unity? It is found in one word... HUMILITY. Each of us should paste this verse on our mirror and meditate on it each morning before face the world, "Do nothing out of selfish ambition or vain conceit, but in humility consider others better than yourselves. Each of you should look not only to your own interests, but also to the interests of others."

What?!? If we do that then the "bad guys" will walk all over us. We can't let that happen!

Stop and think about it. What did Jesus do? He was like a lamb led before the slaughter. To drive this point home Paul breaks into song and quotes a familiar hymn to the Philippians to remind them what Jesus really did. Here was the one person in the whole universe who actually had the right to force everyone to bow down to Him. Yet, He didn't force anyone to do it. Instead, He humbled Himself. He didn't just smile sheepishly and point to the sky in response to a praise. That isn't humility. He actually gave up everything and allowed Himself to suffer injustice at the hand of the enemy. He was ridiculed, falsely accused, beaten, scorned, and murdered. That is how He dealt with the bullies.

One of the many reasons that Jesus died was to demonstrate one very foundational truth in the universe. You cannot repay evil with evil. As soon as you do, you become that which you are trying to overcome. The only thing that overcomes evil is good. What is good? It is the love of God. It is the self-sacrificing, other-serving, God-honoring, pure, blameless, authentic love of God flowing in and through the follower of Jesus.

Yes, the church should unite. But, we should not unite in an angry battalion to blast our culture. We should unite by confessing our sins to each other, bridging ancient walls of hostility between brothers, taking off our clothes of self-righteousness, and putting on the towel of the servant and washing the feet of those who hate us. Only through love and servanthood will the church ever shine like stars in the universe. Until we realize that, we will continue to BE the problem in the world.

Here's a thought. Jesus IS the Supreme Ruler of the universe. Either that is true or it is not. If it is not true, then we are all wasting our time. If it is true, then it's true and there is nothing we can do to change that fact. Jesus does not need us to "defend" Him. I think He can take care of Himself. He did not send His disciples into the world to wipe out the sinners and establish the Kingdom of God on Earth. He sent out the disciples to make disciples, to teach them to obey God. He lived His life to model for us how to do that. The only people that Jesus was antagonistic towards were the ones who thought they were holy. Everyone else He loved and served. As followers of Jesus it is our calling to simply love and serve the Master and serve the world that He made. When we follow that pattern then people will either be drawn to it, or they will reject it. Either way, that is not our responsibility. In the end, every knee will bow and every tongue will confess that Jesus is Lord...that's because He IS Lord.

So, whatever your circumstances today, whether they are good or bad, just remember that God is calling you to walk in humility, to treat others with respect, and to serve others without complaining and arguing. Wouldn't it be great if the body of Christ was characterized by those attributes in the culture? Imagine the impact we could have then.

The answer is one word...Humility.

Lesson 3

- Philippians 2:19-30

Study Questions

Describe Paul's feelings toward Timothy.

Why did he feel this way?

Why did Paul decide to send Epaphroditus instead of Timothy?

What happened to Epaphroditus?

How did Paul want the church to treat Epaphroditus? Why?

Food for Thought

At first glance it seems that this section is out of place. If you remove this text and read from 2:18 directly over to 3:1, it is a smooth transition. Normally Paul would have placed personal greetings like this at the end of the letter. So, why did he stick a note about two men right in the middle of his discussion about unity and humility?

I believe Paul was very intentional about the placement of this text. Look at what he said in 2:14-16,

> Do everything without complaining or arguing, that you may become blameless and pure, children of God without fault in a crooked and depraved generation, in which you shine like stars in the universe as you hold out the word of life—in order that I may boast on the day of Christ that I did not run or labor for nothing.

In today's text we see Paul highlighting two "stars." Notice how he praises Timothy. Timothy takes a genuine interest in your welfare. He's not your typical guy. Everyone looks out for his own interest, but Timothy is truly concerned about the needs of others. Then there is Epaphroditus. Here is a guy who was willing to risk his life to bring comfort and aid to Paul. When he got sick he wasn't worried about himself, he was worried that the Philippians would be worried about him. These two men were true examples of other-oriented, humble, love-gushers.

Look again at 2:3-4,

> Do nothing out of selfish ambition or vain conceit, but in humility consider others better than yourselves. Each of you should look not only to your own interests, but also to the interests of others.

Paul is saying, "You may think that kind of attitude is only for Jesus, or for the apostles. It is easy to rationalize that away and say that it was easy for Jesus to humble Himself because He knew He would be exalted at the end of it all. Or, it is easy for the apostles to live like that because they were hand-picked by Jesus and it is crystal clear for them. But, I lift up Timothy and Epaphroditus to you. Timothy is from my group and Epaphroditus is from your group. Both of these men have no tangible reason to live like 'stars,' and yet they do. If the church is going to be strong and be able to stand firm under any kind of opposition, then it needs more people like Timothy and Epaphroditus."

The challenge for us is two-fold today.

Are we living like these men? Are we concerned more for the needs of others or are we continually trying to cover our own butt all the time?

Are we honoring people like them? Who are the heroes in our culture? We typically honor the people who have worked their way to the top and have created a little kingdom for themselves. We honor athletes, actors, musicians, and wealthy people. Isn't it ironic that, as a culture, we are willing to give money (as a form of honor) to people who already have lots of money, yet the people that God honors we don't even recognize?

Spend some time today asking God to show you the areas in your life where you can become more other-focused and how you can show honor to those who are truly serving the needs of others.

Lesson 4

- Philippians 3

Study Questions

What did Paul have to boast about?

How did he feel about those credentials? Why?

What was Paul's greatest desire? Why?

What is Paul's attitude toward the goal?

What is the ultimate hope of the believer?

What impact does that have for your daily life?

Food for Thought

The Process of Spiritual Formation

In chapter 3 Paul responds to the immediate danger that he sees present in the church at Philippi. Epaphroditus had informed him that there was great opposition coming against the church. The people were starting to cave in under the pressure. They were beginning to lose sight of why they decided to follow Jesus in the first place. They were turning on each other and the foundations were starting to crumble.

In response to this Paul gives them (and us) one of the most beautiful pictures of the Christian life and the purpose for our existence that has ever been written. The passage stands on its own in beauty and profound truth and does not need my elaboration. Yet, in the spirit of the creativity and passion that this passage inspires in me, allow me to paint my own picture of how Paul describes the process of spiritual formation in the life of the follower of Jesus.

Imagine that life is like a dance marathon and the universe is the stage. Do you remember seeing old movies where hundreds of couples would get out onto the dance floor and dance their hearts out for hours, hoping to not get tapped on the shoulder by the judges? In some ways, that is what spiritual formation is like. In this analogy I'm not emphasizing the fact that we can get tapped on the shoulder by the judge (although I think there is a place for that), rather, I am focusing on the fact that life is like a dance. God is both the song and our dance partner.

You may wonder where this analogy came from. Before we explore it, let me explain. In 2:12-13 Paul sets up the analogy. He says,

> Therefore, my dear friends, as you have always obeyed—not only in my presence, but now much more in my absence— continue to work out your salvation with fear and trembling, for it is God who works in you to will and to act according to His good purpose.

Throughout the centuries Christians have argued over the issue of God's will verses man's will. Some have said that man can't do anything to increase his spiritual condition, thus rejecting all talk of sanctification and spiritual formation. Others have said that it is man's responsibility to practice the spiritual disciplines so that Christ can be formed within us in the process of sanctification, thus placing all the responsibility on the human being for righteousness. In this passage Paul, once again, shows us that the truth lies in the tension of the two extremes. Life and spiritual formation is a dance. God is our partner. He does His part and we do ours. God has provided for us the ability to be on the dance floor – that is justification. Paul says in 3:9, "not having a righteousness of my own that comes from the Law, but that which is through faith in Christ—the righteousness that comes from God and is by faith." And then in 3:16, "let us live up to what we have already attained." There is nothing we can do to earn God's love for us, He simply loves us and wants to dance with us. Yet, just because we are on the dance floor doesn't mean we are good dancers. That is where our part comes in. It is our job to listen to the music and follow our partner's lead and allow Him to teach us how to dance well. Paul says, "Not that I have already obtained all this, or have already been made perfect, but I press on to take hold of that for which Christ Jesus took hold of me."

Since we didn't have space to address this important topic in our discussion of chapter 2, I am spring boarding from that passage and combining it with Paul's analogy of the race in this passage.

In this passage Paul shows us four aspects of dancing well with God.

Ignore the Opposition

We must keep in mind that this passage is book-ended by Paul addressing the presence of "dogs" that are working in opposition to the church. It would be silly for us to live in a naive fantasy world where we believed that everyone was really good deep down inside and that we can just all get along with each other if we'd just "give love a chance." The reality of life is that there are people out there, for whatever reason, who take great pleasure in seeing others suffer; especially if the ones suffering are followers of Jesus. We do have enemies, but look at how Paul instructs the church to deal with the enemies. We are to ignore them. As we discussed in chapter 2, our greatest "weapon" is humility. We cannot focus on our enemies, because when we do we take our focus off of our goal.

Let's turn to our dance analogy to flesh this out. If we focus on the "competition" – all the other couples dancing around us – then we will lose the focus on our partner and will probably step on His toe. We need to ignore the opposition and focus on dancing well.

Trash the Costumes

Notice how Paul responds to the "dogs" in this passage. To paraphrase, he says, "They think that all that external stuff is what's important. They think that being a Pharisee, or being from the right school, or wearing the right clothes, or quoting the right confession, or following the right list of rules is what makes someone good in the eyes of God. I had all that stuff, and do you know what? It was a bunch of garbage. It meant nothing. It wasn't until I threw all that stuff in the trash, got down to my simple clothes, and starting really dancing with God that I realized what life was all about."

In the dance competition of life it is so easy for us to be distracted by the "other couples." We think, "Wow, that person looks really good. Their costume is really shiny. They're bound to win." Or, "They have moves like I've never seen, I can't compete with that. Maybe if I just put on a better costume, or move my feet like that I'll be a better dancer."

The truth is that the costume, or the make-up, or the self-promotional pieces do not make someone a good dancer. When the day is done, all that matters is if you've danced.

Let's be careful not to play the comparison game. God does not judge us according to how we compare to that "other" guy. God is dancing with us, one on one. He wants us to focus on Him and Him alone. So, if there is anything in your life that exists as a façade, or is present to try to convince someone else that you are "good," then chuck it in the trash compactor and get back out on the dance floor.

Tune in to the Music

In Paul's metaphor he speaks of striving for the goal. He is using the metaphor of running a race -- probably a marathon -- where the runner keeps the end in mind and uses the idea of finishing the race as the motivator to keep going. That's a great analogy and works really well. However, over the years I've found one problem with the race analogy. It tends to be very linear in nature. It makes it seem like all that matters is the end of the race and the race itself is not important. In our dance analogy we connect to the idea of the "goal" in a different way. The dancer's "goal" is not a point in time and space; instead the dancer's goal is to move in conjunction with the music in a beautiful and meaningful way. As the song emanates in the room, the dancing couple's objective is to flow into the song, let the song flow into them, then move in harmony with one another as they interpret and flow with the song. The goal is harmony and beauty...throughout the entire course of the song. Every step has meaning and purpose. There is no wasted energy. If done well, then every aspect of the dance – of life – is a thing of beauty and full of meaning. That is the goal.

Keep Dancing

I find it fascinating to feel the tenacity, intensity, and passion in Paul's words in this passage. He says that he does not feel that he has accomplished the goal, but that he must press on. He must keep going. He must strive to be better, to work harder, and to become the mature man of God that God wants him to be. Think about that for a minute. When did Paul write those words? It wasn't at the beginning of the race when most people are energized and excited. It was toward the end of the race when most people are moaning and groaning that the race is too hard and they want to give up. Paul knows the secret to spiritual formation....it never stops. There is always another hill to climb and another valley to traverse.

Here is where our dance analogy works nicely. As long as the music is playing, we keep dancing. The goal is not to reach a point in time and space and then stop. What then? The goal is to keep dancing and to dance better with each song. In the beginning we will step on many toes, we will zig when we should have zagged, we will be winded and want to quit. But, the great joy in all of this is that we have a very patient and loving partner. When we step on His toes He simply stops and says, "Let's take it from the top." When we get distracted by the "competition" He gently, but firmly, grabs our chin and pulls us back to focus on His eyes. As we dance we get more fluid and able. Then He throws us a new move and the dance becomes more interesting and invigorating. Before we know it we are doing things that we never thought possible. Then, we keep dancing.

Lesson 5

- Philippians 4

Study Questions

Make a list of the attitudes Paul instructs the church to have. Meditate on this list and see how you are doing in your own life.

Why do you think Paul instructs the church to think on those kinds of things?

What is Paul's attitude toward circumstances in life? Why?

Describe Paul's relationship with the church in Philippi.

Food for Thought

Verse 1 is actually a conclusion to chapters 1-3. The message of Philippians was started and stated in 1:27,

Whatever happens, conduct yourselves in a manner worthy of the gospel of Christ. Then, whether I come and see you or only hear about you in my absence, I will know that you stand firm in one spirit, contending as one man for the faith of the gospel without being frightened in any way by those who oppose you.

The rest of the letter was an explanation of how to stand firm. Here's a quick summary.

We stand firm by:

- Being unified through humility
- Ignoring our oppressors
- Striving to dance well with God

Therefore, my brothers, you whom I love and long for, my joy and crown, that is how you should stand firm in the Lord, dear friends!

There are two parts to the rest of chapter 4

The Anti-Schism Vaccine

Throughout the letter Paul has been talking generically and universally about unity, humility, and spiritual formation. In this passage he brings it home and names names.

"Listen ladies – Euodia and Syntyche – knock it off! Can't you see that your fighting isn't doing anyone any good? It's just adding fuel to your enemie's flame. Here's how you can stop fighting and starting uniting..."

Rejoice

This is the over-arching theme of the book. As the chains rattled on his wrist, Paul could write the word "Rejoice!" Find joy in everything. It is truly a matter of perspective. No matter how bad a circumstance may be, there can be something good that can be found in it. As silly as this may sound, researchers have discovered that there are actually physiological benefits to the act of smiling. When the muscles of the face move into the smiling position it stimulates the parts of the brain that release the positive hormones that bring peace and pleasure. Proverbs tells us that laughter is good medicine. When we can rejoice, laugh, dance, and sing, even in the midst of terrible circumstances we will find victory over the enemy.

Be gentle

Have you ever noticed that you are nicer to your kids (or people in general) when someone from outside your family is present? We tend to be on our best behavior in the presence of someone else. Notice why Paul says to be gentle...because the Lord is near. If we went through each moment of our day with the conscious awareness that the Master of the universe was with us, I wonder how that would impact the "gentleness quotient" in our lives. The truth is that gentleness turns away wrath, and with Jesus present we can be gentle. How many controversies could be abated if we would simply remain calm and be gentle?

Prayer not Pacing.

As human beings we have a tendency to worry. Why is that? When you really think about it, it doesn't make sense. Worry is the act of obsessing over something that you can't change. If you could change the situation you would, then you wouldn't have to stress over it. If you can't change the situation, then what's the point of obsessing over it? Paul tells us to give all that non-productive mental energy over to God. He's the only one who can change it anyway. If He wants to change it He will. If He doesn't want to change it then we have to trust that He has a bigger picture in sight and we have to trust in Him. When we are able to stop pacing the floor in worry and start passing the stress in prayer, then we will find that God will replace the anxiety with peace. We can live in the peace of the knowledge that God is in control and that no matter what happens, we will exist in His love always.

Acknowledge the real battle ground – your mind.

Have you noticed that this whole letter has been about attitudes? Rejoice! Be humble! See the good! The real battle in our lives is the battle of the mind. What we believe about things will dictate how we perceive life and thus how we respond emotionally and physically to the world around us. If our mind is inundated with negative messages that constantly tell us that we are no good, or that the world is going to Hell in a hand basket, that there is no hope, that there is no purpose, then we will probably start believing it and responding accordingly. On the other hand, if we are constantly surrounded by words of encouragement and messages of hope, then we will probably be in a better frame of mind. Here Paul gives us the key to spiritual formation. Be careful what you put into your mind. If we want to be able to see the good and rejoice and be humble and love others, then we need to saturate our

minds with things that are true, noble, right, pure, lovely, admirable, excellent, and praiseworthy.

Spend some time analyzing the things you watch, read, and listen to throughout the course of the week. What messages are you sending yourself and allowing yourself to soak in. Are they leading you to a good dance, or are they causing you to question whether you should be dancing at all.

As we close out this week, keep this picture in mind. God loves you very much. Regardless of your circumstances, His love for you remains constant. He is standing in the middle of the dance floor with His hand stretched out to you. The music is playing; your place has already been reserved on the dance card. All you need to do is step out and start enjoying the dance.

A Blessing for you today:

May your love abound, may you dance with joy, with the ability to perceive the good and beautiful in all things so that you may be able to figure out what sets you apart from the "crowd" and empowers you to be filled with Jesus' luscious fruit in your life.

Colossians

This session we will look at the last two "Prison Letters." There are two reasons that we are studying two letters this session. The first is one of convenience. There are four chapters in Colossians and one chapter in Philemon. That makes 5 chapters. 5 chapters, 5 lessons. Pretty nice. The second reason actually has biblical validity. Colossians and Philemon go together. Colossians was a letter written to an entire church, like all the other letters we have studied so far. Philemon was a letter written to an individual man in whose house the church at Colossi gathered.

One unique aspect of the Colossian letters is that Paul did not plant this church. During his two years of ministry in Ephesus, recorded in Acts 19 "He took the disciples with him and had discussions daily in the lecture hall of Tyrannus. This went on for two years, so that all the Jews and Greeks who lived in the province of Asia heard the word of the Lord." (Acts 19:9-10) During that teaching ministry a man named Epaphras heard the Gospel and took it back to his town of Colossi, 100 miles east of Ephesus.

There are two reasons that Paul wrote this letter. The first is that Epaphras had brought him news that a certain philosophical system had begun to influence the church and was threatening to pull the believers away from their simple and pure walk with Jesus. Scholars have debated for years over the exact nature of this philosophy. From the evidence in the letter it seems to combine Jewish elements of legalism with a hyper-spiritualized system of angel worship and, possibly, emperor worship. Regardless of its identity, Paul saw it as a real threat to the purity and simplicity of the Gospel that he had spent his life proclaiming across the Roman Empire.

The second reason had to do with an escaped slave named Onesimus. This slave had escaped from the household of Philemon in the city of Colossi and had made his way to Rome. While there he came into the relational orbit of Paul and became a follower of Jesus. Paul sent him back with Tychicus and a letter to his master pleading with Philemon to not punish Onesimus, but to receive him as a brother in the Lord.

Lesson 1

- Colossians 1:1-23

Study Questions

How does Paul know about this church?

What are his feelings for the church?

What is his prayer for the church and his purpose in writing?

How is Jesus described?

What has happened to the Colossians as a result of knowing Jesus?

Food for Thought

As we read through Paul's letters we take for granted our place in life. As we read there is the hum of electrical currents buzzing all around us, the constant drone of traffic in the background, and a universe of information at the click of a mouse. We take for granted our freedoms as well. As Americans we have embedded into our psyche the idea (whether real or not) that we have a voice in our own government and that, at some level, our opinion counts. The individual American citizen has been empowered to believe that they at least matter. This ideal of the empowered individual and the personal right to certain liberties is so powerful in our country that even individuals that enter the country illegally feel the right to speak out and expect to be heard.

In Paul's world it was not so. We need to remember that Paul's life was embedded in two overlapping worlds. On the one side he was a Jew, through and through. He was a Pharisee by training. He believed strongly in the special place that Israel held in world history and, more importantly, the special place that Israel's Messiah held in world affairs. On the other hand he lived in a world that was completely dominated by the Roman Empire. We must realize that, from the perspective of the person in the 1st century, there was not a corner of the world that was not living under the shadow of the Empire. If it wasn't under the direct control of the Emperor (which nearly everything was) it was a shadowy "barbaric" tribe that lived on the fringe and cowered in fear at the greatness of Rome. In this world there was no idea of individual rights and freedoms. Every individual came under the authority of someone else. That authority was determined by race, gender, and ethnicity. Conquered tribes were at the bottom of the pecking order and were good only for slavery. Children and women were second-class. Roman citizens sat at the highest level of society, yet only the wealthiest men held any control over the destiny of the Empire. Ultimately it was the emperor who held supreme control over the destinies of every life in the Empire. This fact was very real to Paul as the chains of Roman bondage clinked on his wrist while he penned this letter.

During Paul's life the Empire had become so enamored with itself, and the Emperor so enamored with himself, and religion and politics were so enmeshed with each other, that the emperor was elevated to god-like status. The Romans believed that the gods were distant from humans and cared very little for their well-being. They believed that the force behind creation was so vague and abstract that it practically did not exist. Therefore, humans were really on their own

Colossians

in the universe and were left to the mercy of the gods and fate – not really an encouraging prospect. However, with the rise of the Roman Empire things started to change. Under the leadership of the emperor and Roman military might, great peace and prosperity was brought to the world. Since the entire world had been brought under Rome's control there was no longer any fighting or local squabbles between neighboring tribes. Under the supreme intellect of Roman ingenuity great feats of architecture and civil engineering had drastically improved the quality of life through things like international highways that allowed for speedy trade and aqueducts that brought fresh water to otherwise parched lands. The emperor was truly seen as the great liberator of the world. He brought a "good news" a "gospel" of peace and prosperity to the universe. He was the image of the most high god. He was a god in human form that actually cared about the livelihood of the citizens of the Empire. Everywhere you looked in the Empire you saw great statues of the emperor. His image was carved on the walls and on the coins. Sacrifices were made to him in every town in thanksgiving for his great deliverance. He was the light of hope around which all creation revolved. All authorities were under his control.

Enter Paul. As a Jew he could not tolerate the self-perception of the Empire. No "good" Jew could. That's why there was constant turmoil in Judea. For centuries the Jews had believed that there is one God that created all things and desires to interact with all creation. They believed that they were the chosen nation from which would come the Messiah, the King who would bring all nations under His control and into the worship of the one true God. To the Jews the emperor was an imposter and they would never bow to him. Yet, their Messiah had not yet come. Except for Paul. Paul met the Messiah on the road to Damascus. He was chosen by the Messiah to be His herald; His ambassador to the world. He was sent to proclaim a "Good News" to the world that ran contrary to the "good news" of Rome.

As Protestant Christians we have 20 centuries of historical filters through which we study the life and message of Paul. Our understanding of Paul has been handed down to us through the heritage of the Reformation that happened in Europe during the 16th century. As is true with every generation and every culture, during the era of the Reformation Paul's message was interpreted through the lenses of the day. The Reformers were fighting against the corruption of the Papacy and questioning issues like authority, salvation, church government, etc. Through that process Paul's message was stripped from its own context and the ideas of salvation, justification, and "The

Gospel" were skewed. The "Gospel" came to mean a personal relationship with Jesus that got the individual out of Hell when he died. Everything became spiritualized so that the struggles were about the inner struggle with sin and the eternal destiny of the individual soul, and nothing else. As a result of this Protestant Theology, and its subsequent European domination of the world through colonialization, "religion" became a personalized affair that was to be kept far away from politics and every day life. Eventually "religion" was nothing more than a personal preference and was seen as obsolete.

I realize this has been an extremely brief introduction to a very complex matter; however we don't have space in a study like this to go any deeper into it. Let's put it simply. While it is present in every letter of Paul, in Colossians we are confronted with the politically subversive nature of the Gospel that Paul preached. As you read Colossians, especially this first chapter, try to read it with the Empire and emperor worship in mind. If you were listening to Paul's Gospel and reading Colossians 1, how would you hear these words? In Colossians 1:15-20 Paul gives a wonderful description of Jesus. As American Christians we tend to spiritualize this and, in so doing, dilute its power. Let's look at this passage with fresh, Roman-Empirical lenses.

Who is Jesus?

Image of the invisible God, Firstborn over all creation

Archaeologists have discovered inscriptions that use these very words to describe the Roman emperor. Basically, Paul was saying that Jesus is the true Emperor. He is the image of the one true God. What's even better than the Roman imposter's image is that Jesus is the image of YHWH, the one true God of Israel, and not some abstract force that is detached and impersonal.

When Paul says firstborn, the emphasis is not on the idea of being 'born' as if Jesus was somehow procreated by the Father. The emphasis is on "first." The firstborn was a socio-political-economic station in the empire. The firstborn son of a clan received the inheritance; he was the heir apparent of the estate. The emperor was considered the "First Man in Rome" the "Firstborn" of everything and over everything. Not anymore.

195

Creator of all things, before all things,
holds all things together

Here Paul places Jesus' status higher and beyond the scope of Roman theology. The emperor was merely a man that had risen to god-status because of his ability to bring peace to the world. The gods were "out there" and practically irrelevant. Jesus, on the other hand, was not a man that rose to god status; He was, in fact, the Creator of all things. He was before all things. He is the glue that holds all things together.

From this statement we can deduce some important theological concepts regarding Jesus:

- He is infinite
- He is the Creator
- He is the energy that holds all things together.

Head of the body

Here Paul redefines Kingdom. The true Empire in the world is not the political entity of Rome. Instead it is the church. It is comprised of those who bow and pledge allegiance to the true Lord, Jesus the Messiah. He is the head and we are all parts of the body. We are a living organism that moves and breathes and serves the head.

Firstborn from among the dead

Here Paul makes a very important distinction for the world. There is life after death. We are eternal beings with hope for more to this life. The Kingdom that Jesus rules is the real Kingdom that stands beyond the confines of time and space. The Roman Empire may be strong and mighty, but it is temporal and it will fade. No matter how much they may call it the Eternal City, Rome will someday fall. But the Kingdom of Jesus stands in reality for eternity. His resurrection from the dead was the demonstration of that truth and it was the beacon of hope for all creation that there is more to life than life.

Supreme, Fullness dwells in Him

Jesus is not an abstract God that hovers around the fringes of human existence, just out of touch of our consciousness. Nor is He merely a human that has ascended to some level of godlike status. Instead He is the interface between God and Man. Jesus is the fulcrum through which the "invisible" God has been revealed – made visible and tangible – to the creation.

Reconciles all things, Makes peace through his blood

Now, here is heart of the Good News. The Roman Empire believed it brought peace and prosperity to the world. It did, at one level. It was a wonderful existence if you were a wealthy Roman male and member of his family. In that privileged social status the Roman Empire was the most wonderful thing that you could possibly imagine. Why would anyone not like it? If you were not of that gender, race, and economic standing, however, you had a very different perspective. Life in the Roman Empire was one of oppression, pain, and injustice.

Jesus' Kingdom was different. Here, under Jesus' rule, there was no race, gender, political, or economic standing. In Jesus' Kingdom there was equality. The kind of peace that Jesus brought was not through military domination and forced submission. Jesus is the kind of ruler who gave himself up and allowed Himself to become publicly scorned at the hands of the Empire in order to demonstrate the true path of love. By spilling His blood Jesus modeled for us what the true Kingdom is all about. Followers of Jesus are called to love one another, to forgive, and, in so doing, to enter into the truth of God's realm.

I know this may have been a lot to swallow and, perhaps, a little melodramatic. However, the challenge for us today is two things:

1. Think about how we view the Kingdom of God in relationship to the power structures in our own lives. Do we put more credence in the "thrones, powers, rulers, and authorities" of our local government, thinking that they are the ones who hold our future security in their hands, or do we look to Jesus and His Kingdom to be the definition of our daily lives?

2. Spend some time meditating on the description of Jesus. Do you view Him as the Supreme Ruler of the universe, or is He more like a lucky charm that you keep in your back pocket to either hug when you feel bad or rub when you want to get something good?

Lesson 2

- Colossians 1:24-2:23

Study Questions

How does Paul define the "mystery" of Jesus?

What is Paul's purpose for writing?

Describe the false teaching that Paul is arguing against.

Why did Paul consider this to be a danger to the Colossians?

How has Jesus defeated this teaching?

Can you think of any contemporary parallels to this false teaching?

What would Paul say to it?

Food for Thought

Living in the Mystery, not the Rule

The key word to this section is mystery. Jesus is a mystery. That doesn't mean we can't know Him, it means we can't explain Him. We can know Him and we are called to know Him deeply. However, we are not called to explain Him and codify Him and place Him in a tidy little theological specimen container. That would be impossible. After all, He is the image of the invisible God, the Creator of the universe. He is THAT which holds all THIS together. How could we explain Him? Yet, He invites us to know Him. He reaches out to envelope us in His love and empowers us to walk in Him.

This is one of the main thrusts of Paul's Good News. He was fighting against the human tendency to create categories and systems and laws that serve to explain and control the environment. Whether it was the Jewish distortion of the Torah on the one side, with its countless dietary and social codes of ethics; or the Roman Legal code on the other that attempted to bring order to the world through the chain of command, the church in Colossi was being attacked and tempted to give into the pressure and place its trust in systems. Paul screams out to them, "Don't do it!" Put your trust in the mysterious reality of Jesus. Simply believe that He is the Supreme Ruler and allow Him to transform you from the inside out and learn to walk in the ways of His Kingdom.

In our present situation we find a similar struggle taking place. Many in our culture are starting to join together in what is called the "emerging church." This phenomenon is simply a growing conversation of people who are willing to challenge some of the accepted systems of belief within Modern, Western, Protestant Christianity and revisit some of the primary questions that are presented to us as we encounter the reality of God, Scripture, and Culture. Many other Christians in our culture are frightened by the "emerging conversation" and are claiming that it is heretical. These groups are asking the emerging church to lay out clear-cut "statements of faith" and articulate the minutia of its doctrinal stance, reflecting a belief that the movement is compromising the "truth." This tension, as I see it, seems to reflect the tension that the Colossian church felt. They were surrounded by people who wanted to reduce their faith to a religious system that could be clearly defined and copiously followed.

Just this week, as I was studying Colossians, I received an email that deals with this issue.

What is really wonderful about these statements is that they were written by one of my theology professors from Seminary. His name is LeRon Shulz. I submit this email to you in hopes that it will not only reflect the spirit of what Paul is saying in our current passage, but also encourage your spirit as you attempt to walk in the mystery that is Christ.

"The coordinators of Emergent have often been asked (usually by their critics) to proffer a doctrinal statement that lays out clearly what they believe. I am merely a participant in the conversation who delights in the ongoing reformation that occurs as we bring the Gospel into engagement with culture in ever new ways. But I have been asked to respond to this ongoing demand for clarity and closure. I believe there are several reasons why Emergent should not have a 'statement of faith' to which its members are asked (or required) to subscribe. Such a move would be unnecessary, inappropriate and disastrous.

Why is such a move unnecessary? Jesus did not have a 'statement of faith.' He called others into faithful relation to God through life in the Spirit. As with the prophets of the Hebrew Bible, He was not concerned primarily with whether individuals gave cognitive assent to abstract propositions but with calling persons into trustworthy community through embodied and concrete acts of faithfulness. The writers of the New Testament were not obsessed with finding a final set of propositions the assent to which marks off true believers. Paul, Luke and John all talked much more about the mission to which we should commit ourselves than they did about the propositions to which we should assent. The very idea of a "statement of faith" is mired in modernist assumptions and driven by modernist anxieties – and this brings us to the next point.

Such a move would be inappropriate. Various communities throughout church history have often developed new creeds and confessions in order to express the Gospel in their cultural context, but the early modern use of linguistic formulations as 'statements' that allegedly capture the truth about God with certainty for all cultures and contexts is deeply problematic for at least two reasons. First, such an approach presupposes a (Platonic or Cartesian) representationalist view of language, which has been undermined in late modernity by a variety of disciplines across the social and physical sciences (e.g., sociolinguistics and paleo-biology). Why would Emergent want to force the new wine of the Spirit's powerful transformation of communities into old modernist wineskins? Second, and more importantly from a theological perspective, this fixation with propositions can easily lead to the attempt to use the finite tool of language on an absolute Presence that transcends and embraces all finite reality. Languages are culturally constructed symbol systems that enable humans to communicate by designating one finite reality in distinction from another. The truly infinite God of Christian faith is beyond all our linguistic grasping, as all the great theologians from Irenaeus to Calvin have insisted, and so the struggle to capture God in our finite propositional structures is nothing short of linguistic idolatry.

Why would it be disastrous? Emergent aims to facilitate a conversation among persons committed to living out faithfully the call to participate in the reconciling mission of the biblical God. Whether it appears in the by-laws of a congregation or in the catalog of an educational institution, a 'statement of faith' tends to stop conversation. Such statements can also easily become tools for manipulating or excluding people from the community. Too often they create an environment in which real conversation is avoided out of fear that critical reflection on one or more of the sacred propositions will lead to excommunication from the community. Emergent seeks to provide a milieu in which others are welcomed to join in the pursuit of life 'in' the One who is true (1 John 5:20). Giving into the pressure to petrify the conversation in a 'statement' would make Emergent easier to control; its critics could dissect it and then place it in a theological museum alongside other dead conceptual specimens the curators find opprobrious. But living, moving things do not belong in museums. Whatever else Emergent may be, it is a movement committed to encouraging the lively pursuit of God and to inviting others into a delightfully terrifying conversation along the way.

This does not mean, as some critics will assume, that Emergent does not care about belief or that there is no role at all for propositions. Any good conversation includes propositions, but they should serve the process of inquiry rather than shut it down. Emergent is dynamic rather than static, which means that its ongoing intentionality is (and may it ever be) shaped less by an anxiety about finalizing statements than it is by an eager attention to the dynamism of the Spirit's disturbing and comforting presence, which is always reforming us by calling us into an ever-intensifying participation in the Son's welcoming of others into the faithful embrace of God."

Lesson 3

- Colossians 3:1-4:1

Study Questions

Why should we "set our minds on things above?"

Create a compare/contrast chart that lists the things that must be put to death and the "new clothes" that must be put on.

Restate verse 11 in your own words and in contemporary terms.

What are the implications for the church in our world?

What would/could/should the church look like in light of verses 15-17?

Notice that the only group to whom Paul gives any detailed instructions is the slaves. In light of the Onesimus/Philemon issue, what do you think Paul is trying to communicate?

Food for Thought

A New Set of clothes

Here, and in the previous chapter, Paul draws upon a strong image to describe what it means to walk in the mystery of Christ. He says that we have died, have been buried, and have been raised in new life. That is exactly what Jesus did and that is exactly what He calls us to do each day of our lives. If you will look at the illustration for the letter you will see the image of a watery grave. At the bottom of the grave are all the negative emotions, behaviors, and attitudes that keep us bound up in the darkness and cut off from the life-giving presence of God. Through Jesus' death, and our participation in His death through the "circumcision of our heart" we have drowned those sins. They are washed away, buried in the sea of forgetfulness. In our resurrection, as we participate in the resurrection power of Jesus, we are set free from sin and empowered to walk in the mysterious life of Jesus in His Kingdom.

In describing this new life Paul mixes four metaphors: a plant, a building, a body, and clothing. Let's break these down and glean the lesson from each one.

The **plant**. The plant starts with a seed. Jesus said in John 12:24,

> I tell you the truth, unless a kernel of wheat falls to the ground and dies, it remains only a single seed. But if it dies, it produces many seeds.

Here Paul taps into that imagery and reminds us that it is only through our identification with Jesus' death and burial that we can be transformed into something new. We must die to our own selfishness and pride. Anyone involved in healing, at whatever level, and from whatever perspective, will agree that negative mindsets like greed, anger, hatred, self exaltation, self-preservation, bitterness, etc. will ultimately destroy you and the people around you. Jesus calls us to die to those things. We must do the one thing that seems most counter-intuitive to survival in order to survive. We must die. Give it all away. Only then will you be able to truly walk in freedom and let the love of God flow through you fully. It is then that the seed will spring up from the dirt and produce fruit that will multiply.

As the plant matures it develops a strong root system that digs deeply into the ground. This allows it both to draw nutrients and moisture from the soil and have a firm anchor against the wind. Part of walking in the mystery of Jesus is realizing that it is our primary task to be deeply rooted and established in our relationship with

Him. We must engage in the soul-nourishing disciplines of prayer, meditation, scripture-study, worship, and fellowship in order to be anchored and healthy. Then, in its season, the fruit of that relationship will be produced in our life and it will drop into the lives of the world around us.

The **building**.

I believe the building metaphor speaks the same message as that of the roots of the plant. The taller a building is going to be, the deeper and wider its foundation must be. If we want to have a small building, we dig a shallow foundation in our relationship with Christ. If we want our lives to be erected into a magnificent temple for the glory of God then we must dig deeply into the mystery that is Christ.

The **body**.

Jesus is the head and each part of us is a member of that body. There are no body parts that are more important than another. Each one is different, but all are important. When one hurts, the other hurts. They all work together under the leadership of the head.

Here we must focus on an incredibly important aspect of "body life" in the Kingdom of God. We must also focus on it through the lens of the discussion concerning the Roman Empire that we discussed in chapter 1. The point is found in both verse 11 and verse 23:

11 Here there is no Greek or Jew, circumcised or uncircumcised, barbarian, Scythian, slave or free, but Christ is all, and is in all.

25 ...there is no favoritism.

In the Roman Empire the worth of a person was determined by his or her socio-racial-economic position. That is not the way of the reality of Jesus' Kingdom. In His Kingdom we are all part of the body. Yes, we may be different. We have different skins colors. We have different cultural backgrounds. We even have different theological paradigms to explain this thing called the body of Christ. Yet, we are all members of it and are called to be active participants that are contributing positively to its life and health.

Clothing.

In the final metaphor we see the attitudes that are to clothe this new body. These are the attitudes that are replacing the negative ones lying at the bottom of the watery grave.

As I think about this metaphor I remember those days when I have worked out in the yard all day in the heat. My body is sore, there is dirt caked into my crusted sweat, and I stink. Then I hop into the shower, scrub off all the crud, soak in the rejuvenating power of clean water, and then step out to put on a clean set of clothes. There are few things more refreshing than slipping on that clean shirt and smelling the freshness of it as it goes over your head. Even though you are tired you suddenly feel refreshed. That is how it is when we engage in the mystery of Jesus. He has laid out a new set of clothes for us on the bed, waiting for us to get out of the shower and slip them on.

Finally, there is the most important piece of all the metaphors. There is an overcoat. There is a piece of clothing, an attitude that pulls everything together. Through it all the other things are possible. It is love. It is because of love that Jesus gave up Himself for us. It is through His love that we are empowered to die to our old self. It is in His love that we sink our roots and draw nourishment. It is in the spirit of His love that we tear down the dividing walls of prejudice and cling together in the bond of peace and unity as members of the body. It is out of love for God that we offer it all up to Him as a fragrant offering of thanksgiving.

There is no law that can make you love. There is no religious system that produces love in your heart. There is no theological specimen container that can encompass and explain love. God is love and that is the mystery. We are simply invited to dive into it and live there, now and for eternity.

Lesson 4

- Colossians 4:2-18

Study Questions

Restate verses 2-6 in your own words.

Think of some practical ways this might look in the church of our culture.

Food for Thought

How to Treat the "Outsider"

As we read the last chapter of Colossians I want to look specifically at verse 5-6 and make a few observations. He says,

> *Be wise in the way you act toward outsiders; make the most of every opportunity. Let your conversation be always full of grace, seasoned with salt, so that you may know how to answer everyone.*

First of all I have to admit that I am uncomfortable with the word "outsiders" since it is breeding ground for exclusivism, bigotry, and hatred. However, it is there and there are no lingustical ways around it. The word means to be outside. As I reflect on it, however, I realize that it is an inevitability within the human condition. As people we flock together in like-minded groups. Even within mundane and amoral issues like favorite foods or styles of music we tend to create "in" groups and "out" groups. "We" like classic rock, and "you" like rap, or country, or oldies, or whatever. And, more fundamentally and theologically, there is the reality that we must group together in faith communities for the purpose of fellowship and intimacy. Without intimacy we will die. Yet, in order to gain healthy intimacy we must cluster together with "safe" people with whom we can be transparent, authentic, and allow in to examine our hearts, hold us accountable, encourage us, and simply be family. Even under the umbrella of the body of Christ, we cannot have this level of intimacy with everyone. Not every fellow follower of Jesus is 'safe' for us. Thus we will naturally create "in" groups and "out" groups.

So, how are we supposed to deal with the people that are "outside" of our "in" group? Our natural tendency is to say, "Our group is right and your group is wrong. Go away. We're better. We don't like you." In society there are two basic extremes on the continuum of how people have answered this question. On the one extreme is the view that your own group is superior and has the right to exterminate all other groups. On the other extreme is the view that there are no groups and that we are all just one big group that should equally get along with each other. The former group has obvious problems given our many discussions about the nature of God's love and the Kingdom that Jesus invites all people to enter. The latter group has problems in light of our previous discussion about the need for "safe" groupings for the purpose of intimacy. It is a logical impossibility that all human beings can equally bond in intimacy. So, groupings must happen.

In this passage Paul instructs us on how a follower of Jesus should deal with the reality of "in" groups and "out" groups. The answer should make sense to us after so many weeks of studying Paul's letters. It is one word – GRACE. After all, how does God deal with us? He extends grace to us. He loves us, even when we don't love Him. Even when we were sinners Christ died for us. Grace means gift. How do we deal with the "out" group? We give to them. We extend love to them. We sprinkle salt on them to make their life full of flavor. We redeem the time. We seize the day. There is no time for pettiness and wars. We agree to disagree and we extend grace.

Notice something very important. He doesn't say, "You redeem the time so that you can convert them to become part of your 'in' group." Whoa. Traditionally these verses have been used as mantras for evangelistic and apologetical ministries. They have been used as a type of marketing scheme for how to penetrate the enemy lines with a soft sell and then pounce on them with the "answer" so that they will acknowledge the failings of their group and become part of our group. I wonder if that is what Paul is really saying.

As I read Paul's words I hear him saying that we should pay attention to the other group. We should listen to them. How can you know how to answer someone? Only when you know who they are. In order to be in a position to know how to answer someone you must first be in a relationship. An answer implies a question. A healthy exchange of questions and answers requires an equitable environment in which differing views can be exchanged in dialogue. As any good marriage counselor will tell you, in order for communication to exist there must be empathetic listening and compassionate telling.

These principles can be applied to every level of "in grouping" and "out grouping" that occurs in our lives. Within the local church there will inevitably be groupings of people that lean one way or the other on issues. They should apply these principles to how they treat each other. At the macro level there are those who acknowledge Jesus as Supreme Ruler and explicitly seek to follow Him and there are those who do not acknowledge the name of Jesus explicitly. How should they treat one another? If they followed these principles the world would be a safer place.

Perhaps we could pray that God would allow us to extend to others "outside" of our group the grace that He has extended to us. Let's see how we can serve those people and be salt in their lives and learn from them.

Colossians

Lesson 5

- Philemon

Study Questions

How does Paul feel about Philemon?

What is Paul asking Philemon to do?

Summarize verses 17-21 in your own words.

What tone and/or tactic does Paul take in these verses?

Food for Thought

He's your brother now

Philemon is a wonderful little personal note that Paul wrote to a friend and tucked into the package with Colossians. It is most likely that the "church that meets in your home" is actually the group to whom Paul addressed the letter of Colossians.

Here's the context of the letter. As Paul sat in house arrest in Rome he built up quite a teaching ministry with all the people that came in and out of his home. Perhaps he even sat out on the porch and taught to large groups. His reputation in the city grew and many people from the Jews, the Gentiles, and from the Roman guard came to hear his teaching and decided to pledge allegiance to the true King, Jesus. One of these people was a man named Onesimus. He was a slave that had somehow escaped from the household of Philemon in Colossi and made his way to Rome. Hungry and scared he probably heard about a radical rabbi that taught about the love of God and equality for all people in the Kingdom of Heaven. Naturally Onesimus would have been intrigued so he sought Paul out and came under his teaching. Over time he bonded with Paul and became like a son to him as he came alongside Timothy to serve in Paul's ministry.

Now imagine Epaphras' surprise when he came to visit Paul and saw Onesimus there with him. "Onesimus! We've been looking everywhere for you. Philemon was so upset the day told us that you had escaped. You know that your life is in danger. You have put me in a very dangerous position. I can't hide the fact that you are here with Paul. You belong to Philemon and I have to turn you in. Paul, what should we do?"

Paul looks at Epaphras then looks at Onesimus. He mulls over in his mind the Gospel of equality that he has been teaching all throughout the Roman Empire.

"Well Epaphras, I tell you what we should do. I don't know the people in Colossi since you started that church, not me. However, I've always wanted to visit them. Why don't I write two letters? One to the church in which I clearly emphasize that we are all equals in the body of Christ, under the rule of Jesus the Messiah. Then I write a letter to Philemon. Him I know from our exchange in Ephesus. I will appeal to him from my heart, and put a little loving pressure on him to actually put this stuff into practice. By sending Onesimus back to Colossi we will give a physical, tangible demonstration of what Jesus' Kingdom really looks like. Imagine the looks on the townsfolk's faces when they see Philemon walking down the road with his arm around Onesimus like a son when he should have had him hanging in the stocks for escaping. Instead of setting the example of what happens to those who disobey the Roman laws, we will be setting an example of what happens when we submit to the laws of Jesus and actually love each other. Here, give me a pen. I'm going to write this one in my own handwriting, just to drive home the point."

The challenge for us from this letter obviously has nothing to do with slavery. In our country we dealt with that over 100 years ago. However, it does smack us square in the face when it comes to the issue of equality. Throughout Paul's letters he is challenging the status quo of dominant power structures. He challenges the emperor's right to supremacy. He challenges the power structures of rulers and thrones. He challenges the ethnic prejudices and economic hierarchies. He challenges the power structures of the household in the husband/wife, father/child, and slave/master relationships. He calls for all people to see that we are all equal under the headship of Jesus. We are called to love one another. Imagine how hard it must have been for Philemon to read Paul's letter and let go of the age-old categories of slave and master. What are your categories? Through what lenses to you allow yourself to look down on another person and consider yourself better than them? Is it race? Is it money? Is it politics? Is it ethics? Is it theology? As a follower of Jesus we are called to be like Him and look at that person through the eyes of love. It will be difficult and counter-intuitive, but it is the way of the Kingdom.

Introduction to The Pastoral Letters

This session our journey takes us into a thick bank of fog. Up to this point we have been able to clearly locate each of Paul's letters within the context of his story recorded in the book of Acts. At the end of Acts we find Paul under house arrest, awaiting his day in court. During this period he wrote the four letters we call the "Prison Epistles." But then it just ends. Acts is one of the most frustrating narratives ever written (see note below). It just ends. It leaves us hanging and doesn't tell us what happens to the hero. The fog bank moves in. Historically, things get pretty sketchy from that point on. Tradition tells us that Paul was eventually released from his house arrest in Rome. For the next few years he continued to take the Good News of Jesus' Kingdom to Gentile regions that had not yet heard the message. Apparently he finally made the trip to Spain that he had written about in his letter to the Romans. It also seems (from the content of the letters to Timothy and Titus) that Paul retraced the steps of his earlier journeys and visited the churches in Asia, Macedonia, and Greece. During that time he left Timothy in Ephesus to serve as the leader there and Titus on the island of Greece to serve in leadership there. At some point –traditionally A.D. 64 – Paul was, once again, arrested and sent to Rome. Only this time he was thrown into the dungeon. Eventually he was beheaded in the streets of Rome.

It is during this post-Acts period of Paul's life that the last three letters we will be studying were written. The first two – 1 Timothy and Titus – were written by the free Paul as he was traveling around the countryside. These letters are personal letters written from a mentor to his young protégé. They give sound advice for the difficult task of leading people in the context of the body of Christ. For this reason they have traditionally been called the "Pastoral Epistles" since it seems that Timothy and Titus were the "Pastors" or chief leaders of those churches. The last letter – 2 Timothy – is very different. This was a letter written by an old man in a dungeon. The weathered and wise Paul can see that his end is near and he reaches out his heart one last time to his spiritual son, Timothy, and asks him to come to him before he dies.

Before we dive into these letters I think you should be aware that there is great controversy in the scholarly world over the authenticity of these letters. For many reasons, scholars question whether Paul wrote these letters. First, they do not fall within the storyline of Acts and therefore cannot be verified historically. Secondly, the language style is dramatically different from all the other Pauline letters we possess. Thirdly, there are stark contrasts in the theology presented in the letters. For example, Paul talks very little about the role of the Holy Spirit in the Pastorals where it is dominant in the other letters. Also, Paul seems to have a very structured system of church leadership – bishops, deacons, etc. – that seems absent from the other letters and the evidence of the 1st century church. Finally, there are certain terms – most obvious being the term "godliness" – that is completely absent in all of his other letters.

If we employ good Bible study skills, the first of which is OBSERVATION, we must agree that these points are valid observations. As I read through 1 Timothy again in preparation for our study the term *godliness* jumped out at me. I did the research and, sure enough, Paul does not use it once in all of the other pre-pastoral letters. In fact, the term is hardly used at all in the entire Bible, even the Greek translation of the Old Testament. And yet, Paul uses it 8 times in 1 Timothy alone. As good Bible detectives we must ask the question, "Why?"

There are a few potential answers to why Paul's language would be so different in these letters. First, these letters are different in nature from the others. The other letters were written to groups of people and were intended to be read aloud in a public gathering. The Pastorals were intimate letters written from a loving father to a son (spiritually, that is). From our own experience we know that our vocabulary and tone changes depending upon our audience. If we were writing a speech or a sermon it would sound and feel very different than if we were writing a love letter or a personal diary entry. Perhaps Paul did not intend these letters to go public.

The second explanation – especially for terms like "godliness" – is that Paul's theology may have developed further after he was released from prison. Perhaps he encountered the term "godliness" during his dialogue with the Romans and it was newly added to his repertoire.

Another reason he may have introduced the idea of "godliness" was that it was the term being used by the false teachers whom Timothy was supposed to address. Perhaps they introduced the term as an alternative – and superior – idea to Paul's simple Gospel message. Paul may have felt the need to define the term according to his understanding of the Gospel and set it in its proper context.

The final possibility for the drastic uniqueness of the Pastoral letters is that they were not actually written by Paul. Instead, they were written by one of Paul's disciples from the next generation who was writing in Paul's name in order to address the issues of his own generation (this was a common practice and does not diminish the integrity of the letter).

While I acknowledge the observations that highlight the uniqueness of the letters, I don't feel the evidence is strong enough to abandon the idea that Paul wrote them. For the purpose of this study we will be operating under the assumption that these are genuine letters from Paul to his protégés, during the period of time after his imprisonment in Acts 28 and before his execution in Rome.

1 Timothy

This session we will look at the first letter written to Timothy. We first meet Timothy in Acts 16 where Paul meets him during the first missionary journey. He is a little half-breed kid that sparked something inside of Paul. With a Jewish mother and a Greek father, perhaps Paul thought he was the perfect example of what the Kingdom of God should look like. We don't know why, but Paul "adopted" Timothy and took him along as an apprentice. Apparently Timothy matured quickly and grew very close to Paul's heart. In fact, he is listed as the co-author of the letters to the Thessalonians, Corinthians, Philippians, Colossians, and to Philemon.

He was with Paul in Rome during the house arrest of Acts 28. Now, after Paul had been released from house arrest, it was time for Paul to kick his young apprentice out of the nest so that he could spread his leadership wings and fly. His first assignment was Ephesus. This fact may speed past us, but it would do us good to snatch it out of the air and examine it for a moment. Ephesus. Do you remember what happened in that place? If you don't, go back and read Acts

19. Paul's successful ministry caused a riot in that city that got his friends dragged before a mob and him nearly killed. Many believe that Paul was imprisoned in Ephesus and suffered greatly while he was there. On the flip side, Ephesus was also the hub of the ministry in Asia. Through Paul's teaching ministry there many churches were planted in the satellite communities. At many levels this church held great importance for Paul and the church at large. Now Paul was commissioning Timothy to be his representative and the minister of Jesus' gospel. That couldn't have been an easy task to fulfill.

From the evidence in the letter it seems that Timothy had a few things stacked up against him in this assignment. First, he was young and the "false teachers" were older men. Culturally, it would have been natural for the church to respect the "wisdom" of the older men before they would listen to some young punk sent over by Paul. Secondly, Timothy seems to have had a somewhat timid personality. Can you imagine being a timid guy sent to get in the face of a group of elders that needed a little "doctrinal adjustment?"

Thirdly, it seems that Timothy struggled with frequent physical illnesses. This only complicates any task.

As we read this letter let's keep in mind that it is a personal letter. This is one of those "talks" that a father has with his son just before he leaves him on the college campus for his first semester of school away from home. "Remember everything I've taught you son...you're on your own now, be strong..." Timothy was facing a big challenge and some very specific issues in the church of Ephesus. As we study it we can learn a great deal about what it means to be a leader in the body of Christ. If you find yourself in any type of leadership -- whether it is as an elder, a parent, a boss, or a mentor – hear the spirit of Paul's advice and see what kind of heart Paul encourages Timothy to have as he approaches this important task of leadership.

Lesson 1

- 1 Timothy 1:1-17

Study Questions

Why did Paul urge Timothy to stay in Ephesus?

How are the false teachers described?

How does Paul view the purpose of the gospel in light of his own story?

Food for Thought

The Gospel Message: "Hyper-Grace," not religion

In this passage we are presented, yet again, with a wonderful contrast that is evident, not only in the specific setting of the Ephesian church, but also throughout Paul's ministry. On the one hand is the group of false teachers that is constantly trying to make the Gospel into a legalistic system of rituals and rules. On the other hand is Paul who keeps crying out the KISS principle: Keep It Simple Stupid. The Gospel is simple, it is grace. That's it.

Let's walk through verse 12-17 and let the beautiful message of the Gospel wash over us once again.

- Verse 12 – Paul's attitude toward everything is one of humility and gratitude. He knows he was not worthy of God's love, and yet, there it is, freely given to him. He knows he's not smart enough or strong enough to preach the Gospel around the world, and yet, there he is, walking in the gracious gift of God's strength.

- Verse 13 -- The key word here is mercy. It is at the heart of the Gospel. Look at how Paul describes himself. He was a blasphemer, a persecutor, and a violent man. If anyone deserved the wrath of God it was Paul. Yet, Jesus showed mercy to Paul. Not only did He dismiss the charges against him, He embraced him and called him to be a vital part of His Kingdom. Here's the weird part. Paul wasn't even asking for it. Jesus came into Paul's distorted world, into his hateful heart, and met him there. He forgave him, even when He wasn't asked to, and transformed him from the inside out.

Once again, mercy is at the heart of the gospel. Jesus said in Matthew 9:13

But go and learn what this means: 'I desire mercy, not sacrifice.'

Again, he said to the Pharisees in Matthew 23:23

"Woe to you, teachers of the law and Pharisees, you hypocrites! You give a tenth of your spices—mint, dill and cummin. But you have neglected the more important matters of the law—justice, mercy and faithfulness. You should have practiced the latter, without neglecting the former.

- Verse 14 – The syntax of this verse is a little difficult to translate directly. Literally it says "way too much was our Lord's grace with the faith and love that is in Christ Jesus." The first word is the Greek word *hyper-plaonazo*. *plaonazo* means "too much." When you put *hyper* in front of it the word actually becomes absurd. It is hyper-too much. Jesus' grace skyrockets out of the stratosphere, it is so far beyond comprehension. That is "Hyper-Grace" and that is what the Gospel is all about. It's about forgiving and restoring, not tearing down and condemning.

- Verse 15 – If you were to poll the average man on the street and ask what the general message of the church is to the world, I believe the answer would be, "You're a dirty rotten sinner and you are going to burn in Hell!" That is sad. Look what Paul reminds us of here. Jesus came into the world to save sinners. The hyper-grace Man took the plunge into the muck to rescue us, not to rub our noses in it. Paul should know; he was the chief muck slinger. Yet, Jesus took the clean water of the Kingdom and washed him clean. Jesus said of himself in John 3:17,

  For God did not send His Son into the world to condemn the world, but to save the world through Him.

- Verse 16 – Paul was chosen to be the example of what God is all about. God is all about saving people. The key phrase here is found in two Greek words: *apassan makrothumea* Each of these words is loaded with theological significance. *apassan* (or *pas*) means "all." It was used to describe the fact that God is all encompassing. All things come under His dominion. He is the all in all. *makrothumea* means "long-suffering." It means that God will wait, and wait, until the very last minute to make sure that everyone has a chance to repent. He will give us as many chances as we need because He loves us. He said to Moses as He gave the law in Exodus 34:6-7,

  The LORD, the LORD, the compassionate and gracious God, slow to anger, abounding in love and faithfulness, maintaining love to thousands, and forgiving wickedness, rebellion and sin. Yet He does not leave the guilty unpunished; He punishes the children and their children for the sin of the fathers to the third and fourth generation.

God is not standing there, waiting for us to mess up so that He can zap us. He knows we are messed up. He loves us and longs for us to come home to Him. He longs to cleanse us in His love and allow us to shower each other with His love. That is the Gospel. It is not about rules and regulations and "appeasing the gods" or "meeting the standard." It is about receiving the hyper-grace of a loving Father, who waits, and waits, and waits, for us to come home.

- Verse 17 – As Paul meditates on the hyper-grace of God that He has personally experienced, he can't help but slip into worship. That is the heart of worship. When we come face to face with the Almighty Creator of the Universe and realize that He loves us in spite of our selfishness, pride, greed, lust, and crud, we can't help but fall on our face and worship Him in total thankfulness.

My prayer for us today is that we can live in the experiential knowledge of God's grace. When we realize that we are the recipients of the gracious love of God we can't help but overflow that love to everyone we meet. There is no room for categorizations, prejudices, alienation, and self-righteous abuse. There is only room to be the conduits of Hyper-Grace.

Lesson 2

- 1 Timothy 1:18-3:15

Study Questions

For whom should we pray? Why?

How should men pray?

How should women carry themselves?

Summarize the qualifications for overseers and deacons in your own words.

Why do you suppose Paul would have to create this list?

Food for Thought

Pray for "all men"

Roll up your sleeves, buckle your seatbelts, and tighten your chinstraps because this section will be a bumpy ride! Three of the most hotly debated topics of the late 20th century American church are contained in today's reading: The relationship of church and state, the role of women in the church, and the nature of the public worship service. Are you ready for this?

Obviously, in a short commentary like this we cannot plunge the depths of these very important topics. Allow me to quickly water-ski over all three.

The Worship Service

Some Study Bibles label this section "Instruction for Worship" thus leading the reader to believe that these verses are telling the church how to function during that one hour time slot on Sunday morning in the sanctuary. I think that is an unfortunate and misleading label. The key to this passage is found in 3:14-15

Although I hope to come to you soon, I am writing you these instructions so that, if I am delayed, you will know how people ought to conduct themselves in God's household, which is the church of the living God, the pillar and foundation of the truth.

In our modernized view of the church we read the words "in God's household" and automatically envision the beautiful sanctuary with its padded pews, jumbo-tron video screen, worship band, and hefty mortgage. That is the farthest thing from Paul's mind when he penned the word. A household was a family. It was the master of the house, his wife, children, and servants. That was the typical household of the Roman Empire. The household of God simply means all the people that share the common bond of being followers of Jesus. That is the church. It is the living body of the living God. He is the Master of the household and we are all His bride, His children, and His servants – all wrapped up into one.

So, 1:18-3:14 are not instructions on how to behave during a time slot on Sunday, rather they are specific instructions for Timothy on how he should instruct the household of God in Ephesus to be all the time.

Once again, we must keep in mind the nature of the letters. This letter was not Paul's attempt to write a textbook on "Exactly How to Run the Church Everywhere for All Times." This was a personal letter to Timothy giving him instructions on how to lead in Ephesus until he could return and knock some heads around. You see, Paul personally knew the people in Ephesus. He knew the quirks and the hang-ups. He knew where they were theologically sound and he knew where they had serious blind spots that were going to get them into trouble. This point is evident in 1:20 where Paul specifically mentions two men by name. I think it would be helpful for us if we viewed this passage through these lenses and realize that Paul is focusing on the specific hotspots in the Ephesian church that he knew Timothy was going to face.

Church and State

If you were not a Roman citizen life in the Empire was pretty tough. The Romans had conquered your land, ousted your leaders, commandeered your land, enslaved your people, imposed their religion on top of yours, and taxed your income. The Jews weren't the only people group that was constantly trying to oust the Romans. Most non-citizens carried with them a low-grade resentment toward their oppressors. To follow Jesus was a welcomed alternative to the imposed emperor worship that permeated their culture. Jesus was a good King. He promised deliverance, forgiveness, liberty, and justice...for ALL people. The emperor only promised these things for the citizens of Rome. Everyone else was simply fodder for the Empire.

In light of this underlying resentment Paul's words through Timothy would be a hard pill to swallow. He wants us to do what? He wants us to pray for the emperor? Isn't he the devil? Isn't he the anti-Christ? Paul reminds them of a foundational principle of the kingdom of God: God wants ALL people to come to him. God wants us to pray for ALL people, even the emperor. God loves the emperor. He loves the centurion. He loves the temple prostitute. He loves the tax collector. Pray for them. Remember, it's hard to hate someone that you are authentically praying for. It seems that this was an issue in Ephesus that Timothy needed to address.

Gender Issues

It is important that we don't sever this passage from the previous section. We must read it as a flow. In 2:1 Paul's instruction was that requests, prayers, intercession, and thanksgiving be made for everyone... in 2:8 he continues the idea by clarifying how we should pray. The emphasis here is "without anger or disputing." Apparently there was a lot of "in grouping" and "out grouping" going on in Ephesus. People were getting angry

with each other and there was great tension. One of the greatest areas of tension in the church was the issue of the liberation of women that came with the Gospel of Jesus. For the first time women were considered to be valuable, as Paul taught in the letter to the Galatians when he said that in Christ there is no male or female, neither slave nor free. We've discussed this issue before in our study of 1 Corinthians 14. The male-dominated society was having difficulty with this. Elsewhere in the culture there was the rise of a radical feminist movement in which women were the high priests and sexual immorality was part of the religious practice. The church was afraid that the women would "go wild" with their new-found freedom and disgrace God and themselves. In verses 11-15 Paul gives a corrective to both extremes of the women's lib issue. To the women-rule side he says, "No, remember that Adam came first and Eve was a helpmate. There are no grounds for woman domination." To the men-rule-because-Eve-was-the-one-who-sinned camp Paul says, "Hold on boys. First of all, in my letter to the Romans I reminded them that I attribute sin to Adam. Secondly, it was a woman who brought our salvation into the world. Mary had Jesus and there was no man involved. Go figure. I'd say the score was settled and we're all even, so stop being such jerks."

As we've discussed elsewhere, I believe Paul was telling the women of Ephesus to tone it down and not embarrass themselves. Allow the Holy Spirit to work and don't be stupid about liberty. Take your time and be educated properly before you start strutting your stuff.

In the 21st century we don't have those issues. We are brothers and sisters in Christ, equal children in the family of God. Women have access to education and we all bring unique gifts to the table. Let God lead, the Holy Spirit empower, and us try to keep up.

Leadership

Apparently there was another issue going on in Ephesus. There was a question of leadership. Who should be an elder and a deacon? As we will see in chapter 5-6 it seems that some of the troublemakers in the church – the "false teachers" – were actually elders. That would make Timothy's job especially difficult. One of the accusations that Paul brings against the false teachers in chapter 6 is that they were using their spiritual authority as a means of getting rich. In chapter 3 Paul reminds Timothy that leadership in the church is not something to be taken lightly. It is an important responsibility and must be given to a person with a pure, servant's heart.

Don't be too quick to make someone a leader. Once a person is in a place of leadership it is hard to get them out. And, if the leader is corrupt then the whole community is going to suffer.

Given the amount of ink we've used already today, we don't have the space to dissect the qualifications for leadership. I think they are pretty straightforward and worth digesting. The question for the church today is whether our leaders are qualified and equipped for the job. The corollary challenge to the church is two-fold:

1) is our standard for leadership in alignment with the servanthood model of Jesus and Paul or is it being influenced by the success-at-all-costs model of corporate America, and

2) are we providing adequate resources to truly equip our leaders to shepherd God's flock and lead us into the heart of God?

Lesson 3

1 Timothy 3:16-4:16

Study Questions

How is the mystery described?

How is the false teaching described in 4:1-6?

Where is the believer's hope placed?

Restate Paul's instructions to Timothy in 4:6-16 in your own words.

Where is Timothy's focus supposed to be?

Food for Thought

Godliness is Mystery, not Method

I believe today's passage is the heart of the message to Timothy in this letter. The key phrase is "beyond all question the mystery of godliness is great." The mystery of godliness. Throughout the ages people of all cultures have asked the basic question of what it means to be godly. Every culture has a sense that humanity is messed up, that there is a higher power of some sort, and that the higher power sets the standard for what is "right" and what is "wrong." All the religions have devised ways to "appease the gods" in order to be in good standing with them. They devise religious systems and rituals that will instill "godliness" in the adherents and so insure safety in life and safe passage to the afterlife. It is no different with Judaism and Christianity. The rabbis in the first century had created the ideal formulas for "godliness" that, if followed, would usher in the Messianic Kingdom.

We all do it. That's because we're human. We are finite beings who need rules to follow, whether we like it or not. Even the people who claim "no rules" follow their own rules religiously.

In Ephesus Timothy was faced with a group of older men, perhaps even elders in the church, who were trying to establish a set of external rules for the church to follow in order to insure "godliness" among the body. One of Paul's biggest struggles, and the heart of his Gospel, was that true godliness doesn't look like that. You can hear Paul breathe in deeply and pause before he lets the word resonate on his tongue. "Godliness. Ah yes, the ever elusive ideal. How do we attain it? That is all of our quest. How true it is...this is a deep and profound mystery."

Mystery. That is the key to it all. The truth is that godliness is not found in a set of rules. It is not found in how many Bible verses you've memorized. It is not found in how often you attend church, or how many "souls you've saved." It is not found in the kind of food you eat or don't eat, or the movies you watch or don't watch, or the clothes you wear or don't wear, or the music listen to or don't listen to. That is surface stuff. Godliness isn't about what you do. It isn't even about who you are. Look at how Paul answers the question of mystery. He quotes an enigmatic poem.

> *Who was made visible in the flesh*
> *Was made right in the spirit*
> *Was seen by messengers (angelos)*
> *Was announced in nations*
> *Was trusted in the world*
> *Was taken up in glory.*

What does that mean exactly? The first word of this poem is a masculine, relative pronoun. A pronoun represents a real noun somewhere else in the passage. To whom is "who" referring? It is referring to the word "mystery." Here's the beauty of the Good News. The path of godliness is not a "what" or a "how," it's a "who." Isn't it interesting that Paul does not name the who? From the poem itself it is plain to see that Paul is referring to Jesus, yet he does not name Him. Hmmmm.... Mysterious, isn't it?

Let's jump down to 4:9-10. Mark this in your Bible. Highlight it. Underline it. Star it. Here is the key.

> We have put our hope in the living God, who is the Savior of all men, and especially of those who believe.

Read that a few times. How does that set in your theological grid?

Let's break it down.

- **We have put our hope in the living God.** We have not put our hope in our ability to adhere to a set of rules and regulations, insuring our godliness. We have not put our hope in our church, denomination, or creed. We have not put our hope in the abstract idea of "god" or "goodness" or "love." We have put our hope in the LIVING GOD. We have a relationship with the dynamic presence that gave us life. The living God is our Father, our Mother, our Master, our Gardener, our Source. He can be known and we can be known by Him and He can transform us from the inside out. That's mysterious and lovely and terrifying.

- **Who is the savior of all men, and especially those who believe.** Wouldn't you expect this phrase to say, "who is the Savior of those who have prayed the sinner's prayer, been baptized, have publicly proclaimed the name of Jesus, and are faithfully moving forward on a path of positive spiritual growth?" Yet, that is not what it says. He is the Savior of all men. Does that mean that all people are saved? I don't know. I don't think I can answer that question, nor is it my business to answer it. It may not even be my business to ask it. What I do know is that God does not want anyone to be lost. As we discussed earlier, He is *makrothumia* – long-suffering – and is a Father that does not want to see His children walk away from His love. I think it would do us well to soak on that idea for a while.

Let's finish today by looking at Paul's personal challenge to Timothy and see if it might not be a personal challenge to all of us as well. Paul gives Timothy a series of imperatives:

> *Train yourself to be godly.*

> *Set an example for the believers in speech, life, love, faith, and purity.*

> *Do not neglect your gift.*

> *Be diligent so that everyone may see your progress.*

> *Watch your life and doctrine closely.*

Timothy had the charge to be the leader of one of the biggest churches of Paul's ministry. Yet, even with that responsibility, where did Paul urge Timothy to focus his attention? On his own relationship with God. Train yourself to be godly. In light of our previous discussion about godliness we know that Paul was not telling Timothy to jump through religious hoops and rituals. He was telling Timothy to work on his relationship with God. Here is the key to leadership in the church and the key to basic spiritual health and growth in the body of Christ. Worry about your own heart, keep your focus on your source of light and life, and let the overflow of your heart be what touches other people's lives. People don't care what you say about God. They want to see God at work in your heart. If the love of God is not oozing out of your heart then you can point your finger all you want at someone's sin, and be as "doctrinally correct" as you want to be, but if the Spirit of God's love is not washing through you then they will see right through your charade and walk away.

I pray that we can be the kind of people that love God deeply and walk authentically and humbly in the world, demonstrating the Kingdom of God through our actions of love and hospitality to all people.

Lesson 4

- 1 Timothy 5:1-6:2

Study Questions

What attitude should Timothy take when he is called to rebuke someone? Why?

What was the problem that had arisen among the ministry to the widows? What are some parallels of this in our own culture?

How should the church treat an elder? Why?

How should the church treat everyone (including elders) according to verse 21?

How should slaves view their masters? Why?

Food for Thought

Rebuking with respect

Today's reading brings balance to the last lesson. In lesson 3, the message was all about not pointing the finger at others and keeping your eyes on your own stuff. You may have asked the question, "But aren't we supposed to exhort and admonish our brother if they fall into sin?" That is what Paul addresses today.

Timothy was the leader of the church. You can't be a good leader if you only look at your own life, as if you had blinders on, and never examine the flock. That's just silly. There is a time and a place where a leader has to do the tough job of "rebuking" people in the church that are in need of a reality check. Let's look closely at Paul's instruction on this matter. In 5:1-2 he spells out the guidelines. There are basically four kinds of people Timothy will have to deal with: older men, older women, younger men, younger women. There are two key words for how to deal with them: family and purity.

Family. We need to remember that the church is not a corporation. It is not a business or a club. You don't sign up and get a membership card that can be revoked at any time. We are part of a family. Family is a beautiful and an ugly thing all at the same time. You're stuck with family. In your biological family you have a mother, father, and siblings whether you like it or not. Even if you change your name and move to another country they are still your family. The same is true in the church. We may have thousands of sects and denominations in the world, but as hard as we try to deny it, we are still brothers and sisters in Christ. So, if you're stuck with somebody you have a choice. You either figure out how to get along, or you stay miserable. Paul reminds Timothy of the old proverb, "You catch more flies with honey than you do with vinegar." When you see a brother that has fallen into a pit, does it do any good to go over there and yell at him, "I told you to watch where you were going!!!" Of course not. If your child has been playing with a knife that you specifically told her not to play with and she cuts herself, do stand there and say, "We'll you can just stop that bleeding yourself because I told you not to play with that knife. Serves you right." Of course not. You rush over there and stop the bleeding. You get her healthy. Then you kindly, but firmly establish the fact that her natural consequences have taught her the lesson you've been speaking in words.

Purity. Before we go off on someone about their "sin" we need to stop ourselves and check

1 Timothy

our motives. Why are we about to rebuke them? Are we trying to establish dominance in the relationship? Are we trying to make them suffer for some pain they have inflicted on us? Are we just frustrated with our belief that the world is going to Hell in a hand basket and we are taking it out on the closest "sinner" we can find? Or, are we authentically demonstrating love to our brother or sister in an attempt to restore them to complete health?

There were many people that needed rebuking in Ephesus. Timothy was charged to do the rebuking. Let's look briefly at some of the problems that were going on.

Rebuking lazy widows

In the ancient world to be a widow was to be in a dire strait. Women couldn't own property; therefore they could not generate income. The only way a woman could have anything was through her marriage. If the husband died, then the woman could potentially be left out on the street. The government didn't really care about them. Fate had thrown its dice and they lost.

Next.

But the Gospel of Jesus urges the church to care for the down and out. We are supposed to help those in need. We are supposed to care for the orphans and widows. It was not different in Ephesus. The church had taken well to the task of caring for the widows. There was a problem, however. The church in Ephesus ran into the same problem that every charitable organization faces on a daily basis. There is a certain breed of person who loves a handout. The sin that grips this person's life is laziness. If there is a bleeding heart out there who will take care of them and make it so they don't have to work, then they'll say "yes" every time. These kinds of people make it difficult for the truly needy to get the help they need.

Paul's instructions to Timothy were to weed out the lazy widows. The challenge to them was this, "Are you truly needy? Is it possible that you have children that can take care of you? Is it possible that you could find work somewhere? Is it possible that you could remarry and be reestablished within society?"

The challenge for us today is similar. Our country is unique in that it has governmental systems that actually want to care for the poor and needy. Unfortunately, there are people who take advantage of the system. The burden of this problem falls both on the lazy person, and on the family. Many times we turn our family members over to the government and think, "they're not my

problem," when we could actually be giving them the help and support that they need. Thus freeing up resources for those who have nothing. The challenge is also to the family of God, the church. Should we allow the government to be the leader in taking care of the poor? The government does it because the church doesn't. Ouch.

Rebuking straying elders

5:17-25 are difficult to interpret. We don't have time to break it all down. Let me summarize what I think Paul is saying. It seems that there were problems among the elders of the church in Ephesus. Timothy had the difficult task of rebuking some of them. In this passage Paul instructs Timothy about how to treat elders.

Good elders need to be treated with respect. They feed and care for the flock, and they deserve honor and compensation. Don't be flippant with them.

However, don't show partiality toward elders and soft-peddle around them just because they are an elder. There is no favoritism in the body of Christ. Everyone is simply using their gifts, and your gift is teaching, so tell it like it is.

Don't be hasty to make someone an elder just because they are a prominent person in the community. They may have ulterior motives and, once in the position, may make your life miserable and drag you into legalism and sin. Give it time before you appoint someone. Let their lives be displayed before you for a long time before you hand over the mantle of authority to them. Time will show their true colors.

Rebuking defiant slaves

The issue of slavery is similar to the gender issues we discussed in chapter 2. Slavery and the domination of women was simply a fact of life in the first century. The truth is that the 20th century is the first century in the history of humanity where a world power did not own slaves and where women had the right to own land and vote. Does the fact that these social systems existed in the first century make them right? Does the fact that Paul addresses these social classes and does not boldly say to abolish them mean that they are supposed to be a part of the Kingdom of God? No, I don't believe it does.

Here's what was happening in Ephesus. The Gospel of Jesus was a liberating message for slaves. Do you remember the letter Paul wrote to Philemon? He reminded Philemon, the slave owner, that Onesimus, the slave, was no longer property, but was a brother in Christ. Can you imagine what that message would do to the heart and mind of a slave? "Yee-Haa! I don't have to work for the man, anymore. Down with the system! Slaves revolt!" Before you know it the Christian slaves are behaving very un-Christ like to their masters. It was probably causing chaos in the socio-economic arena of the city.

As Americans we know how difficult it is to transition from a slave-based economy to one of equality. It doesn't happen overnight. People are willing to kill and destroy over these things. 600,000 men lost their lives in the civil war. Thousands of black men, women, and children have been ruthlessly murdered simply because they were born black. Paul knew this about human nature. His advice to the slave was to slow down. Yes, the seeds of freedom have been sown, but let God bring them to fruition. If you force your hand there were be needless bloodshed that will be counterproductive to the Kingdom of God's love. Instead, learn to love your master and serve him well. Position means nothing anyway. You never know how far God's love can go if you give it a try.

Lesson 5

- 1 Timothy 6:3-6:21

Study Questions

What are the pitfalls with people who love controversy?

How are the false teachers described in 6:3-5?

What does Paul consider true "great gain?" Why?

How should we view riches? Why?

What was Timothy supposed to make his life's focus? Why?

Food for Thought

Redefining "Gain"

There are two challenges for us today.

The Gospel is not for sale.

At this point I must insert a personal story. Four years ago I left a well-paying job as a pastor at a mega-church. Walking away from the security of that position was, humanly speaking, a very scary thing to do. I really didn't have a job to go to; I simply had a sense that God was calling me to something different. It's four years later and God has miraculously supplied all our needs. Yet, in spite of God's great provision, I still allow my human fear and need to control my own destiny get in the way. Since you are reading these words you are probably aware that I spend a great deal of my time studying the Bible, creating illustrations to teach the passage, writing these daily studies, and posting them on the web. For the past few years I have been trying to figure out how I could make a living through selling this curriculum. That way I wouldn't have to be dependent on the church and have my relationship with my spiritual family be clouded by a paycheck. Over the past several months this dream of creating a curriculum development company came to a head and we were pumped about getting published and taking seminars on the road, the whole nine yards. Then, two weeks ago, by the grace of God, the reality hit us. We can't do it. Financially it would be nearly impossible to make a living selling Bible study materials. We took our prize pony out behind the shed and put her down, right there. It's over.

I'd be lying if I said that I wasn't sad for a few days. Now what, God? What do you want from me? Here's the message that I heard loud and clear, "Steve, the Gospel is not for sale." I realized that I was heading down the wrong path. I can't sell this stuff. It was right then and there that I decided to give it all away and be content with where I am and who I am. I may not be a big, successful pastor, or a best-selling author, or a famous artist, but that doesn't matter. I am a child of God. He has freely given me gifts and I will freely give them away. I have to say that a deep sense of peace has taken residence in my spirit since that decision. I'm not sure where my paycheck will be coming from, but I know that God is faithful and that he has placed me within a loving and faithful spiritual community.

Contentment

I believe this is one of the most difficult words for an American to digest. Contentment means being authentically satisfied with your current physical circumstances. America was built on ambition and drive. Bigger, better, faster, stronger! We work hard so that we can find the flow of upward mobility. The size of our house, the speed of our car, the beauty of our spouse, the depth of our portfolio; these are the things that make our mark in the universe. Without them we are nothing. When we hear the word contentment it feels synonymous with laziness and apathy.

Paul reminds Timothy to not get caught in that torrent of thought. It is so easy for spiritual leaders to allow materialistic standards of success to drive their decisions in ministry. We think that success is measured in numbers: numbers of people, numbers of programs, numbers of buildings, and numbers of dollars. Many leaders just plain see ministry as a way to make money and be wealthy. Paul reminds Timothy that material wealth means absolutely nothing. "But godliness with contentment is great gain." What is godliness again? It is a dynamic relationship with God. When we walk with God, we truly have all that we need. He will supply our needs; we don't have to worry about that. We simply need to walk with Him, be courageous enough to obey His calling, and willing to work hard. The rest is up to Him.

Today the challenge is simple to say, but difficult to live. Are you content? Are you grateful for what you have been given? Are you using all that you have been given for the benefit of the body of Christ, or are you hording it and constantly making plans on how you will "get ahead" in life?

Let's take Paul's challenge to heart today, "flee from all this and pursue righteousness, godliness, faith, love, endurance, and gentleness."

Titus

"Everyone from your town is a liar!" How'd you like that to be the way everyone perceived your hometown? It would make it pretty difficult to do business abroad, don't you think? That is the reputation of the people among whom Paul's second protégé was left to work. Last session we saw that Timothy was left in Ephesus to straighten out some messes there. This session we turn our attention to Titus who was left on the island of Crete to try to bring order to this unruly bunch.

We don't know much about Titus. Interestingly enough he is never mentioned in the story of Acts. However, there are two significant places where Paul demonstrates his long-term relationship with Titus. In Galatians 2 Paul describes the time he went to Jerusalem to discuss the issue of Gentiles and circumcision. He took Barnabus and Titus with him. Titus, being a full Greek, did not feel compelled to be circumcised after that meeting. The second place we meet Titus is in Paul's second letter to the Corinthians. Titus was one of the messengers that Paul sent back and forth between Ephesus and Corinth during those intense correspondences.

From this evidence we can surmise that Titus was a Greek who had become a follower of Jesus. We don't know where he was from, but he was in Antioch with Paul. We also know that Paul trusted him implicitly to be his representative during his missionary journeys. Finally, because of this letter, we also know that Paul entrusted Titus to carry out a very similar charge that he had given to Timothy. Titus was the leader of the church on the island of Crete.

As we mentioned last session, this letter was written after Paul's release from the house arrest found in Acts 28. During his post-Acts ministry Paul apparently spent some time planting churches on the island of Crete and left Titus there to do the follow-up.

If you have the time, it is an interesting study to compare the letter to Timothy with the letter to Titus. In many ways they are very similar. Both are personal letters written from a mentor to a protégé. Both deal with issues of leadership in the church. Both deal with specific issues of social ethics and conduct among the body of believers. Both give the challenge to the young leader to refute the false teaching that was bubbling up in the church and to shut down those who were creating opposition to the message. Yet, there is one very obvious difference between them. The letter to Titus seems much less personal that that to Timothy. 1 Timothy had a great deal of passion and compassion oozing between the lines. While the letter to Titus delivers the same basic content, it seems much more dry and to the point. There is no way of knowing the reason for this difference; it only awakens our interpretive radar to state the observation.

Sound doctrine

In the introduction to the Pastoral Letters we mentioned that there are some unique terms and phrases in these letters that are not used in any of Paul's other letters. The unique phrase found in Titus that we will focus on is "sound doctrine." While this is always a relevant topic, regardless of context, it seems an especially appropriate topic for our current state of affairs in the local church of the Western world. There is great debate about what is "sound doctrine" and how it should be presented and/or defended. In Paul's day he was constantly being challenged by the religious establishment and accused of being a heretic, an anti-Moses (Law) apostate, and a mamby-pamby liberal thinker. The situation on Crete was no different. Titus was faced with a group of teachers that desired to pull the church away from the simple message of Jesus into a complex set of rules, regulations, hyper-spirituality, and "correct doctrine." In an attempt to counteract this movement and equip Titus to stand firm against this movement, Paul quotes two different "confessions" that had already become established in the early church to remind Titus of the heart of the Gospel. As we read through these studies we will examine what 'sound doctrine" really is and how we are to appropriate it and exemplify it in our every day lives.

Lesson 1

- Titus 1:1-9

Study Questions

Why did Paul leave Titus on Crete?

List the "qualifications" for being an elder.

For being an overseer.

How does this list compare to Paul's instructions to Timothy in 1 Timothy 3?

Food for Thought

Leading the Church

If one of the biggest challenges facing Titus was that of discerning "sound doctrine," challenging false teachers, and sifting through what is right from wrong, then it makes sense that Paul would begin with the qualifications of a leader. There is a cliché that says, "Speed of the leader, speed of the team." This is especially true in the church. If you were to take all of the churches in America and line them up along a wall with a brief description of their personality, and then look at the senior leader of that church, you would probably find a strong correlation between the leader's profile and that of the church. Whether it is right or wrong, I don't know, but churches tend to take on the personality of the senior leader. So, you had better be sure you know who those leaders are before you put them into place.

During our study of 1 Timothy we blew past this topic in lieu of others. Today we will take the time to look at this famous passage and see what it takes to be a good leader of the church. Of course, one of the biggest issues in our current church culture is whether being an "elder" in the church is a male-only club, or whether it is open to women as well. This is not the time to go down that road. All we can say with certainty is that the Greco-Roman-Judaic world was definitely a male-only club and Paul was certainly operating within those cultural parameters. Other than the issue of being the husband of one wife, all of the other traits have no gender boundaries. I ask that, for this discussion, you remove that controversy from this list of leadership qualities and simply read it for the essence of the kind of character that is needed to be entrusted with the spiritual leadership of God's people.

It starts at home

In our English translations it appears that Paul begins a new thought in verse 6 and lists the first quality of the elder. This is not the flow of the Greek, however. The sentence actually starts in verse 5 and runs through the end of verse 6. Here is a literal translation:

> Because of this I left you in Crete, in order that you might straighten out the things left undone and appoint elders by city, as I directed you to do, if someone is unreproachable, a man of one woman, having faithful children, not in accusation of dissipation (unrestrained pursuit of pleasure) or unsubmissive.

Then he starts a new sentence and says:

It is necessary for the overseer to be unreproachable...

There are two observations that we can make from this section. First, as we observe the grammar, it appears that there are a couple of ways to translate and interpret verses 5-6. The first way is to do what most of the English translations do and separate it into two separate sentences, thus making it appear that Paul was listing the first quality of an elder in an equal manner to verse 7. The second option, which seems to fit more with the original syntax, seems to read like this: "I left you to appoint elders in every city; this is assuming there are men in that city who are good family men that have no unruly wives or children." In other words, Titus did not need to feel the pressure to appoint an elder if there weren't any qualified candidates in the church. Given the nature of the Cretans and their distorted views of sexuality and order it was highly possible that there weren't any candidates in many of the regions at that time.

The second observation has to do with the key words. In verse 5 Paul told Titus that he left him there to appoint "elders" in every city. The Greek word is *presbuteros* and literally means "older man." It was common practice, both in Jewish and Greco-Roman cities to have a group of elders appointed to govern the daily affairs of the community. Every synagogue had elders that provided leadership in the faith community. Paul was simply working within the established traditions and acknowledging the need for some father figures in the growing community of Jesus followers.

The second key word gives us a reason for a slight pause. In verse 7 Paul switches words. He does not say that the *presbuteros* should be above reproach, he says the *episkopos*, or overseer, should be above reproach. If you sound out those two Greek words --- *presbuteros* and *episkopos* – you may recognize them. Two entire church denominations have been formed over the argument that stems from this passage. The Presbyterians (*presbuteros*) believe in a government that is governed by a board of men called elders that each has equal power to make decisions: leadership by committee. The Episcopalians (*episkopos*) believe that there should be a singular leader (bishop – another translation of *episkopos*) that has absolute control of the leadership mantle. So, the question is whether Paul was a) making a distinction between the elder and the bishop as two different roles in the church, or b) using the words interchangeably in that the act of overseeing the flock was the duty of the elder.

Obviously, in light of two very large denominations that each take differing opinions on the subject, there is no clear cut answer. I think the important thing is that the church needs leadership. And, more importantly, that leadership needs to of a high quality of person. Here's what is most important in this first section. A good leader of the church needs to first be a good leader at home. Paul puts it more clearly in his instructions to Timothy in 1 Timothy 3:5

If anyone does not know how to manage his own family, how can he take care of God's church?

Let's stop right here and place a challenge to all church leaders. Your first responsibility is to raise up your children in the Lord. You are the priest of your family. You are to love your wife more highly than yourself and provide a nurturing environment for her where she can thrive and grow and become the woman God intended her to be. She needs to feel safe, protected, valued, honored, and spiritually nourished. You are the god-image that is being imprinted on your children's minds and hearts. Are they seeing an authentic human being that is striving to love and honor God, that loving corrects and comforts them, or do they see an absent father who puts his work and status above his family? Too many pastors have been sucked into the meat grinder of church life and the allure of 'successful ministry' and have lost their families in the process. Too many wives and children have turned away from their faith because of the "other woman" named the church. While this may seem like an unfair burden to place on a leader's shoulders, it is still the truth. I am not calling for leaders to be super-heroes. Just the opposite. I'm calling for leaders to leave the superman costume in the comic book and be a real person that allows his leadership to begin authentically in his home and then to naturally overflow into the church. If things aren't going well at home, don't cover it up for the "sake of the church." Deal with it. Get healthy. Don't play hurt, because then everyone suffers. God can handle the church without you for a while. If you are doing well at home, then the rest will fall into place.

What he is not

In verses 7-8 Paul sets up a contrast. In verse 7 he says what an overseer should not be and in verse 8 he says what an overseer should be. It seems that he is making a contrast between what the world's standards of leadership are versus what Jesus' standards of leadership are within His Kingdom. Look at the list of what the leader is not and compare it to our standards of successful leaders in corporate America, the military, or the sports world.

He is not

Overbearing

Quick-tempered

Given to drunkenness

Violent

Pursuing dishonest gain

  Hmmm.....

What he is

Now let's look at the positive list

He is to be

Lover of the stranger (Hospitable: this means a lover of strangers; one who takes in the outcast and makes them feel welcome)

Lover of good

Of sound mind

Just

Holy/devoted

Self-controlled

One who holds to the teaching of the faithful word

If you were to post this list up in some leadership circles you would probably get a moment of silence, then a loud outburst of laughter. "You are talking about a man, right?!?" We must remember that much of the machismo and "tough guy" models that have been developed in our culture do not come from wisdom, but come from fear and survival instincts. The way of Jesus teaches us a deeper truth, that, in the long run, it takes deep, still waters to truly lead a group of people through the chaos that is inevitably the stuff of life.

What he is to do

Finally, Paul concludes with the "why" of this list of character traits. There are two things that the leader is supposed to do. The leader is to

1. *Encourage others with sound doctrine*

2. *Refute those who oppose it.*

We will spend the rest of the session discussing what "sound doctrine" is. For now let's focus on the two important qualities of the leader. The leader is a feeder and a protector. It is no wonder why Jesus chose the image of a shepherd to describe leadership in His Kingdom. A leader must feed the sheep to keep them healthy. He must also ward off the predators that seek to harm the sheep. Isn't it interesting that both of these qualities seem to be orbiting the issue of teaching? What we believe determines who we are and how we behave. It is the job of the leader to ensure that the flock is getting a truthful and accurate delivery of the message of Jesus. It is so easy for the message to become distorted through the lenses of time, language, culture, and politics. The leader's job is to make sure that the message stays pure and relevant. That the food stays fresh and the water clean, so that the sheep will be healthy. He is to be aware of the spiritual "junk food" filled with preservatives and byproducts that many try to slip into the sheep chow or use to lure the sheep away. The point for today is that the number one responsibility of the leader is not to attend board meetings, or build bigger buildings, or get the lighting just right on the stage. The primary responsibility of the leader is to be on his face before the one true Shepherd, digesting the Word for himself, then serving it up in healthy portions for the church to nourished, equipped, and protected.

Lesson 2

- Titus 1:10-16

Study Questions

How does Paul describe the opposition that Titus was facing?

How does Paul feel about the opposition? Why?

What does their false teaching seem to be about?

How is Titus supposed to deal with the false teachers?

Food for Thought

There are two questions on the table for our discussion of Paul's letter to Titus. The first is "what is sound teaching." The second is "How do you deal with people who are teaching your people things that are not in agreement with sound teaching?"

This passage deals mostly with the second question. In verses 10-16 it is easy to detect Paul's frustration with his ever-present nemesis –the circumcision group. We have encountered this philosophy many times as we have read through Paul's letters. Let's make some observations about Paul's instructions on how to deal with these people.

They exist. Let's face it, people love to argue. No matter where you go, no matter who you are, no matter what side you take, or what you say...someone will disagree with you and want to correct you. If you want to be in leadership you had better get used to it.

It is OK to not like them. What?!? I thought Jesus said to love your enemies? Sure he did. You can love your enemies with the love of God and authentically desire their best interest, but that doesn't mean He said to have intimate community with your enemies. That is actually impossible. We must keep in mind that Paul is talking to Titus about leading the intimate community called the church. The only way for intimacy to work is for the people in the church to connect at a fundamental level of belief, faith, and practice. If there is not unity on the essentials of faith and practice then there will be disunity – disease – in the body and it will get sick. It is OK to ward off dangerous elements to the flock that you are protecting. Obviously Paul had no problem with this.

They are dangerous and must be silenced. Notice what effects Paul said these people will have on the church. Whole households will be destroyed. There is debate over what exactly Paul meant by the word "household" but it is most likely that he is referring to the local house church. At that time all the churches met in homes and functioned as a family, or household, of God. This house church was the base of intimacy for the body in which people could become vulnerable with one another as they came as equals to the table of God for communion with Him and each other. Here they prayed for each other, met each others needs, and truly became involved in one another's lives. Imagine how destructive it would be if one or two people started sowing seeds of doubt regarding the integrity of the leader of the truth of the teaching. Soon people would begin retracting back into their prison of self-protection and the intimacy of the church would be destroyed as brother turns on brother. This must not happen and it is the job of the leader to protect the church from allowing the roots of these weeds to set in and take over the garden (sorry for the mixed metaphor!).

The goal of rebuke is not hate, but correction. Notice that Paul doesn't begin with hatred and expulsion. First he says to rebuke them so that they will be sound in faith. Even in the midst of protecting the flock there is still the attitude of loving teaching. The definition of rebuke is "to expose error for the purpose of repentance and reconciliation."

Beliefs impact perception. In verse 15 Paul exposes a deep and profound truth. He says to the pure all things are pure. Now, we need to be careful with this verse. Many have taken it too far and reasoned, "Hey, Jesus made me pure by Grace, so that means that I can do anything I want and, since I've been made pure, it is pure as well." With this philosophy they have indulged in all sorts of self-destructive behavior with no remorse. I don't believe that is what Paul is saying. We must remember that the immediate context to what Paul was referring when he said "all things" was most likely the issue of dietary laws. Under the new covenant, in light of Peter's vision of the sheet full of animals, it was no longer necessary to distinguish between clean and unclean animals. While we need to keep that context in mind, and do not want to err to the extreme, I do think he is referring to more than just the issue of meat. He is reminding Titus that the point of the Good News of Jesus is not about external behavior modification through the adherence of enforced laws, but rather, it is the inner transformation of the heart to the point where a persons perceptions come in line with the purity and heart of God, thus making all behavior pure because it flows from a pure conscience. Jesus said it is not what goes into a man that makes him unclean, but what comes out of a man. Two people can do the same action and, depending upon the state of their heart, for one it is sinful and for the other it is not.

Actions speak louder than words. The final observation for today is simple. When people come into the church and start boldly proclaiming that they have "the truth" and that everyone is deceived or wrong, don't get too flustered. Simply wait and watch. What kind of attitude does their belief ignite in their heart? Does it soften and open their heart so that they exude the love of Jesus to all people? Or, does it harden their heart and cause them to hate people and draw hard lines of "in" and "out" over which they are the judge? In the end, the true colors will show through and you will either see the face of Jesus, or you will not. He will let you know.

Lesson 3

- Titus 2

Study Questions

How do you define the phrase "sound doctrine?"

Where do you get your definition?

Create a chart that shows Paul's instructions for each type of person.

What have you learned from these observations?

Restate 2:11-14 in your own words.

What is the heart of the Gospel according to these verses?

Food for Thought

As we look at chapter 2 today we will deal with three topics. First, we'll tackle the definition that we have been dancing around this session – what is 'sound doctrine.' Second, we will look at the 'sound doctrine' as it applied to the household. Third, we will look at one of the first "confessions" that had become established in the church that attempted to encapsulate the heart of the 'sound doctrine' of the Good News of Jesus.

Sound Doctrine

Let's first define each word. "sound" is the Greek word *hugiaino*. It literally means "healthy." In the Greek world health was defined as being balanced. All excesses were avoided. So, a teaching that is 'sound' is one that is rational and balanced and reasonable.

"Doctrine" is a loaded word in our culture. In the New Testament the word is *didaskalia* and simply means "teaching."

Over the millennia of Western Christianity the battle has raged over what is 'sound doctrine.' Of course, every denomination and sect believes that their particular interpretation of scripture and its subsequent theological construction is the basis for all sound doctrine -- thus aligning them with the apostle Paul -- and that all other views fall into the category of the empty talkers and deceivers that must be silenced. Hence, the Crusades, the Spanish Inquisition, the 100 years war, various ethnic cleansings, countless church splits, etc, etc, ad nausea.

Why does this happen? Perhaps one reason this has happened throughout history is due to the interpretation that reads the phrase "sound doctrine" to mean "absolute, definitive truth that is unalterable and completely reflects what is "right" and "wrong" for all time; therefore, if you disagree with any part of it you are going burn in the eternal fires of Hell and if you agree with it you will pass through the pearly gates and live in Heaven forever." If this is how you define "sound doctrine" then it is easy to see why so much is at stake to make sure you are on the correct side of the "sound" line.

What if this definition isn't quite right? What if we defined it according to the definition of the words – healthy teaching? Teaching that is healthy; that produces health in the body of Christ. Do you see how this changes the focus? Healthy teaching is not as concerned about absolute correctness as it is about promoting healthy body life in the Kingdom of God. Jesus didn't present a Gospel of propositional truths and new theological constructions. He taught in parables and enigmatic methods that deemphasized propositional truth and reemphasized ethical behavior. Ethics were not based upon "correctness according to law" but were based upon Jesus Himself. Our standard is not a humanly constructed system of do's and don'ts; it is the standard of the person of Jesus as He modeled Kingdom life for us.

Perhaps our standard of healthy teaching should not be the academy – the logical dissection of theological models – but rather the fruit of the branch from which it stems. Jesus said He had one command for us to obey; the command to love. If we remain in Him we will bear fruit, and that fruit is love. If a person's teaching fosters hatred, or fear, or animosity, or bitterness toward another, then it seems pretty safe to say that it is not healthy teaching that promotes unity and growth in the body of Christ.

Healthy teaching should promote, first and foremost, the love of God demonstrated in the world. It should promote peace and unity in the body and service to the world. It should inspire the church to be the blessing to the world that God has always intended His family to be so that all people, in every nation, can see, first-hand, that God is a loving God that desires to lavish them with His Grace and enjoy life with them. He seeks to set them free from hatred and bitterness and war and oppression and famine and suffering. He invites them to sit at His table and feast, and it is His church that is called to do the inviting and the presenting of the hors d'oeuvres tray. That is healthy teaching. That is sound doctrine.

Sound doctrine in community

In 2:2-10 we run into the controversial subject of gender, generational, and social-class issues again. Here Paul instructs Titus on how he should teach men, women, and slaves. The following commentary does a good job of helping us to make sure we have on the right lenses when we read this passage.

Because the Romans suspected minority religions, especially religions from the East with ecstatic elements to their worship, of subverting traditional family values, minority religions often followed the philosophers in exhorting adherents to follow "household codes." These codes instructed patriarchs of households how to treat each member of the household, especially wives, children and slaves. Under the broad topic of "household management," such codes also extended to treatment of parents, duties to the state (3:1) and duties to the gods. Because the church met in homes and was viewed as a sort of extended family around the household of the patron in whose home the believers met, the instructions naturally extended to categories of relationships in the church.

Early Christian adaptation of Roman social relations was important for the church's witness to society and for diminishing preventable opposition to the gospel (2:5, 8, 10). Modern readers often recognize only the traditional values of their own culture (e.g., traditional family values of the nineteenth-to mid-twentieth-century U.S. middle class), but one should recognize that Paul addresses instead the traditional Roman values of his day (including the household slavery of his day, which differed from many other societies' models of slavery).

A "confession" vv. 11-15

Throughout the letter to Titus Paul uses the phrase "these things" to summarize a passage he has just stated. Many scholars believe that this phrase indicates that Paul has just quoted a commonly accepted "confession of faith" that had been developed in the early church. In other words, during the 30 years since the time of Jesus, His followers had already developed many hymns and poems that were intended to preserve the core teaching of and about Jesus for the purpose of uniting the church. We call them "confessions" because the person who recites them is confessing to all people that he believes the words to be true. With this in mind let's break down the confession that Paul is proposing to contain the core truth of the Good News of Jesus.

For the grace of God that brings salvation has appeared to all men.

The heart of the Gospel is grace. Grace is a gift. To whom has this grace been presented? All men. Too many times we want to horde God's grace and believe that it was a gift just for us and people who look and feel just like us. The problem is that when we horde a gift it ceases to be a gift. Grace is to be given, always...everywhere.

It teaches us to say "No" to ungodliness and worldly passions, and to live self-controlled, upright and godly lives in this present age. God's grace is not license to sin. People who advocate grace for all people are promoting 'wild living." Far from it. God's salvation is salvation from our own self-destructive patterns. He has presented His grace to the

world to set them free from all the muck. Notice how it doesn't say it "forces" us to say "no." It teaches us to say "no." This is the gracious process of spiritual formation and God's patient leading in the lives of anyone who wants to follow.

while we wait for the blessed hope—the glorious appearing of our great God and Savior, Jesus Christ,

Throughout the Old Testament the hope of Israel was that God would send the Messiah to sit on David's throne and reestablish the Kingdom in the world, and that through that Kingdom, peace would be restored to the nations. That hope was still alive in the heart of Paul. As Christians through the ages our focus has tended to be on the death of Jesus and whether or not we said the right words in the right prayer in order to secure our position in Heaven when we die. That never seems to be Paul's (or the early church's) emphasis. Their hope was not in the past, but was focused on the future. Their hope was in the fact that God loved the world so much that He would someday bring peace to the world through the glorious appearing of Jesus. That is the mission of the Kingdom of God, both now and in the future. The people of God are to bring the love and shalom (peace) of God to all nations.

who gave Himself for us to redeem us from all wickedness

Jesus' death set us free from wickedness and all the junk that keeps our backs turned from God. He did it for us. It is done. We have been bought back.

and to purify for Himself a people that are His very own, eager to do what is good.

The purpose of the whole deal is to reconcile the estranged relationship between God and man. How wonderful it is that man was the one who turned his back on God, but God was the one who paid the price. God does not want to torch us and torment us, He wants to purify us, draw us close to Himself, and grow us up to be the mature children that we were originally intended to be.

That's it. There are no doctrinal statements over theories of atonement, or eschatological views, or theories of inspiration. God loves us. He paid the price; He wants to make us whole. We can't wait until He returns and sets everything aright. Until then we wait and serve, in love. That's healthy teaching.

Lesson 4

- Titus 3:1-2

Study Questions

Using the infinitive verbs (a verb with "to" in front of it; to play; to run) make a list of all the ways Paul wants the Christians on Crete to be.

Meditate on this list and ask God to show you areas in your own life where you can grow according to this list.

Food for Thought

A worthy checklist

Today we are going to meditate on two simple verses. Here Paul gives a list of character qualities that describes how a member of God's family should be and should conduct himself in the world. It would do us good to hold this list up as a mirror and make sure that our behavior towards all people reflects these qualities.

(This is my translation, based on the observation that this list is organized around the infinitive form of the verbs.)

Remind the people:

To be submissive toward authorities and rulers

There's that crazy word again – submit. The Greek is h*upotasso* and it means to place under something else. In the first century the church lived in the shadow of the Empire. There is a great mysterious tension in the message of Jesus that Paul preached to the world. On the one hand he claimed that Jesus is the Supreme Ruler of the universe, far above the Emperor. Yet, on the other hand, he instructed the church to submit to the emperor and the local magistrates. Why would he do that? Why didn't Paul call for a political revolution to overthrow the evil Empire and free the slaves, feed the poor, and liberate the oppressed? Why? Because Paul knew that a violent course of action would be counterproductive to the Gospel. We don't fight violence with violence. We don't fate hatred with hatred. Paul knew the truth of Jesus' parable concerning the mustard seed. The Kingdom of God is like a seed. When you plant the authentic seed of God's love in the heart of one individual, and that love grows inside of them and transforms them to the point where they love even their enemies, then that love becomes contagious. The love spreads, and eventually entire systems change from the inside out. The Roman Empire was a stark reality in the church's life. It wasn't going anywhere. It was far better to humbly submit, than to needlessly draw attention and stir up anger and pointless persecution.

To obey

Ouch! There's another very un-American word. We don't want to obey. We want to be free spirits who create our own destinies and do what we like. That's because we forget that we aren't God. There is a Father and ruler of the universe. Just because He's gracious and loving doesn't mean He's permissive and overlooks sin. God loves us so much He established basic principles for us to follow. If we act unkindly toward one another it will eventually turn back on us and become disastrous to the community. If we would all simply acknowledge our place as equal members in the world and obey Jesus' command to love one another, then things would move along smoothly. As soon as we allow pride and greed to get in the way, then we start hating and hurting one another.

To be prepared to do all good

What does it mean to do "good?" We have a tendency to define "good" as "right" as if we are supposed to figure out the rules and follow them legalistically in order to be "good." The term "good" in this passage is the term *agathos* and has the sense of that which is best or useful. When we are challenged to do "good" in the Kingdom of God we are challenged to do that which is best for the other. We need to be always prepared to look out for the interest of others, and, putting their needs above our own, seek to serve their best interest.

To blaspheme/slander no one

The old saying "sticks and stones may break my bones, but words will never hurt me" is just plain wrong. Words are lethal. One of the most hateful and hurtful things we can do towards someone is to speak harshly against them and spread seeds of hatred about them in the minds and hearts of others. The Greek word here is *blasphamao* from which we derive the word "blaspheme." So many Christians are crying out against those who "blaspheme" the name of the Lord, yet, in their crying they blaspheme other humans in far more destructive ways. If we would simply keep our tongues in check and ask God to allow us to see others through His eyes, then we would cease the verbal bloodshed and begin the healing process.

To be non-fighters, gentle, demonstrating all meekness to all men.

Three great men modeled this style of world transformation: Jesus, Gandhi, and Martin Luther King Jr. Paul instructed the church in Rome to

Do not repay anyone evil for evil. Be careful to do what is right in the eyes of everybody. If it is possible, as far as it depends on you, live at peace with everyone. Do not take revenge, my friends, but leave room for God's wrath, for it is written: "It is mine to avenge; I will repay," says the Lord. On the contrary: "If your enemy is hungry, feed him; if he is thirsty, give him something to drink. In doing this, you will heap burning coals on his head." Do not be overcome by evil, but overcome evil with good." (Romans 12:17-21)

Stop right now and try to imagine something. Imagine what the world would be like if every Christian in the world demonstrated these attitudes. Do you hear the silence? Do you feel the sense of peace rush through the world like a wave of healing water? It begins with us. We cannot control others or change the world. Yet, we can control our own heart. We can ask God to take over our lives and give us the strength to submit to him, obey His command to love, and to live in other-oriented peace with all people. The Kingdom of God on Earth.

Lesson 5

- Titus 3:3-15

Study Questions

How were we before grace affected us?

How are we after grace affected us? Why?

Why did God pour out His grace?

Who deserves His grace?

What does it take to receive His grace?

Why does Paul want Titus to stress "these things?"

What is Titus to avoid? Why?

Food for Thought

Look at verse 8. There's that phrase "these things" again. Remember we said that phrase was a signal that Paul had just quoted a "confession" of the early church. That means verses 3-7 are another snapshot of the Gospel. This snapshot gives us a before and after scenario of the effects of Jesus' message on our lives. In verse 3 we see the before:

we too were

foolish,

disobedient,

deceived and

enslaved by all kinds of passions and pleasures.

We lived in

malice and

envy,

being hated and

hating one another.

If we analyze this list we see the plain effects of sin-sickness on the nature of humanity. The first four traits have to do with a person being isolated from himself; living in a prison of darkness, delusion, and self-hatred. The second four traits demonstrate how sin isolates us from each other. When we look through sin-sick eyes we see the other person as a threat, the enemy, someone to be distrusted and despised.

We must emphasize the most insidious aspect of sin and its effects on the world – isolation. We have been separated from God, from each other, from ourselves, and from nature. We are alone in the dark cosmos and live in a world of fear. That is the human condition. That is Hell. And that breaks God's heart.

Then we move on to verse 8 and encounter one of the greatest words in the Bible --- BUT! It's a contrasting conjunction. But wait! There's more! The story isn't over! Look what comes busting through the prison gates; what comes gushing forth over the dam in verse 4-7! Let's stop and relish each delectable morsel of this delicious picture of God's Kingdom.

But when the kindness and love of God our Savior appeared,

Kindness and love. This is the God we serve. When sees people wallowing in the darkness of verse 3, He doesn't say, "Serves you right. That's what you get for rebelling against me!" Just the opposite. He reaches out and says, "I love you and do not want you to wallow in your own muck. Give me your hand, I'll pull you out."

He saved us, not because of righteous things we had done, but because of His mercy.

> Mercy. No one, anywhere, has ever been good enough to earn God's favor. We don't earn it, we simply accept it. Wouldn't it be great if we could turn to the next guy who is wallowing in muck and treat him the same way God has treated us?

He saved us through the washing of rebirth and renewal by the Holy Spirit,

> Washing, rebirth, and renewal. Not punishment and payback. God is the author of life and He desires to redeem all things. He desires to see people made clean and refreshed and renewed as they enter into an authentic relationship with Him. It's as if God's Spirit is a fresh river of water that is constantly flowing around us. We can either resist it, or let it carry us along. As followers of Jesus, being carried along in the river, it is our job to be a conduit of the refreshing water of the Spirit.

whom He poured out on us generously through Jesus Christ our Savior,

> God poured this soul-cleansing water on us when we were dirty. He didn't tell us to get cleaned up before we could come and drink at His "Member's Only" drinking fountain. Jesus was the vessel of this soul-cleansing water. We are called to follow Jesus' example, and so we are called to overflow cleansing water on people through our lives, not stand off to the side and condemn them for being dirty.

so that, having been justified by His grace, we might become heirs having the hope of eternal life.

> In our world when we hear the phrase "eternal life" we automatically think of pie in the sky in the great by and by. We think eternal life is something that begins when we die. Think about that for a minute. If something is eternal it has no beginning or end. If "eternal life" is something that begins when we die, then how can it be eternal?
>
> In John 17:3, Jesus said, *"Now this is eternal life: that they may know you, the only true God, and Jesus Christ, whom you have sent."* What if eternal life is not a state of existence after we die, but is the process of entering into the dynamic flow of God's presence and His Kingdom right now? God's life is eternal and our hope is in the fact that we can participate with Him in it, right now. We can step into the stream and flow in the Spirit of God's love and be conduits of that love in the world that so desperately needs to be washed in its cleansing power. What would happen

if we took our eyes off of the afterlife and pointing the fingers at all the "sinners" in the world and starting living in the hope of our present interaction with the eternal life and became the conduits of its healing power in our world right now?

If we understood the Gospel in this light then we would have to agree with Paul as he says in verse 8,

> *This is a trustworthy saying. And I want you to stress these things, so that those who have trusted in God may be careful to devote themselves to doing what is good. These things are excellent and profitable for everyone.*

We are to be devoted to doing what is good; that is, what is good and in the best interest of the other; what is beneficial for everyone.

Notice the contrast that Paul makes in verses 9-11. What is the greatest evil and threat to the Kingdom of God? Divisiveness. Why is this so dangerous? Well, what is divisiveness? It is that which divides. When things are divided they become isolated from the other parts. What is isolation? It is the result of sin. It is Hell. That is why Jesus could look at the Pharisees and say, in Matthew 23:15,

> *"Woe to you, teachers of the Law and Pharisees, you hypocrites! You travel over land and sea to win a single convert, and when he becomes one, you make him twice as much a son of hell as you are.*

As we end this session of study, let's pull back from the trees and look at the forest of this letter Paul wrote to Titus. Titus was living on an island that was under the shadow of the Roman Empire. They were a conquered people. They were a divided people. They had the reputation of being liars and brutes. They lived in rigid social roles where the aristocracy was divided from the poor, men were divided from women, and masters were divided from slaves. Fear, greed, envy, and power governed every flow of society. What did the Kingdom of God look like in this mess? Was Titus called to go on a rampage and blast all the atrocities in the social system? Was he supposed to start taking names of all the sinners and bring justice on their heads? No. He was called to love. He was called to bring "healthy teaching" to the body of Christ and remind the church that their role in the world was to be the conduit of God's soul-cleansing Spirit to all people. And they were to do this through their actions and attitudes toward everyone.

2 Timothy

We've come to the final leg of our journey. It's been 30 years since that zealous persecutor of the followers of the Way set out on a murderous rampage to the city of Damascus and met the risen Jesus in a burst of bright light. Since that time he has traveled across most of the known world, planting churches among the Gentile people. He has been accused of blasphemy and heresy. He has been ridiculed, flogged, stoned, exiled, falsely accused, imprisoned, and released. During those journeys he wrote at least ten letters to the churches that he had planted; encouraging them, rebuking them, and instructing them on how to practically live out the Kingdom of God in their own town.

As we have seen over the past two sessions, Paul was released after the house arrest recorded in Acts 28. In his post-Acts ministry he traveled throughout Asia, Macedonia, Greece, and (most likely) made the journey all the way to Spain. During those post-Acts journeys Paul wrote to his two protégés, Timothy and Titus, to encourage them in their leadership posts.

This week everything has changed. At some point along the way Paul was arrested again. This time

he was not treated with dignity and placed under house arrest. This time he was thrown into the dungeon and treated like a common criminal. It is from this dungeon that Paul writes his final letter to his beloved "son" Timothy.

In order for us to grasp the depth of this letter it would be good for us to step back and look at the political climate of the Empire at this time. Early on in Paul's career (approx. A.D. 54) there was a power shift in the Empire from Emperor Claudius (Caligula) to Nero. Nero was 17 when he came to power and it is believed that he claimed his throne because of murder and treachery perpetrated by his mother. Nero was a narcissistic emperor who cared more about playing in the games and entertainment than about distributing justice throughout the Empire. With each passing year of his reign, tension and animosity toward Nero among the Senate and the army grew higher. Shortly after Paul's first imprisonment and release from Rome there was a tragic event that took place in that city. Nearly half of Rome burned to the ground. Nero's opponents blamed him for the fire and even accused him of setting it himself. Here is a quote from the Roman historian, Tacitus, that describes the events.

> *And so, to get rid of this rumor, Nero set up [i.e., falsely accused] as the culprits and punished with the utmost refinement of cruelty a class hated for their abominations, who are commonly called Christians. Nero's scapegoats were the perfect choice because it temporarily relieved pressure of the various rumors going around Rome. Christus, from whom their name is derived, was executed at the hands of the procurator Pontius Pilate in the reign of Tiberius. Checked for a moment, this pernicious superstition again broke out, not only in Iudaea, the source of the evil, but even in Rome... Accordingly, arrest was first made of those who confessed; then, on their evidence, an immense multitude was convicted, not so much on the charge of arson as because of [their] hatred for the human race. Besides being put to death they were made to serve as objects of amusement; they were clothed in the hides of beasts and torn to death by dogs; others were crucified, others set on fire to serve to illuminate the night when daylight failed. Nero had thrown open his grounds for the display, and was putting on a show in the circus, where he mingled with the people in the dress of charioteer or drove about in his chariot. All this gave rise to a feeling of pity, even towards men whose guilt merited the most exemplary punishment; for it was felt that they were being destroyed not for the public good but to gratify the cruelty of an individual." (Tacitus, Annales, xv.44)*

The A.D. 60's were a very difficult decade for both the Christians and the Jews. Ever since the days of Jesus tension was rising in Jerusalem and the people were straining terribly under the yoke of Roman occupation. There were continual uprisings and revolts in the city and claims of Messiahs that had come to reestablish the rightful King on David's throne. The tension grew so great that a war between Rome broke out in 66 and lasted until 70. That war ended with the total destruction of the Temple in Jerusalem at the hands of the Romans. The Jews were utterly defeated and dispersed throughout the world, not to be reestablished as a nation until 1948.

It was during the heat of this war that Paul was arrested. Paul had two things working against him at this time. He was stuck right in the middle of the conflict. On the one side the Jews hated him because they felt he was a sell out to the Romans. He taught his followers to "submit to the King and the rulers and authorities." That was treasonous speak for a true Jewish patriot. He also claimed that Jesus was the Messiah, but what kind of Messiah would allow Himself to be crucified at the hands of the enemy and then not do anything to overthrow their evil power? Paul was a threat to all that was good and decent and he was a hater of God. On the other hand, he was not very popular with the Romans either. First of all, many of the human torches that lit up Nero's garden party were probably disciples of Paul. He was a ring-leader of this new-found Jewish cult that Nero had so brutally chosen to be his scapegoat. To kill both Paul and Peter would be a great feather in Nero's cap. To further justify Nero's anti-Paul sentiments, the Romans considered Christians to be nothing more than a renegade version of the Jewish religion, which had always been a thorn in their side. Since the war was raging against the Jews, why not kill Paul and send a strong message to his followers. These Christians were just a civic nuisance as they continually refused to pay homage to the deity of Caesar and participate in the cultic practices of emperor worship or civic life. The Empire would be better off without them.

As you read this last letter to Timothy, try to put this political context into your lenses. When you read the words "suffering" and "endure hardship" try to smell the burning flesh of the human torches and the screams of the women and children being mauled by wild beasts in the coliseum, or feel the rats nibbling on your toes as you hear the dripping echo through the dank prison cell.

Try to feel the depth of human loneliness when you read the words,

> *Everyone in the province of Asia has deserted me.*

> *Do your best to come to me quickly, for Demas, because he loved this world, has deserted me and has gone to Thessalonica. Crescens has gone to Galatia, and Titus to Dalmatia. Only Luke is with me. Get Mark and bring him with you, because he is helpful to me in my ministry. I sent Tychicus to Ephesus.*

> *At my first defense, no one came to my support, but everyone deserted me.*

Then, try to grasp the depth and maturity of faith when, from the bottom of the pit, Paul claims these words,

For I am already being poured out like a drink offering, and the time has come for my departure. I have fought the good fight, I have finished the race, I have kept the faith. Now there is in store for me the crown of righteousness, which the Lord, the righteous Judge, will award to me on that day—and not only to me, but also to all who have longed for his appearing.

As you read this last letter, may you be encouraged in your times of difficulty and gain perspective for what life in the Kingdom of God is all about.

Lesson 1

- 2 Timothy 1

Study Questions

What is Paul's attitude toward Timothy?

Given the message of verses 6-7, what may have been happening in Timothy's heart?

Why is Paul suffering?

Restate Paul's instructions to Timothy in your own words.

How might Paul be feeling given the message of verse 15.

Food for Thought

We can summarize chapter 1 simply. Paul was saying to Timothy, "everyone has abandoned me and I'm suffering terribly. I know it looks grim, but don't give up. Don't let your pilot light go out."

For today's thought, let's focus in on verses 6-7. This scene is like a classic boxer movie. The hero of the story is the underdog that no one believed would last 2 rounds with the reigning champ. Now it has been 12 grueling rounds and the hero is still hanging in there. The reigning champion has been punishing our hero's body round after round, even knocking him to the ground more than once. Round 13; more punishment. Round 14; the hero takes more abuse, but holds on. Here it is -- the final round. The hero's eyes are swollen shut. He cries out to his manager, "Cut me, just cut the eyes so I can see!" He can barely stand from all the abuse. He's about to go under. His light is about to go out. But then, memories of his family flash through his mind. He reconnects to his main purpose for beginning the fight. BAM! Like a bolt of lightning he is recharged. As the hero's tiger-eyes lock on target, the champ can sense the difference in his opponent.

DING! They come out fighting and the hero is a new man. Punches start flying. Before you know it the champ is on the ropes and our hero is wailing on him with unbridled fury. SLAM! The champ hits the ground and our hero raises his hands in victory while the crowd goes wild.

OK, so maybe that was a bit melodramatic. The point is that many times we can come to a place in our life when it seems our pilot light is about to go out. No doubt Timothy was feeling a bit punch drunk and staggering in the corner. His mentor was in prison. All of his faithful ministry partners had abandoned the mission. Almost all of the Christians had fallen away under Nero's brutal attacks. Paul's opponents took advantage of the situation and went in for the kill, trying to wipe out Timothy in Ephesus. Any one of us would have been tempted to bail at that moment. "It's just not worth it! Do I really want to die? Do I really believe in this Jesus stuff? Wouldn't I be better off to just go back home and work in the fields?"

Where are you right now? If you are feeling weary from the journey then let's take some encouragement from Paul's words to Timothy.

Fan the Flame

Over the centuries many people have debated over the issues of works vs. faith. Some people say we can't do anything to increase or improve our walk with God; it all has to come from Him. Others say that you have to do everything and work your way into Heaven. This little phrase sheds some light on the controversy for us. First of all, the controversy exists because we have framed the question incorrectly. This is not a "salvation issue" in the sense of "will I get into Heaven when I die." The issue is about spiritual growth. God has given us all the gift of life. He loves us and wants us to grow. But, just like the embers of the fire, it takes some effort on our part to fan the flame. If we don't do anything with the ember then it will never burst into flame. But, if we gently blow on it and get the oxygen rich air circulating around it, things will start happening and, before you know it, combustion will take place again.

So, the question is how do we fan the flame? The answer is simply stated – Spiritual Disciplines. Before you roll your eyes and dismiss this as just another discourse about the need for spiritual disciplines and the mantra, "if we would just get more disciplined and get our act together then maybe things would shape up around here," I ask you to stop and consider a metaphor for a moment.

I realize the following metaphor strays from the immediate context of 2 Timothy 1, but I believe it is related to the idea of fanning the flame and it has been rumbling around in my mind for a while and I want to share it with you. So here goes…

Life is a lot like sailing. God the Father is like the open sea. He is infinite and unpredictable. The Holy Spirit is like the wind. Jesus is like the North Star. The church is like the ship, and the Bible is like the compass. There is one more piece to the analogy that needs a little context. It comes from the story *Voyage of the Dawn Treader* in *The Chronicles of Narnia*. Lucy, Edmund, and Eustace are on a voyage across the sea toward the land of the Emperor-Over-the-Sea. As they get closer to his land they notice that the water and the air start to change. The water becomes sweet and more like light. There is a presence that both quickens and calms the spirit. It is a beautiful place. The sea of life, in our analogy, is like that.

The destination of this journey is the heart of God's love. The direction of God's love is "north" and Jesus is the one fixed point in the universe that leads us to that place. We are all sailing – every one of us. The power that propels the ship is the Spirit.

Let's stop there for a moment. The Spirit is the wind. If you have ever sailed or read about the great sailing vessels of the 18th and 19th centuries, then you know the kind of relationship that the sailor has with the wind. The wind is the power,

the energy, for the boat. Yet, the wind is also the power that can destroy the boat. When the wind is not blowing, the sea is calm. That's nice for taking in a sunset and having a nap, but it leaves you dead in the water. When the wind blows it causes the sea to become rough. The sailing is difficult, but the boat begins to move. There are two things that a sailor must do in relation to the wind. First, he must fear it. If you do not respect the awesome power of the wind; if you take it for granted, then it could destroy you. Secondly, he must learn to tap into its power so that his boat can be propelled through the water.

In this spiritual journey of life (remember, it's all spiritual) we are invited to sail into the heart of God's love. The only way that we can successfully do this is to learn the art of sailing. That is the purpose of the spiritual disciplines. We must learn how to read the stars, having the North Star (Jesus) fixed in the center. We must learn how to use the compass (the Bible) and the Sextant (theology) to continually figure out where we are. We must learn how to hoist the sails and turn the rudder (prayer and worship). Finally, we must realize that we cannot operate the vessel alone and it takes a crew to make it work (fellowship). We are a community at sea. We must sail together. If we don't know how to hoist the sails, read the instruments, and work together, then we will be blown against the reefs of despair, division, hatred, greed, bitterness, resentment, etc. But, if we can respect and work within the wind, then we can sail across the infinite expanse and voyage deeper into the heart of God.

Now, I don't know if that metaphor helped or not. Perhaps we can flesh it out further later on. For now, let's see how it applies to Timothy and to us. If our pilot light is going out and our spirit is down to a smoldering ember, then we need to engage in the spiritual disciplines and let the wind of God's Spirit reignite our hearts and reengage in the wind.

Timidity vs. Power

In verse 7 Paul goes on to encourage Timothy by reminding him of the truth. We do not need to be timid. We do not need to be intimidated by the big brute in the opposite corner of the ring. We do not need to be deflated when we see people running away from the ministry or attacking us. We need to remember that the Spirit that lives in us is not a weak Spirit.

Let's meditate on the three things that the Spirit gives us for the journey:

- **Power.** This is the Greek word *dunamis*. From it we get the word dynamite. The Spirit is the power for the journey. Looking at our sailing analogy again, we see the truth in this. The fact is that we cannot cross the sea and journey into the heart of God in our own strength. The sea is too vast and we are too limited. However, the wind is power. The wind blows however and wherever it wants and our job is to learn how to ride it. Sometimes it is a tail wind and we drive straight ahead and cover incredible ground. Other times it is a headwind and we must tack back and forth. We travel for days and only make a short distance. Still other times it is a wild storm and we hold on for dear life. That is the way of the Spirit. It is power. God has given it to us to move ahead.

- **Love**. This is the destination itself. The beauty of God and the spiritual journey is that the destination is both a present reality and an ever-increasingly-realized future. Our destination is the heart of God's love where we will ultimately be swimming in the sweet water of life, but, during the journey we have the wind of God's love blowing through us and giving us the very breath we need to live. It's all about love. If it isn't about love, then it is a reef that threatens to rip out our hull and cause us to take on water.

- **Self-control**. The Greek word here is *sophronismos* and is somewhat difficult to translate. It can be translated "making understanding or wise," then "admonition," also "discretion," "moderation," "discipline." In this context I think it brings us full circle; it means being disciplined. The Spirit gives us the ability to be disciplined. The disciplines give us the skill to harness the power of the Spirit so that we can move forward in love and into love.

Power. Love. Discipline. When we believe that we have been given these things then we do not need to be afraid of anything. Even if all the ships around us are crashing on the rocks, with the proper navigational skills, we can ride through the storm that is currently raging and come out the other side in one piece.

Timothy was feeling discouraged. Perhaps you are as well. It is my prayer, along with Paul's prayer for Timothy, that you would be encouraged as you read this final letter of Paul's and find a way to reignite your flame.

2 Timothy

Lesson 2

- 2 Timothy 2:1-13

Study Questions

Why is Paul's charge to Timothy in verse 2 so important?

What is the meaning of the three metaphors Paul uses: soldier, athlete, and farmer?

Reflect on the hymn Paul quotes in verses 11-13.

Restate this passage in your own words.

What is Paul communicating to Timothy?

Food for Thought

There are two challenges for us in this passage.

Pass it On

As Paul sits in the dungeon he has come to the end of his ministry. Imagine what would have happened if Paul's ministry was all about him. It would have ended in that dungeon. In leadership there is a temptation to grasp onto a position of power and influence and hold onto it. When a leader falls into that trap they begin to believe that, as the leader, they are supposed to the "answer man," the "go-to guy" who has his act together and can lead the troops fearlessly. If a leader has this mindset they feel threatened when younger people begin to emerge and display leadership gifts. Young people tend to be free thinkers and innovators and are not afraid to challenge previously accepted traditions. If the leader believes that his leadership is based upon his ability to control the power position then he feels motivated to silence, remove, or discredit the emerging leaders. That is sad.

Thank God Paul did not behave this way. Much of Paul's energy was spent in the process of making disciples that would be able to carry on the mission of being and bringing the good news of Jesus' Kingdom to the world. Timothy and Titus were two of these disciples. We know the depth of Paul's work with them through the fact that he calls them his sons. This was not a ten-week, once-a-week workbook program that Paul led Titus and Timothy through on their fast-track to spiritual growth and leadership. Paul brought these young men into his life and took them with him as he did his ministry. They ate together, worked hard together, and played together. They were arrested with him, they healed his wounds after he had been beaten or stoned, and they prayed diligently for the people they were trying to reach. In the end, Paul left behind a new generation of leadership that could carry the torch.

Here's the beautiful thing. The process of passing it on and making new disciples and leaders is in the DNA of the whole deal. In 2:2 Paul encourages Timothy to "entrust [it] to reliable men who will also be qualified to teach others." Timothy was supposed to turn around and do for others what Paul had done for him. Why is this pattern part of the DNA? Because that is what Jesus both modeled and commissioned His disciples to do. At the end of Jesus' ministry He told His rag-tag band of followers "as you are going out among all nations, make them into learners, teaching them to obey my commands."

Notice how I translated it "make them into learners." That's because the word we translate "disciple" is the Greek word *mathetes* and it means "one who learns." I love that image. Notice what Jesus did not say. He did not say, "Go out there and give everyone all the answers so that they can have their doctrine down pat and know everything they need to know about God and the universe, and force them to obey me or else." He said to make people into learners. As learners we never stop growing. We never stop asking questions and discovering new layers of God's infinite truth. The teaching process is not one in which we indoctrinate people to become clones of a limited, finite confession. The teaching process is one in which we teach people about the ways and teaching of Jesus and empower them to obey His command to love everyone and empower them to follow His example in their everyday life. That is the purpose of teaching, discipleship, and spiritual formation. Jesus passed it on to Paul. Paul passed it on to Timothy. Timothy passed it on, and on, and on to us. Now it is our turn to pass it on.

No Whiner-babies

The great irony of life is that human beings enjoy entrenching themselves in their own perspectives, building institutional walls around it, and then hating everyone who disagrees. That is one of the main reasons we continually kill each other in war after war throughout history. Then, when someone comes along and says, "Hey everybody, why are we killing each other? God created us all to live in love and unity. Let's rise above all this noise, follow the ways of God, and walk in love" the crowd tends to turn on that messenger and kill him. That is what Jesus experienced, that is what Paul experienced, and that is what Paul is reminding Timothy that he will experience as well.

Paul uses three metaphors to drive home this point; a soldier, an athlete, and a farmer. What do these three metaphors have in common? They share two things. First, they all have a higher purpose for which they are living; the soldier serves his nation, the athlete wants to win the contest, the farmer wants to harvest healthy crops. Second, it takes hard work to see the vision realized; the soldier must train and risk his life for the cause of the nation, the athlete must make sacrifices and endure the pain of training to win the contest, and the farmer must sweat and toil to till the soil and make the ground receptive to growth. That is the way it is with the Kingdom of God. Our higher purpose is to say "no" to the distortions of our human institutions, pettiness, pride, etc. and walk above the noise in the love of God. As we

challenge certain institutions and inbred hatred we will undoubtedly be misunderstood, abused, and maybe even physically harmed or killed. Jesus walked this path. Paul was walking this path. Paul was warning Timothy that he, too, may walk this path if he wants to bring the Kingdom of God to the world. Many of Paul's followers had already fallen away under the persecution. Paul was reflecting Jesus words in Luke 9,

If anyone would come after me, he must deny himself and take up his cross daily and follow me. For whoever wants to save his life will lose it, but whoever loses his life for me will save it. What good is it for a man to gain the whole world, and yet lose or forfeit his very self? If anyone is ashamed of me and my words, the Son of Man will be ashamed of him when he comes in His glory and in the glory of the Father and of the holy angels. I tell you the truth, some who are standing here will not taste death before they see the kingdom of God.

As we used to say in the gym, "No pain, no gain." It's not that we, as followers of Jesus, are masochists and are seeking to live a life of pain. That's really distorted. The point is that, before we head out to live in the way of Jesus in the world – loving everyone and being willing to be misunderstood by the religious establishments – we need to be prepared to take the heat for it...because the heat will come. Here's the good news, though. If you are truly walking in the way of Jesus, if you have hoisted your sail into the wind of the Spirit of God, then the pain won't matter to you. When we are being transformed by the love of Jesus we will be able to look at our accusers and see them through eyes of compassion, and love them.

So, as we close today, be encouraged. Let's make sure that we are investing in other people's lives by modeled and instructing them in the way of Jesus, and let's be prepared to take whatever heat people may want to send our way in the process.

Lesson 3

- 2 Timothy 2:14-3:9

Study Questions

What is the main problem Paul has with the false teachers?

How is the false teaching described?

Contrast the way the false teachers behave with the way Paul tells Timothy to behave.

What should Timothy avoid? Why?

Food for Thought

They say the letter "i" destroyed the church. In A.D. 1054 the church was divided between the East and the West over a single word in the Nicene Creed. The topic was the nature of Christ in relationship to the Father. In the Greek-speaking East they wanted the word to be *homoiousious* which meant that Jesus was of "similar substance" to the Father. In the Latin-speaking West they wanted the word to be *homoousious* which meant that Jesus was of the same substance as the Father. The only difference in these words was the letter "i." The two sides of the church could not come to agreement so the pope in the west ex-communicated the pope in the East and the pope in the East ex-communicated the pope in the West. Thus was born the Roman Catholic Church in the West and the Greek Orthodox Church in the East.

These kind of theological squabbles have been going on forever. The Jewish rabbis of Jesus' and Paul's day loved to sit around and argue about the spelling of words in the Torah and the difference of their vocalizations. Small "schools" of thought would form around the subtle variations of these issues. No church movement or religious grouping has ever been exempt from this type of thing. These battles have continued to rage during the Protestant era. Protestant theologians and church leaders have delighted over arguing about issues like whether Jesus' body was physically present in the Eucharistic bread or only symbolically present; whether baptism should be by immersion or sprinkling; and, my favorite, lapsarianism vs. supralapsarianism (if you don't know what that is you can either a. look it up, or b. consider yourself fortunate).

This issue is at the heart of Jesus' message and the ministry of Paul. In our passage today Paul reminds Timothy to keep this deep truth in perspective. The good news is about Jesus and the reality of His mission in the world. Jesus called us to receive the love of God and be a conduit of that love to the entire world. He didn't call us to dissect it, codify it, quantify it, compartmentalize it, package it into theological bullets, and then shoot it at each other. He called us to live the life of other-oriented, self-sacrificing, go-the-extra-mile-for-your-brother kind of love. Timothy's ministry was surrounded by "teachers of the Law" who loved nothing better than to sit around and harangue him about his use of the scripture and coerce him into following a distorted and legalistic adherence to the Laws of Moses and the exclusivistic ethos of the Jewish culture.

Paul explained this dichotomy through the metaphor of vessels. Here's a paraphrase of his advice to Timothy.

"Look, Tim, here's the deal. There are two kinds of leaders in the world. They are like dishes in the kitchen. Some of the dishes are used to serve up the food and feed the family. Others of the dishes are used to pile up the garbage and store it until trash day. Which do you want to be? If you want to sit around arguing, splitting theological hairs, and jockeying for theological dominance in self-glorifying power plays while the majority of the people are wallowing in pain, then you can be the trash can. If, on the other hand, you want to keep things simple and do the work of being the vessel of Jesus' love, then you will be able to feed the hungry souls that desperately long for God's nourishment.

Here's how you be a good vessel

> Don't fight, simply
>
>> Be kind
>>
>> Teach clearly
>>
>> Don't hold a grudge
>>
>> Instruct your opponents with gentleness, always with the intention of bringing about reconciliation and healing."

Unfortunately there is a lot of mudslinging and name-calling going on in the church. That is unfortunate. We are all brothers and sisters in the family of God. The fighting does nothing but deplete the soul and cause pride, bitterness, envy, and self-protection to isolate us from each other, God, and the world. Let's keep our minds and hearts focused on the person and mission of Jesus. Don't get me wrong. I'm not advocating an anti-intellectual, naive, "why can't we just get along" approach to spirituality. Just the opposite, in fact. I'm advocating a deep study of the scripture, culture, and the heart of God that will produce in us a sincere humility. When we stay open to the idea that we are perpetual learners and eternal sailors on the waves of God's infinite love, we will be awestruck and humbled to the point that we have no grounds to sling-mud or point fingers. We simply throw our sails to the wind and love unconditionally, trusting that God is in control and that we are called to simply enjoy the ride of a lifetime.

Lesson 4

- 2 Timothy 3:10-4:5

Study Questions

What does Paul claim will be a certainty in the life of the person committed to living a godly life? Why?

What were the 'scriptures' for Timothy?

Of what use were they for him?

What is Timothy supposed to preach? Why? What is this?

Food for Thought

Having grown up in a predominantly Baptistic tradition this passage is extremely familiar to me. Preach the Word! That was always the battle cry of the "good Christians." If you moved to a new town and were looking for a new church your litmus test as to whether that church was worthy of your attendance was always, "Do they preach the Word?"

What does that mean, exactly? When you hear and use a phrase so often it can tend to lose its meaning. What does it really mean to "preach the Word?" As I've analyzed this I realized that, for me, it basically meant "does the pastor preach verse by verse through whole books of the Bible from the pulpit every Sunday?" At another level, it also meant, "does the pastor believe that the Bible has absolute and timeless rules for behavior that must be followed exactly in every culture and does he interpret the Bible exactly the way I do in every area of my systematic theology?"

Through these lenses I have always read 2 Timothy 3:10-4:5 as a homogenous unit that basically said,

> *Timothy, remember that the scripture is the Word and the Word is the most important thing you have because it tells you how to live. Now, get out there and preach the Word so that everyone can know the rules and live exactly like you do!*

This time through the text I must confess that my understanding of Paul's instruction to Timothy has radically changed. Let's look at it closely;

- **Context of being tortured by word-arguers.** We must remember that this passage flows from the previous passage in which Paul is telling Timothy to steer clear of the people who love to argue over the "letter of the Law" and split theological hairs. These people tend to establish power structures around their interpretations and take joy in destroying those who disagree. Paul was suffering at the hands of these people and warned Timothy that he, too, would suffer greatly at their hands as well.

- **Scripture.** The Greek word is *gramma* and it literally means "letters, or writings". The "Holy writings" that Timothy had known from infancy was the Jewish literature that was comprised of three parts. First, there was the Law of Moses – Genesis, Exodus, Leviticus, Numbers, and Deuteronomy. Second, there was the "Prophets" which was all the other books of what we consider to be the Old Testament. Finally, there was the Rabbinic Literature – these were the accepted interpretation of the Law that had been passed down to the people and generally accepted as authoritative in many cases. Paul encourages Timothy that the study of these writings is a good thing. It is profitable and it will prove instructive toward a life of righteousness.

- **Preach.** The Greek word is *keyrussein*. It is a mistake simply to render *keyrussein* by "to preach." Fundamentally *keryssein* is the declaration of an event." It is similar to the word "witness." People in the New Testament who "preached" were people like the blind man who said, "All I know is that once I was blind and now I can see." That is the true sense of what it means to preach or to declare the truth of an event.

- **Word.** The Greek term that we translate "word" is *logos*. This is very different from the *gramma* that Paul referred to earlier as being useful. John, at the opening of his Gospel, said, "In the beginning was the *Logos*..." That *Logos* was Jesus, not the Law of Moses or an abstract philosophical idea of the Greeks. The *logos* was the person of Jesus and the reality of His life, teaching, death, and resurrection.

Allow me to paraphrase this passage to expose my new understanding of what Paul was saying to Timothy.

Look, Tim, the teachers and scholars love to study the "Holy Writings." After all, that's how they make their living. They spend all day and night parsing the verbs and arguing over whether it should be in the pluperfect or aorist tense. They create divisive and destructive battle lines around their hermeneutical gymnastics and theological hobby-horses. Stay away from that kind of thing. It leads to nothing more than arrogance, hatred, and the antithesis of Jesus' Kingdom. These men will hate you for your simple message and they will make you suffer. You can be sure of that. Don't worry, though; just stay the course.

Now, don't get me wrong. The "Holy Writings" are good and very important. Study them well. They were designed to inform you and instruct you about the righteousness that defines God's heart. The principles and models that you will glean from knowing them inside and out will definitely equip you to handle the challenges you will face in leadership in the church.

But, Tim, remember what is really important. Remember the reason that I have put my life on the line. I'm not willing to die for theology. We don't serve letters that have been scribed on papyrus; we serve the Word – Jesus Christ. Declare the awesome and simple truth that the Logos has become flesh and has made life in the eternal now accessible for all of us. Know Jesus, walk with Jesus, be Jesus to the world, both when you feel like it and when you don't. Then, and only then, when the reality of Jesus oozes out of your pours, will you truly be encouraging and instructing the people. Teach them with your life and with your ability to bring wisdom to the moment. This is healthy teaching – sound doctrine – that promotes the Kingdom of God on Earth. People will ridicule you and hate you for it, but keep your head and don't get distracted. Spread the good news by being a servant to everyone and, in so doing, being a conduit of God's love.

Lesson 5

- 2 Timothy 4:6-22

Study Questions

How would you describe Paul's emotions in vv. 6-8? Why?

Spend some time meditating on Paul's words in verses 6-8. Given the fact that he is in a dungeon and about to die, what thoughts, feelings, and/or questions do his words spark in you?

Spend some time reflecting on the life of Paul and the writings that we have been studying.

What has God taught you through this journey?

Food for Thought

As we read the final words of Paul I would like to make some random observations and comments:

It all seems anti-climactic. Let's be honest, we love the stories where the hero overcomes the obstacles, kicks butt, and gets the girl at the end of the movie. We love to cheer and feel vindicated. Paul's story doesn't end that way. After this letter was sent off to Timothy things got worse. Until one day the big Roman brute with a hood over his head rattled the iron of Paul's cell door. "Get up, Christian!" He grabbed the tired body of Paul, dragged him out of the cell, up the stairs, and out in the street. There, on the street, in front of the casual passers-by, as a common criminal, our hero's neck met the blade of the executioners axe and his life was snuffed out. Within that same time period another leader named Peter was crucified upside down in Rome. In fact, all of the original apostles (with the exception of John) along with thousands of others, were mercilessly murdered at the hand of Nero.

What does it all mean? Is this the "good life" that I can have right now? Is this the life of fulfillment and hope that is "Good News" for the nations? Did God really intend for His most faithful servants to die horrible deaths? Honestly, I don't know exactly what it means. What I do know is that life is not easy, and the Gospel is not a promise of easy-living and comfort. The world we live in is hard and people are operating under various levels of distorted perspectives that cause us to do terrible things to one another. It happens and we need to be prepared to deal with it.

There's a bigger perspective. OK, so if the last point was the last point then there would really be no point. If it were the final word then the "good news" would be "life stinks, then you die." Somehow I don't think that is the message that Jesus brought or that Paul died for. Perhaps the "Good News" of Jesus' message is, "life stinks, if you want it to." If you look at life through purely physical lenses, and the basis of your happiness is the acquisition of material goods, political/social position, power, and self-gratification, then yes, life does stink. Jesus came to remind us that life is more than that. We are spiritual/physical beings created by a loving God who invites us to enter into His presence now and experience the deep fulfillment of receiving and giving His love. It is possible to live life above circumstances and operate in the higher value of God's Kingdom, bringing love and hope to all people regardless of status. Paul knew that he had served Jesus faithfully and that he would know the fruits of his labor both in the knowledge that he had brought others closer to their knowledge of God's Kingdom and in the promise that he would ultimately participate in the resurrection of Jesus and know the eternal purpose for life with God.

If we believe this with all of our heart, then we, too, can face any circumstance. I was recently reminded that no one can make you do anything. No one can make you be sad, or angry, or happy, or fulfilled. You choose how you react. Now, it is dangerous to be too flippant or simplistic about this because our feelings are a complex interplay of hormones and neurochemical reactions in our brain. However, life is ultimately a matter of choice, and choice is informed by our core beliefs, and our core beliefs are formed by our exposure to, processing of, and assimilation of the truth of reality in the universe. Simply put, we will only make good choices when we diligently seek to understand the nature of God, the universe, ourselves, and truth. God promised that if we seek Him we will find Him. Paul found Jesus (Jesus found Paul) and his mind was transformed to the point that he could even see imprisonment in the Roman dungeon as a good thing.

Wow.

Our study is over

We have come to the end of a 16-session journey through the life and writings of Paul. Through this study I hope that you have gained some more insight into the life and times of Paul which, in turn, have helped you to hear Paul's words through new ears, read his instructions with new eyes, and respond to his challenges with a new heart.

More important than understanding Paul's letters, I hope that you have gained a deeper understanding of Jesus, His message, the purpose of His Kingdom, and a model for how to apply the principles of His Kingdom within specific cultural contexts.

In keeping with the message of 2 Timothy, remember that our study of the Bible is not for study's sake. It's not for the purpose of becoming smarter students. We study so that we can allow the Holy Spirit to transform us and make us "good vessels" of God's grace upon which the delicious feast of His love can be served to the nations.

More Titles from Vibble Books

The Overflow Principle

The Overflow Principle is a 7-week introductory small group Bible study that explores how to grow in the love of God and overflow God's love to the world. The study explores how to obey Jesus' commands to love God and love neighbor. We love God with a whole heart - the mind, spirit, and body. Then we overflow God's love to the natural spheres of relationship that surround us; first to our comfortable neighbor, and then, most importantly, to our uncomfortable neighbor.

The Life of Jesus

In this study you will follow Jesus' life story as it is recorded in the four gospels of the New Testament - Matthew, Mark, Luke, and John. All four Gospels have been combined to create one continuous story. The study is divided into 15 Sessions with 5 lessons each. On your own you will read the text, answer the study questions, and chew on the 'food for thought'. There is also a "just for kids" section to involve the whole family. Ideally you will gather with others in a small group or house church to discuss your findings and encourage each other to follow the teachings of Jesus.

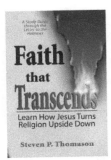

Faith That Transcends: A Study Guide to Hebrews

In the 1st century, a group of Jewish people adopted the idea that the rabbi Jesus was, indeed, their long-awaited Messiah. However, His teaching turned their worldview upside down and left them confused, discouraged, and persecuted. The writer of Hebrews, with the heart of a shepherd, lovingly helps them rethink some of their old-school doctrines and opens up a whole new world of possibilities.

We need that guidance today.

In this 13-lesson study of Hebrews you will glean the principles from their journey, and learn how to apply them today. Perhaps it is time to turn from a faith that clings to tired traditions and find a Faith that Transcends.

Printed in the USA
CPSIA information can be obtained
at www.ICGtesting.com
LVHW011804121023
760795LV00010B/145